American Catholic Women

MAKERS OF THE CATHOLIC COMMUNITY

The Bicentennial History of the Catholic Church in America
Authorized by the National Conference of Catholic Bishops

Gerald P. Fogarty, S.J., ed. *Patterns of Episcopal Leadership*

Joseph P. Chinnici, O.F.M. *Living Stones: The History and Structure of Catholic Spiritual Life in the United States*

Margaret Mary Reher. *Catholic Intellectual Life in America: A Historical Study of Persons and Movements*

Dolores Liptak, R.S.M. *Immigrants and Their Church*

David O'Brien. *Public Catholicism*

Karen Kennelly, C.S.J., ed. *American Catholic Women: A Historical Exploration*

American Catholic Women

A Historical Exploration

Karen Kennelly, C.S.J., Editor

The Bicentennial History of the Catholic Church in America
Authorized by the National Conference of Catholic Bishops
Christopher J. Kauffman, General Editor

MACMILLAN PUBLISHING COMPANY
NEW YORK

Collier Macmillan Publishers
LONDON

Macmillan Publishing Company
866 Third Avenue, New York, NY 10022

Collier Macmillan Canada, Inc.

Library of Congress Catalog Card Number: 88-18108

Printed in the United States of America

printing number
1 2 3 4 5 6 7 8 9 10

Library of Congress Cataloging-in-Publication Data

American Catholic women : A historical exploration / edited
  by Karen Kennelly.
        p.   cm. — (The Bicentennial history of the Catholic Church in
  America)
    Bibliography: p.
    Includes index.
    ISBN 0-02-917302-7
    1. Women in the Catholic Church—United States—History.
2. Catholic Church—United States—History. 3. United States—
Church History. I. Kennelly, Karen. II. Series.
BX1407.W65C37 1989
282'.73'088042—dc19   88-18108
                                                            CIP

This book is dedicated to all the women, the ordinary and the extraordinary, the named and the nameless, whose presence is evoked in these pages. By their lives and deeds they expand our vision of woman as Catholic in our society, who she has been, who she is, and who she can become.

Contents

List of Contributors

DEBRA CAMPBELL, assistant professor of religion at Colby College, has written several articles on Catholic women and lay activism.

MARY EWENS, O.P., author of *The Role of the Nun in Nineteenth Century America*, is associate director of the Cushwa Center for the Study of American Catholicism at the University of Notre Dame.

JAMES J. KENNEALLY, author of *Women in American Trade Unions*, is professor of history at Stonehill College.

KAREN KENNELLY, C.S.J., provincial of the Sisters of Saint Joseph, Saint Paul Province, has written extensively on notable women in the Catholic community.

COLLEEN McDANNELL, lecturer, University of Maryland, European Division, is the author of *The Christian Home in Victorian America*.

MARY J. OATES, C.S.J., is professor of economics at Regis College in Winston, Massachusetts, and the author of many articles on women in the Catholic community.

ROSEMARY RADER, O.S.B., on leave from the faculty of religious studies at the University of Arizona and currently president and prioress of Saint Paul's Priory, Saint Paul, Minnesota, has written several books and articles including works in Catholic women's studies.

General Editor's Preface

The Second Vatican Council developed a new apologetic, a fresh articulation of faith suitable to the diverse peoples of the world. The Council also marked the turn from the atemporal transcendental character of the neoscholastic theological synthesis to a historical approach to the role of culture in the development of dogma, an approach influenced by the historical-literary methodology fostered by Catholic biblical exegetes. Implicit in the Council Fathers' call to discern the "signs of the times" is the need of the historian to provide a lens to improve our vision of the signs of past times. New models of the church, such as the "pilgrim people" or the "people of God," stressed not the institutional structures but rather the people's religious experiences.

Concurrent with these general trends in apologetics, systematic theology, and ecclesiology was the dramatic rise in consciousness of the ethnic particularities throughout the world. Just as the movements in the Catholic church were based upon a dynamic of historical consciousness, so the rise in ethnic awareness was steeped in the historical dynamic of national and regional identities.

Of all the students of American Catholicism, James Hennesey, S.J., stands out for his singular contribution to the dialogue between theologians and historians. In several studies he has focused on the role of the Christian historian in the process of discerning the authentic tradition of the church. To sharpen our focus on that tradition he juxtaposes a quotation from John Henry Newman with a text from the conciliar decree on Divine Revelation.

Newman in 1859:

> I think I am right in saying that the tradition of the Apostles, committed
> to the whole Church in its various constituents and functions *per modum*

unius [as one unit], manifests itself variously at various times, sometimes by the mouth of the episcopacy, sometimes by the doctors, sometimes by the people, sometimes by liturgies, rites, ceremonies and customs, by events, disputes, movements, and all those other phenomena which are comprised under the name of history. It follows that none of these channels of tradition may be treated with disrespect; granting at the same time fully that the gift of discerning, discriminating, defining, promulgating, and enforcing any portion of that tradition resides solely in the Ecclesia Docens [the teaching Church].

The Council Fathers in 1965:

What was handed on by the apostles [the tradition] comprises everything that serves to make the People of God live their lives in holiness and increase their faith. In this way the Church in her doctrine, life and worship, perpetuates and transmits to every generation all that she herself is, all that she believes.

Of course this implied religious task of the church historian must be grounded in the rigorous principles and scholarly methodology of the profession. Writing religious history is by its very nature different from writing, say, economic history. Both must avoid a priori reasoning and evaluate the sources of their discipline with a precise analysis. Just as the economic historian must be conscious of the biases embedded in her or his social-class perspective, so the church historian must explore her or his place at the intersection of faith and culture. Without such a hermeneutical exercise of self-exploration one can neither adequately struggle against biases nor develop clear principles for understanding the past. During several group meetings with the six primary contributors to this work such a hermeneutical process developed. Since all of us have been influenced by recent trends in ecclesiology and historiography, each has a sense of her or his place at the intersection of faith and culture. Though some focus on the institutional church and others analyze the movement of peoples, all are professionally trained historians and are sensitive to Newman's notion of the diverse manifestations of tradition.

We conceived this topical approach of the six-volume history as the most effective means of dealing with an enormous amount of material. In a sense this project was an attempt to weave the American fabric of tradition into distinctive patterns. Although I designed the overall project, each of the primary contributors, either author or editor-author, was responsible for the particular design of his or her book. We seven historians met several times over a three-year period. In this case the term "community of scholars" is no exaggeration; a remarkable climate of honesty, candor, civility, and humor prevailed in our discussions. Though each volume stands on its own, the six achieve an unusual unity. There is a common beginning in most of the books. Commemorating the bicentennial of the appointment of John Carroll, each of the books opens during the federal period when Catholics achieved some semblance of ecclesiastical organization. We anticipate that a fresh synthesis of colonial Catholic history will be published at the quincentennial in 1992 of Columbus's arrival in the New World.

Throughout these volumes one reads about the persistent need for Catholics to forge their religious identities within the ethos of the new nation. In its origins the nation tended toward enlightenment and toleration; Catholics in Maryland and Pennsylvania reflected an open cosmopolitanism symbolized by the leadership of John Carroll. There was a conscious effort to embrace religious liberty and pluralism as positive factors; a denominational civility characterized the era. Subsequently, periodic outbursts of militant anti-Catholicism and nativism during the periods of immigration led Catholics to identify their loyalty to the United States in terms of good citizenship, but they retreated from the culture into ethnic enclaves; these were the preservationists who nurtured their particular Old World cultures in defense against this hostility. Isaac Hecker and the Americanists, such as John Ireland, forged a transformationist identity, one that was derived from the Carroll era and was based upon the spiritual compatibility of Catholicism and American culture.

Preservationist and transformationist are more appropriate concepts than ideological terms such as conservative and liberal because they are rooted in the religious and social contexts. Though today the lines are blurred between these identities, they are still viable conceptually. Today's preservationists are defensive against what they perceive as the antireligious tendencies of the culture and are searching for a wholeness in their view of the past. Transformationists tend to mediate religion in the terms of the culture and, like Isaac Hecker, see the movement of the Spirit not in opposition to modern society but within strands of the larger national ethos.

The "Romanness" of the American Catholic identity has seldom been a problem. During periods of conflict and controversy leaders in both camps have appealed to Rome as symbolic of their general loyalty to the papacy. American notions of religious liberty, denominationalism, pluralism, and voluntarism were not legitimated by Rome until the Second Vatican Council. While many Americans have consistently held that this attitude by the Vatican represents the inherent conflict between Roman authority and American democracy, Catholics have tended to consider the assumption that there is such a conflict to be another malicious manifestation of the anti-Catholic animus. While very loyal to Rome, Catholics have shared with other

Americans a pragmatic sense, a sense that Martin E. Marty refers to as a kind of experimentalism. While Catholics articulated a loyalty to Rome as the center of their changeless religion, paradoxically many had derived from their American experience a spirituality and a religious worldview that accept change as a fact of life. Marty quotes Jacques Maritain on American experimentalism: "Americans seem to be in their own land as pilgrims, prodded by a dream! They are always on the move—available for new tasks, prepared for the possible loss of what they have. They are not settled, installed. . . . In this sense of becoming and impermanence one may discern a feeling of evangelical origin which has been projected into temporal activity." In a sense this Catholic insistence on changeless faith, while their religious behavior is protean, allowed many leaders to hold to an Americanist vision and even a modernist methodology (applied not to Scripture but to evangelization) after the condemnations of Americanism and modernism.

Catholic identities derived from race, gender, and non-European ethnic groups are distinctive from the Roman, transformationist, and preservationist identities. Black Catholics were so marginalized that there was no sizable number of black clergy until the mid-twentieth century. The general periodization, particularly "immigrant church," is simply meaningless to their experience. The racism of the vast majority of people was reflected in the church. Many black Catholics now identify with Afro-American culture and the exodus experience basic to liberation theology. French Canadians and many Hispanic people also have developed their distinctive identities. Their non-European origins marginalized them in a church dominated by assimilationists of the more affluent classes. As with the black Catholics, their identities are deeply influenced by their historically rooted outsider status.

These six volumes struggled against exclusivism based on race, ethnicity, and gender. While chapters in these books deal with race and major non-European ethnic groups, an entire volume focuses on gender. I consulted with several Catholic feminists before deciding on a separate book on women in the Catholic community. Some might ask why not each of the other five books deals with this subject. Because there are so few secondary works on Catholic women and because not each historian could do ground-breaking research in women's studies, it became evident that an entire book should be devoted to this topic. As a consequence of a corollary decision, specialists in particular areas wrote separate chapters in the book because one author could not do justice to a general history of Catholic women. Of course, many Catholic women were drawn into the issues discussed in the other five volumes, but many behaved in a countercultural manner and opposed the dominant ecclesiastical identity represented by the conventional notion of the "ideal Catholic woman." In the shadow of patriarchy many women formed spiritual identities that did not fit religious and social categories.

Dolores Liptak, R.S.M., and Karen Kennelly, C.S.J., help us to understand the varieties of ethnic and female identities; David O'Brien and Gerald P. Fogarty, S.J., elaborate on the public forms of Catholicism and episcopal leadership; Margaret Mary Reher and Joseph P. Chinnici, O.F.M., locate various Catholic identities on the intellectual, spiritual, and devotional planes.

These six historians have been sensitive to regional variations, to differing contexts of urban development, and to the need to expand beyond the boundary of the stated theme of each volume into such frontiers as the micro-history of neighborhoods and parishes, the rural Catholic experience, meanings of the Catholic rites of passage and of Catholic "habits of the heart." The design of the project and the bicentennial deadlines limited the historians' range to the broad national contours of their topics. Though there is unavoidable overlapping in the treatment of persons and movements, the particular points of view preclude redundancy. More significantly, these books focus on the distinctive character of the American aspect of the Catholic community and represent various blends of original research and a unique rendering of topics derived from secondary literature.

From design to production I have had the good fortune to work with excellent historians and other fine people. To Justus George Lawler, the literary editor, to Charles Buggé, our liaison with the United States Catholic Conference, to Elly Dickason and Charles E. Smith of Macmillan Publishing Company, to Virgil C. Dechant and the late John M. Murphy of the Knights of Columbus, to Archbishop William D. Borders of Baltimore and Archbishop Oscar H. Lipscomb of Mobile, chairmen of the bicentennial committees of the National Conference of Catholic Bishops, and to John Bowen, S.S., Sulpician archivist and consultant, I am exceedingly grateful for their participation in making this six-volume set an appropriate tribute to John Carroll and to all those people who formed the Catholic tradition in the United States. I am particularly indebted to the inspiration of John Tracy Ellis in this the fifty-first year of his priesthood. May we always cherish his tradition of scholarship, honesty, and civility.

Christopher J. Kauffman

Acknowledgments

The National Conference of Catholic Bishops in 1981 established an ad hoc committee to plan for an appropriate observance of the 200th anniversary of the appointment in 1789 of John Carroll of Baltimore as the first Roman Catholic bishop for the United States of America. It was quickly determined that an important component of that observance should be a serious and substantial effort to shed added light on the growth and development of the Catholic church in Carroll's native land for these two hundred years. A subcommittee for publications was formed and the six volumes, *Makers of the Catholic Community*, are the result of its initiatives.

Grateful acknowledgment is made to the Knights of Columbus and their Supreme Knight, Virgil C. Dechant, who provided a generous grant that underwrote the scholarly efforts necessary to such a venture. For more than a century the work of the Knights of Columbus has epitomized much of the Catholic life that fills these volumes just as their presence and spirit have given discernible form to the faith and external witness of the Catholic church in the United States.

The Order has a rich tradition of fostering historical studies. In 1921 the Fourth Degree established the K of C Historical Commission. It presented its awards to Samuel Flagg Bemis and Allan Nevins, historians who later became notable figures. The commission also sponsored the publication of the K of C Racial Contribution Series: W. E. B. DuBois, *The Gift of the Black Folk;* George W. Cohen, *The Jews in the Making of America;* and Frederick F. Schrader, *The Germans in the Making of America.* Coincidentally, these books were also published by Macmillan. The K of C microfilm collection of the manuscripts of the Vatican archives, which resides at Saint Louis University, is a remarkable testimony to the Knights' promotion of scholarship. In 1982 a scholarly history of the Order, *Faith and Fraternalism*, by

Christopher J. Kauffman, was published, a book that has been widely noted as a solid contribution to social and religious history. Hence, *Makers of the Catholic Community* is a significant mark on the long continuum of the Knights' role in historical scholarship.

For six years the NCCB Ad Hoc Committee for the Bicentennial of the U.S. Hierarchy has given consistent and affirmative support for this series, and the Subcommittee for Publications has provided the technical insights and guidance that were necessary to the finished work. All who have thus contributed time and talent deserve recognition and gratitude. The members of the committee were: Archbishop William D. Borders, chairman; Archbishops Eugene A. Marino, S.S.J., Theodore E. McCarrick, and Robert F. Sanchez; and Bishops John S. Cummins, F. Joseph Gossman, Raymond W. Lucker, and Sylvester W. Treinen. The staff consisted of Rev. Robert Lynch and Mr. Richard Hirsch. Members of the subcommittee were: Rev. William A. Au, Ph.D.; Msgr. John Tracy Ellis, Ph.D.; Sister Alice Gallin, O.S.U., Ph.D.; Msgr. James Gaffey, Ph.D.; Rev. James Hennesey, S.J., Ph.D.; and Msgr. Francis J. Lally.

Most Reverend Oscar H. Lipscomb
Chairman, Subcommittee for Publications

Foreword

The process of doing women's history has been portrayed appropriately as quilting, that is, stitching together the fragments or patches of women's past retrieved from the stories hidden beneath the layers of a male-dominated society. The patch-quilt metaphor certainly applies to the historiography of Catholic women in the United States. Indeed this book tells the stories of hundreds of hitherto invisible Catholic women who, as individuals and as participants in groups and movements, represent almost every point on the religious spectrum. The reader will be struck by the diversity and originality of these stories; there are radical trade unionists, conservative Catholic journalists, models of the cult of domesticity, women religious who defied categorization and patronization, political suffragists and religious dissenters seeking ordination. The quilt is formed by these and other stories, many of which fall into what has been called compensatory history, a catalogue of biographical portraits placed within various thematic perspectives that serve as a counterbalance for their traditional neglect by historians.

There is a distinctively American character to these stories. The frontier movements and European emigrations to the United States had a "liberating" effect upon Catholic women as they engendered a breakdown of traditional roles of nuns, of single women, and of mothers. As the readers encounter the wide diversity of women's activity they should recall the less structured conditions of society characterized by movement, change, and periodic shifts of economic and social reform. Both American and European Catholic women lived in male-dominated religion and culture, but, as this book testifies, the American women's experience has unique features that have profoundly contributed to the character of the Catholic community in the United States.

Karen Kennelly, C.S.J., designed this book with each chapter's focus upon women in a particular sphere. Because these spheres were

not entirely exclusive and because the institutional church threads
its way into almost every chapter, some repetition was unavoidable.
Though much of the contextualization of these stories is cut from the
same cloth, each chapter contributes numerous patches to this particular women's quilt, one that forms a unique pattern in the history
of Catholic people in the United States.

                                        Christopher J. Kauffman

CHAPTER
1
Ideals of American Catholic Womanhood

Karen Kennelly, C.S.J.

*T*he Roman Catholic church marks its second century of official existence in the United States of America with about 27 million women constituting 51 percent of its baptized membership, but none among the ranks of its ordained leadership. In the atmosphere of a democracy, such a discrepancy between numbers and representation would ordinarily foment open rebellion. American Catholic women are certainly in the midst of a process of questioning and challenging the status quo in the church as well as in society. Accompanying and informing this questioning is a redefinition of identity and roles that began for women with their coming to the American colonies and continues to the present day.

Each period of the church's history in the United States—the colonial, the Anglo-American of the early Republic, the immigrant, and the modern—has had its outstanding women. Their story is told in the pages that follow. It is a story of putting down roots and spreading branches, of becoming deeply immersed in the American reality and permeating it with a Catholic approach to domestic, economic, and political life.

Margaret Brent (1601–1671), immigrant to the Catholic proprietary colony of Maryland, modeled a way of life few women of her time (or later) could hope to attain. A member of the Catholic landed gentry

1

in England prior to coming to Maryland in 1637, she became known for her piety, her good business sense, and her astuteness in matters of law (she argued 134 court actions from 1642 to 1650 and usually won). Brent is credited with making the first request for woman suffrage: She came before the Maryland Assembly January 21, 1648, as Leonard Calvert's attorney, and asked to be given voting rights in the assembly commensurate with her legal responsibilities.[1] Her request was denied, and although Brent earned the respect of her peers for her work as executrix for the governor of the colony and attorney for the proprietor, she made no lasting impact on the legal status of colonial women.

Catholics lost the political and religious freedoms they had enjoyed in the proprietary colony with the passage of discriminatory laws in 1654 and with establishment of Anglicanism in 1692. Catholic women, along with men, were disbarred as lawyers and excluded from office. Irish-Catholic servants were the object of restrictive legislation in 1699 and 1717, and Catholic churches were closed by order of the Maryland Assembly in 1704. Catholic women were further affected by laws requiring a surviving Catholic spouse, or a Protestant with children marrying a Catholic, to give up his or her children. Such children were to be taken away from the Catholic and given to parents who could raise them in a Protestant atmosphere.

Catholic women accommodated themselves and their exercise of religion to this land of tenuous freedom by carrying out devotions in the home which substituted for the liturgical celebrations normally conducted in a parish church. Diaries, journals kept by itinerant priests, and reminiscences contain suggestive references in this regard, describing mothers and fathers as leading daily Bible reading and other devotions in the home. Women were generally responsible for teaching children to pray and for preparing them to receive the sacraments. Women's example and influence were often remarked on as having attracted converts to the faith. Their ability to organize and run schools, orphanages, and hospitals, usually though not always as members of religious communities, was both demonstrated and acknowledged as essential to the growth of the church and the fulfillment of its mission in colonial American society.

John Carroll's appointment as bishop in 1789 ended a century-and-a-half without a hierarchy but initiated little immediate change in Catholic life and thought in America. Elizabeth Seton (1774–1821) exemplifies the Catholic woman's place in church and society as the Anglo-American church emerged from its colonial antecedents. A convert, Seton had to make a painful shift in identity and role when she moved from Anglican to Catholic; from popular socialite and respected wife and mother, to widowed and poverty-stricken member of a despised religious minority. She set up a school in her home as a means of supporting herself and caring for her own four children, ultimately founding a religious community composed of herself and the women attracted to her and her work and initiating the parochial school system of the United States.

Seton's story had its unique aspects but in its broad outlines was to be repeated again and again, with variations, as Catholic immigrants arrived in larger and larger numbers and as the church of the immigrants evolved. As the nineteenth century wore on, women's stories—their place in Catholic tradition and in American society—started to attract the attention of clerical and lay commentators. An ideology of woman took shape in Catholic circles, a piece here and a piece there, sometimes published in books and popular magazines, sometimes communicated privately, friend to friend, priest to penitent, teacher to student. The resultant body of thought—or perhaps more appropriately, collection of ideas—gave Catholic women a distinctive model of "true womanhood" to emulate and a set of standards by which to judge the merits of feminist causes.

The first coherent ideology of woman to be formulated by and for American Catholics was anything but original and was by no means distinctively Catholic. Put briefly, it was a domestic ideology, alike in content to its Protestant American counterpart, which enthroned woman in the "God-appointed sphere" of the home. Irish-Catholic clergy and laity, represented most conspicuously by the priest-author Bernard O'Reilly, propagated this domestic ideology of woman among Catholics during the last quarter of the nineteenth century.

O'Reilly, whose instant best-seller, *Mirror of True Womanhood*, came out in 1876 and had gone through seventeen editions by 1892, had an eclectic taste encompassing French, Spanish, and Italian models of the "advice book" genre as well as devotional literature of European origin, most notably, the lives of the saints and the *Imitation of Christ*.[2] Drawing freely from these sources as well as from popular literature of the day, O'Reilly presented a model of "true" womanhood for American Catholic women to admire and emulate.

Woman, according to O'Reilly, was by nature the more spiritual of the two sexes, being prone to all that is most heroic, and endowed by the Creator with unlimited power for good or for evil. Mothers were living images of God in their unsleeping watchfulness and unfathomable tenderness. The home was woman's God-appointed sphere, a place where true woman held sway, a place where woman could be queen and become a saint. She was mistress and sovereign there, not only by the nature of things, but by the supremacy of her own goodness.[3]

In a passage hinting at the very conservative stance from which the author was dispensing his advice, O'Reilly concluded that modern theories about "Woman's Rights" and the "Sphere of Woman" have no basis in the ideal womanhood he is describing: "No woman animated by the Spirit of her Baptism . . . ever fancied that she had or could have any other sphere of duty or activity than that home which is her domain, her garden, her paradise, her world."

Certain virtues came naturally to woman in this ideal picture. Her salvation was seen to depend on the fulfillment of her nature and the practice of the virtues of generosity, fidelity, devotedness, and self-sacrifice. According to O'Reilly, she possessed "a deep sense, characteristic of her sex, of all that is most divine in humility as in charity," and had "by nature the power, the art, and the disposition to please, to soothe, to charm, and to captivate." For woman, to practice generous hospitality was the first impulse of nature, driving her to practice the "out-door" charities. "Every mother . . . has a deep interest in the poor round about," and sacrifice was to be seen as a trait of every woman: "Woman's entire existence, in order to be a source of happiness to others as well as to herself, must be one of self-sacrifice." And again, "Practical and continual self-denial [is] the very soul of womanly virtue."

Having laid a basis for his subject through this sort of idiosyncratic interpretation of scripture and natural law, O'Reilly went on to expand his advice and extend his depiction of true womanhood by commenting on the moral influence of woman and the proper education of girls and of boys. He ascribed great moral power to woman, asserting that the moral ills of the century stemmed from "the early lack of strong moral home-culture, to the neglect of woman's holy influence over boyhood, or to the baneful influence of women ill-trained or taught to look upon pleasure and enjoyment as the prime end of life." Society must look to "the mighty influence of Christian motherhood training an army of true women to withstand and cry down untrustfulness, dishonesty, and corruption, and an auxiliary army of true men." Argument by analogy led O'Reilly to the even more profound claim that "Just as Mary . . . gave the Saviour and salvation to the world, just as the Church . . . evermore performs the divine office of motherhood here below toward the nations,—even so a true woman in every home is the saviour and sanctifier of man."

Mothers needed no special schooling to acquit themselves of this high calling. Instinct would suggest to them the best educational methods, if not all the necessary content, to be used with children. In O'Reilly's words, the mother's "own sense of piety, her womanly wit and instinctive knowledge of child-nature will teach her the best methods to be employed" to help children grow in knowledge of God and piety. The object in educating girls ought to be "to rear women thoroughly enlightened in all that can make them love the faith of their baptism and enable them to explain it and defend it; to rear mothers able to be the first and most successful teachers of their children in all that pertains to faith and the true life,—the life of the soul."

O'Reilly, a professor at Laval at the time he wrote *The Mirror*, had some distinctive theories about the education necessary for American Catholic girls. As girls grow older, he asserts, specifically when they reach the age of thirteen, mothers should be prepared to give them a home course in apologetics, setting forth the history of the heresies and schisms that threaten the authority of the church. Although he grants that only "educated women" who have more opportunity for study than working-class women will have the knowledge of doctrinal differences necessary to instruct their daughters at this level, O'Reilly states that he still feels this obligation applies to all mothers. Beyond this, he feels it is incumbent upon mothers to surround their daughters with good art and good reading material, and to stress the value of time. "Every day and hour idled away . . . is an opportunity thrown away for self-improvement." Even the "little lost moments" could be put to good use in the pursuits of needlework and the practices of devotion. Mothers need not worry about teaching apologetics to sons, but rather should generally emphasize religious patriotism, respect for their mother, and service and devotion to their sisters. He observes that it is an evil to let girls be servants to brothers, calling it a "fatal mistake" for mothers to induce or permit such a thing.

This idealistic and domestic view of womanhood was not compromised by the author's acknowledgment that occasional circumstances might necessitate work outside the home for some women or induce others to choose religious life rather than marriage. O'Reilly reduced the working woman's lot to the realm of the exceptional, and incorporated women religious into his domestic ideology by depicting them conducting schools where the "true Christian mothers who are to bear the priests as well as the citizens of the future" could be educated. Perhaps more than anything else O'Reilly's domesticated, maternal nun demonstrates the degree to which he accommodated traditional Catholic thinking about woman and womanhood to the American Protestant cult of "true womanhood."

A very different contemporary voice articulating an American Catholic perception of woman was that of Isaac Hecker (1819–1888) whose career in the Catholic church began with his conversion and baptism in 1844. Hecker had the kind of inquiring mind and restless spirit that compelled him to address every issue that aroused public interest during his lifetime, including the so-called woman question. In addition, he was very interested in the relationship between the

sexes and the relevance of sex for spirituality. Ordained to the priesthood in 1849, he expressed his convictions about woman through interactions with the many women who subsequently came to him for
advice and spiritual direction as well as through his encouragement
of women writers.[4]

It is clear from Hecker's early writings that he was utterly convinced of the fundamental equality of the sexes and troubled by the
inequities that necessitated the struggle for women's rights. Women
and men were, he felt, equally susceptible of the movements of the
Holy Spirit, equally called to holiness and to oneness in Christ. Hecker
was impatient with what he regarded as artificial and mistaken at-
tribution of certain qualities to men or women, tangling on this score
with the author of an article on "Femality" who identified women
with "love" and men with "truth." "I am inclined to think," wrote
Hecker, "that the two sexes should be in the same individual being,
that the same individual should unite in her being both sexes." Jesus
himself, Hecker asserted, had united in his person qualities often attributed to both sexes, being a person of "light and warmth, head
and heart, understanding and impulse."[5] About the same time that
he penned these observations, Hecker wrote across a diary page,
without note or comment, "Man requires a rebirth of the feminine
in him."[6]

Although Hecker never developed in any public forum his idea of
male and female qualities integrated in human personality, his own
spirituality evolved along those lines, so much so that one modern
student of Hecker has concluded that his was a matriarchal rather
than a patriarchal consciousness.[7] Hecker's advice to women confi-
dants reflected a similar insight, as when he told a woman friend in
1867 that "the perfect blending of great manliness with the extreme
tenderness of a woman's heart is to be Christlike."[8]

Given these views, it is at first glance surprising to find Hecker in
opposition to woman suffrage. His conservatism in this regard
stemmed from a conviction that the Catholic church gave "full scope
to women's capacities and powers," most particularly by affording
women in all walks of life the means to holiness and a full expression
of their personalities, and by holding out to women the opportunity
to join religious communities.[9] Just as romantic and idealistic as O'-
Reilly in his own way, Hecker argued that the demand for suffrage
would not be heard if women had the place in society and religion
that the church had provided in times past and could still provide.

The frequency with which women correspondents and friends
challenged Hecker's position on the suffrage issue is a sign of the candor and honesty he fostered, as was also the consistently even-handed
editorial policy of *The Catholic World*. This journal, founded and edited

by Hecker, featured articles from every point of view on the woman question by an exceptionally large number of Catholic women writers, many of whom he discovered and encouraged.

The closest Hecker himself came to promoting women's rights was in connection with his efforts to develop a spirituality and forms of religious life suited to American conditions. In his own interactions with women as a confessor or spiritual director, he made it his aim to empower them to rely more and more on the Holy Spirit as their guide and less and less on him, thus rejecting the dependence upon directors characteristic of European Catholic tradition. His correspondence with Jane King and Mrs. E. M. Cullen affords ample evidence of this approach.

In his unsuccessful efforts over the years to identify someone who could found a religious community for women comparable to the Paulists, the community he had established for men, Hecker repeatedly urged the necessity for a fresh start free from European customs. Among other ideas, he suggested an entirely new kind of community for laywomen without vows; a more conventional vowed community "untrammeled by [European] customs, regulations and routine," and thus free to work directly among the sick, the poor, prisoners, etc.; or finally, a female counterpart to the Paulists, that is, a community of women who could devote their energies to an intellectual and literary apostolate.[10]

Among the women with whom Hecker worked to implement his goal of founding Americanized communities were Elizabeth Carey and Sara Worthington King Peter. Carey came closest to realizing Hecker's dreams. A Bostonian convert from Unitarianism, she pursued the idea of organizing laywomen to engage in work among the poor despite the reservations of her spiritual director, Robert Fulton, a Jesuit at Boston College. This priest regarded Hecker's idea of an American community as a good one, but admitted "as a matter of conscience" that he could not keep up with Hecker's "startling innovations" and feared he could not encourage Carey to cooperate with a new foundation "which should so far desert safe tradition, as I fear yours might."[11]

Fortified by Hecker's support, Carey heeded her director's cautions to the extent of placing the women in her projected community under the direction of the local bishops, but introduced the innovations of setting aside two hours in the daily horarium for literary work and study and omitting "all petty rules of behavior . . . as unsuited to the American nature and quite unnecessary in a country where every virtuous woman is respected and protected." It was Carey's hope that such a community would not only suit the American woman's circumstances and inclinations but would enable her to adjust to future apostolic challenges in a country where "social changes succeed each other so rapidly, and any order of today" needs to be "sufficiently elastic to adapt itself" to the changed needs of tomorrow.[12]

Neither Carey nor Peter succeeded in founding a new type of American congregation, although Peter ultimately established a community of Franciscans who lived at her Cincinnati home, combining hospital service and contemplative prayer. Hecker contented himself with arranging for the Little Sisters of the Poor, mostly Irish, to settle in the neighborhood of St. Paul's, the Paulist parish in New York, while continuing to believe that American women, provided with a suitable rule of life, could "do more good than three shiploads of foreign nuns" to advance the cause of conversion. Failure to realize this aim did not deflect Hecker from an unswerving belief in the Catholic church's capacity to liberate women and to give them, in religious communities, the scope for leadership and apostolic action that their abilities warranted.

As mentioned, part of Hecker's contribution to the Catholic position on woman came through the writers whose work he published in *The Catholic World*, particularly Catholic women whom he encouraged to publish. Blanch Elizabeth Murphy, in a four-part series appearing in 1872 and 1873, reviewed the historic role of women in the pre-Christian and Christian eras, noting the efforts of women, especially through religious orders, to open new opportunities for service to the poor and for educational and intellectual development. She deplored the frequency with which a woman's sex became a barrier to her aspirations, and attacked the economic conditions that forced women into unsuitable and poorly paid work. The most important reform in Murphy's opinion was to widen opportunities so that women could make choices and come to appreciate their own worth: "Woman's work should be defined . . . by her capabilities," a sentiment heartily endorsed by Cullen.[13] Murphy tempered the ardor with which she backed an enlargement of woman's sphere of opportunity by asserting that the liberated woman would be a good wife, better able by reason of self-esteem to choose a worthy husband and to fulfill the highest expectations of a husband.

Representative of women espousing in the pages of *The Catholic World* a decidedly conservative position was a Mrs. Smalley, whose article in January, 1872 preceded Murphy's. Smalley contended that women should cultivate reverence and submission in order to "win the respect of him who is her head as Christ is the head of the Church." Woman suffrage was to be rejected as a betrayal of the role of wife and mother and a movement in which woman had everything to lose and nothing to gain. Smalley's sentiments were echoed frequently by others throughout the remaining decades of the nineteenth century, most notably by Catholic journalists Eleanor Donnelly and Katherine Conway.

Hecker's oldest friend, Orestes Brownson, had early set forth the most extreme version of the conservative case in his article, "The Woman Question," published in the May, 1869, *Catholic World*.[14] According to Brownson, women were made for men, they were to be subject to their husbands, and they were endowed with virtues and capacities suited only for family and domestic life. Suffrage, a matter of trust granted for the common good on grounds of expediency and practicality, was in no way a right of women and would have deleterious effects on family and society if exercised by them. The vote should not under any circumstances be granted to them. The real solution to the "woman problem" for Brownson was the revival of traditional values: women should be trained to love the home and find pleasure in its duties.

Articles such as those by Smalley and Brownson prompted Hecker's Catholic women friends to assert their own contrary views and challenge Hecker to clarify his own. "Women's rights appear to me," wrote Mrs. E. M. Cullen in 1868, "to be a cry against the disabilities which woman feels both politically and socially. . . . All I ask for in women is that they should be free to do whatever God has given her (sic) the capacity to do, without any social or political disqualifications."[15] Cullen, an intelligent, witty, and outspoken woman, was always willing to offer Hecker unsolicited advice. When he suggested on another occasion that men could not receive spiritual advice from women, her sharp rejoinder led Hecker to withdraw his objection.[16]

Quite a different Catholic voice on the woman question during the last part of the nineteenth century was that of a member of the United States hierarchy, John Lancaster Spalding (1840–1916). Spalding, consecrated in 1876 for the bishopric of Peoria, Illinois, was a popular speaker and essayist who gained considerable respect during his lifetime for his dedication to social reform. He consistently included equal rights for women not only among but at the top of his reform agenda, and gave practical support to Catholic women in their struggle to widen their opportunities for higher education.

Spalding concurred with O'Reilly, Hecker, and virtually all other Catholic spokespersons of the day in defending the church's historical record with respect to women. With the others, he professed to find within scripture and the person of Christ the reasons for all past improvements in woman's lot and the justification for further improvement or reform. After all, had not Christ himself embraced male and female without distinction in his love, and placed the highest ideals of sanctity within the grasp of both sexes on equal terms? "As a person, woman's origin and destiny are the same as [man's]. . . . In souls there is no sex."[17] Spalding thought that religion and knowledge had done much in the past to remedy man's inhumanity to woman, which he called the "deepest stain" upon the human race and "that great blot upon the page of history." The time was rapidly approaching when, in the great vision of Paul in Galatians (3:28–29), there would be made no distinction either in the world or in Christ between slave and freeman, between man and woman.

It seemed to Spalding as a reformer that although much progress had been made, much still remained to be done. He left no doubt in the mind of the man- or woman-in-the-pew as to where the line of duty lay. No one claiming to be Christian, declared this zealous pastor, lecturer, essayist, and labor dispute mediator, could deny the justice of woman's cause: "Whoever is thoroughly imbued with the spirit of Christianity must sympathize with all movements having as their object the giving to woman the full possession of her rights." Distinctions between men and women that Spalding found intolerable have a strikingly modern sound. Seldom absent from addresses he delivered during his episcopacy were critical references to sex stereotyping of occupations; unequal pay for equal work; discriminatory civil and criminal laws when it came to property rights, punishment for crime, and voting; and the double standard in matters of sexual morality. These he labeled social evils no Christian should tolerate, an unfinished Christian reform agenda.

Spalding sounds as idealistic as O'Reilly and as utopian as Hecker in some passages, as in an 1878 commencement address at a men's college in which he described the ideal society the graduates should aspire to create. Such a society, he said, would be permeated by love; in it, the poor would be protected, famine would be no more, drunkenness would be an evil of the past. For such a society to be perfect, cruelty to children and child labor would have to cease. The ignorant would need to be educated. War would be condemned as "public murder," and the prevalent system of industrial competition would be considered worse than war. Finally, in this ideal society, women would have the same rights as men.

Making allowances for the lofty tone of commencement addresses, which has not changed much since, we still have in Spalding's speeches and essays the most comprehensive Catholic agenda of the time with respect to women's rights. He spoke bluntly to the evils as he saw them: "No law that is unjust to [woman] should exist in Christendom. She should not be shut out from any career that offers to her the means of an honest livelihood. For the same work she should receive the same wages as a man, and should hold her property in virtue of the same right that secures to him the possession of his own. For wrong-doing of whatever kind she should not be made to suffer a severer punishment than is inflicted upon man. The world will continue to be unjust to her until public opinion makes the impure man as odious as it makes the impure woman."[18]

Spalding rejected in no uncertain terms the premises underlying O'Reilly's domestic ideology, often contrasting the ideal of "true womanhood" with woman's reality as he observed it, or poking fun at the romanticism and delusions of literature, as in his comment, "The poets have sung divinely of woman, but man has treated her inhumanly"; and, "The objection so frequently raised, that political life would corrupt woman, has, at least, the merit of grim humorousness. Could it by any chance make them as bad as it makes men? To tell them they are queens of the home, to whom the mingling with plebeians is degrading, is an insult to their intelligence. We have forsworn kings and queens, both in private and in public life, and at home women are, for the most part, drudges."[19]

Spalding was a supporter of woman suffrage, speaking out openly in favor of it as early as 1884. His advocacy of higher education for women also dates from the 1880s and was more significant in terms of theory and outcome. An exalted view of the importance of education and of the role of woman as educator characterized Spalding's position on this issue. His argument went as follows: Education is for life in this world and the next; it is the "universal means" God gave human beings to nurture life and to attain ultimate happiness. So important is a genuine education, that religion itself, as the worship of God in spirit and in truth, depends upon it. If we are persuaded of this, and aspire to the very best education for all, reasoned Spalding, we must make it our number one priority to give women the best possible education. Why women over men? Because their rightful education as persons was at the time being neglected, and because an educated mother would ensure educated men.

Philosophical concepts pertaining to personhood and motherhood thus lay at the heart of the feminist education theories that Spalding expressed in numerous talks and in an 1890 plan for a teachers' college for women, finally realized in 1911 as Catholic Sisters' College. His notion of woman as mother being the "aboriginal God-appointed educator," whose care for children within the home was vital for all social progress, related him to the German idealists, while his notion of person linked him with Aristotelian-Thomist ideas on personhood. For Spalding, woman as person has the same right as a man to become all that she may be, to know what may be known. To realize her full rights as a person, women needs an education, which is her birthright regardless of her sex or her state in life.[20]

Spalding cannot be taken as representative of American Catholic bishops in his aggressive and comprehensive stands on the woman question or in the philosophical and theological premises for his views. Nonetheless, his is obviously a significant and arresting voice among the hierarchy, few of whom addressed themselves to women's issues except when implored by people on either side of the suffrage debate to state their views. Most akin to Spalding in his thinking was John Ireland, (1838–1918) bishop and later archbishop of St. Paul, Minnesota, from 1875 to 1918. The two made common cause in the woman-related temperance movement and in the promotion of higher education for Catholic women. They, along with Bernard McQuaid, bishop of Rochester, New York, were singular among the American hierarchy for lending their names to the list of supporters of woman suffrage in a statement issued in 1902 by the National American Woman Suffrage Association.[21]

Ireland focused his efforts on behalf of women on the goal of affording Catholic women equal access to higher education. In this he was inspired by a belief in progress, which he articulated on numerous occasions. A progressive, democratic America had given birth, Ireland thought, to a type of woman society had not before known. He did not hesitate to introduce into his homiletic vocabulary the feminist "new woman" concept and to argue for a new education from a liberal, progressive viewpoint: "In this new world of ours there is, in a true and honorable sense of the word, the new woman. . . . Beyond a doubt the sphere of woman's activities has widened; woman's influence reaches much further than before; and for such new conditions she should be prepared by an intellectual training higher and more thorough than has heretofore been necessary."[22] An editorial that appeared in 1891 in the official St. Paul diocesan newspaper was more explicit on the higher education theme: "The requirements of the time," wrote the priest-editor, "demanded a collegiate institution of the kind we mention. The world has changed very much for women of late years. Almost every department of business, of literature, of science, or art is thrown open to her. The education of the past suited the past narrow sphere of woman; the education of the future must be as broad as the wide field opened up to the gentler sex."[23] Ireland looked to women's religious communities for implementation of this college vision, placing particular confidence in a congregation headed by his sister and assisting that group with money and moral support when it initiated plans for a college in 1891.[24]

Archbishop Ireland's solid belief in women religious as educators had been earned by the nuns with whom he was best acquainted,[25] and was fully shared by the dean of the American hierarchy, Cardinal James Gibbons. Though not in favor of woman suffrage, Gibbons encouraged a teaching congregation of women in the Baltimore diocese to introduce collegiate level studies in their local academy in the early

1890s. Before the end of that decade he withstood the protests of German-American clergy, and papal officials to whom they had complained, and backed another religious community of women in their plans to open a college for women in the District of Columbia.[26]

Representative of a contrasting conservative outlook among American hierarchy was the bishop of Fall River, Massachusetts, William Stang. Teaching moral theology to seminarians at Louvain in the 1890s had exposed Stang to European thought on the woman question. His textbook, *Pastoral Theology*, published in 1896, brought several new strains into the mainstream of American debate, most especially Alphonsus Ligouri's legacy relative to woman. Following the lead of this influential seventeenth-century Italian moralist, woman as temptress began to make her presence felt in American seminarian training, especially in manuals instructing priests in the hearing of women's confessions. Passages such as the following struck the theme: "A dangerous rock which the priest encounters in the stormy sea of the world is the hearing of woman's confessions."[27]

Stang also revived an older church tradition of regarding woman as the "devout sex" *(devotus femineus sexus)*, as exemplified in a section of *Pastoral Theology* advising priests on how to work with women religious in the parish: "The priest who looks upon [the nuns] merely as troublesome women, as a necessary evil in the parish, has lost sight of the supernatural in them, and fails in one of his most important pastoral duties, which obliges him to care first for those who are nearest and dearest to God." Stang advises priests to hold a nun's transcendent vocation in high regard by studying the sisters' rule, reading deeply in ascetic and moral theology, practicing mental prayer and asceticism, and begging help from God in order to be a worthy confessor for the devout sex. Unfortunately, Alphonsus Ligouri's dark view of the flesh and the body, and of woman, gets in the way of this laudable concept. Stang goes on to caution priests against catering to feminine excesses of piety when ministering to the laywoman: "There are some silly women who would go to confession daily, if there were a priest silly enough to hear them. They are regular ninnies, especially when they are young and giddy." Priests must be on their guard to enforce brevity with the devout sex, especially as "men may be waiting for their confessions, and one man at the confessional is worth ninety-nine pious women." Stang advises the wisdom of "keeping pious persons of the devout sex humble and simple-minded," and expresses the fear that unless this path is followed, priests will encourage production of *devotulae*, "the target of our moralists."[28]

Stang's Ligourian approach to moral theology had the effect of reinforcing a radical dichotomy between woman as nun and woman as sexual partner in or out of marriage. It was evidently possible for woman to attain sanctity only as a celibate, even though church tradition named her a member of the devout sex.[29] Women fit into a rigid domestic order, the family being described as a microcosm and mirror of society in its composition and hierarchical pattern of authority. The father's authority is derived from God; enforcement of proper father–family, husband–wife, parent–children, and lord–servant relationships are absolutely necessary for a well-ordered society. Stang's opposition to the expansion of women's rights upon his return to the United States to fill the Fall River bishopric was predictable. In essays published in 1905, he unhesitatingly gave as his opinion that women were intended by God to be wives and mothers and did not therefore need to vote or to be as educated as their husbands, to whom they should be subordinate. There was no necessity for women to read newspapers and novels, occupations for which higher education would presumably fit them, for "smartness is not becoming to a woman."[30]

It is tempting when considering the views of the American hierarchy on the woman question to identify an official church position, or at least a majority and a minority opinion. The most one can conclude from the record of the day is that a spectrum of views on the woman question was represented, with those against woman suffrage often receiving more publicity than those for it as the campaign for a federal amendment waxed and waned. The resounding defeat of the 1915 state referendum in Massachusetts has been taken as a clear indication of the negative influence of Catholic antisuffrage forces, but, as later chapters in this book will document, support for woman suffrage among the Catholic clergy was persistent.

Passage of the referendum a second time around in New York state, in 1917, prompted John A. Ryan (1869–1945), then America's most respected Catholic commentator on social justice, to address himself publicly to the suffrage issue. Ordained a priest for the diocese of St. Paul, Ryan had gone on with Archbishop Ireland's encouragement to become the country's foremost interpreter of Catholic social thought and proponent of justice in the marketplace. He suffered no delusions on the need for women to work outside the home and built into his legislative reform agenda protective laws for women and children. The compelling necessity for reforms of this nature persuaded Ryan to support woman suffrage and to excoriate Catholics who seemed always to be against everything and for nothing.[31] Ryan contended that women, because of their experience as homemakers and wage earners, had potential for exercising the right to vote for the improvement of society. He felt it was shortsighted of Catholics in their obsessive fear of socialism and radical politics to oppose the feminist movement and its suffrage goals. The movement had an undeserved extremist reputation, for one thing—extremist elements when present being more a function of class and "unrepresentative" leaders than of women as a whole, in Ryan's view. Beyond that, women, especially Catholic women, were predictably conservative, "fearful of sudden and great changes," and generally loath to overthrow the existing order, whether of the "family, the state, or industry." Moreover, Ryan argued, women's instincts were sounder than men's when it came to issues affecting the home and morals, and women's experience working in factories rendered them every bit as able as men and sometimes more so when it came to understanding legislation necessary to improve wages and working conditions.

Other interesting facets of Ryan's position on the woman question were his insights into the laywoman's potential compared to that of the nun and his perceptions of how class affected women's political behavior. He called attention to the impressive capacity for charitable work laywomen demonstrated, and noted that they exercised a missionary zeal unattainable to most except through the religious life by their successful exercise of the profession of teaching and nursing. Ryan urged laywomen not to stop there, but to go on to work for civil and social reform through political action and by entering the new profession of social work. To go no further than charity in alleviating society's ills and to use one's vote against the supposed evils of socialism, feminism, and all other forms of extreme radicalism rather than for constructive reform would be to fail in one's duty as a citizen and to be no better Catholics than Catholic men, who all too often fought wrong views but did nothing to discover the social, civic, and industrial evils that ought to be removed and vote for positive measures. Ryan's ideal Catholic laywoman was one with a social conscience who could grasp new opportunities and seek appropriate outlets for her missionary zeal in the home or in the workplace, as well as in the convent.

As for class, Ryan contended that one of the fundamental justifications of democracy was that the members of every social or industrial class understood certain of their own needs better than did members of any other class. This principle was strikingly true, he thought, of the wage-earning woman whose experience had helped her acquire political consciousness. These women, along with others drawn from the elite class, were leaders of the American feminist movement. The radical views they held were understandable given their class origins. To reject the movement, or woman suffrage, for fear of the radical politics of the leadership taking over the country was misguided and self-defeating.[32]

Ryan's collected essays, first published in various scholarly and semipopular journals between 1909 and 1918, bring us to the eve of the Nineteenth Amendment passage and the conclusion of this chapter. Those of the American Catholic hierarchy who had opposed giving the vote to women did a quick about-face when the amendment passed in 1920. Their unanimous, if at times begrudging, endorsement of woman suffrage imparted to the American Catholic critique of the woman question an appearance of solidarity that it had never previously possessed (and actually still lacked).

If this exploration of Catholic voices on the subject of woman proves anything, it is that the democratic context of American society and Catholic women's experience of themselves in that society favored the emergence of a multiplicity of views on this as on many other issues. Diverse opinions flourished among Catholic clergy and laity, women and men, in the presence of a rich tradition and in the absence of any coherent, official church teaching on woman as well as in response to expanding opportunities for women in the nineteenth and early twentieth centuries.

Advice literature written for the laity cast an aura of rightness and necessity over the domestic role of woman, an aura only partially dispelled by later Catholic proponents of an enlarged sphere of action for the devout sex. Advice literature written for the clergy, in the form of manuals of pastoral theology and the like, cast a pall of suspicion over women in the world.

At the same time, a breakthrough was achieved in the growing acceptance of higher education as a necessity for women and the founding of the first Catholic colleges for women. Woman in the convent constituted an ambiguous factor in the Catholic approach to the woman question—the nun's record of past and present accomplishment was a bright jewel in the church's crown, its brilliance often blinding commentators to the lack of progress in church and society toward full equality of the sexes. A beginning was made, chiefly through advocacy of protective legislation and suffrage, toward recognition of woman's need and right to be in the marketplace. Her sexual freedom, seen by later feminists to be a concomitant right, had yet to emerge as the polarizing issue it was to become among American Catholic feminists.

CHAPTER
2
Women in the Convent

Mary Ewens, O.P.

*O*n May 1, 1980, the statue of a nun, dressed in her habit, kneeling, with hands clasped in prayer, was dedicated in Statuary Hall, in the nation's capital. It was the figure of Mother Joseph Periseau, a Sister of Providence, who led a band of five pioneer sisters from their Montreal motherhouse to Fort Vancouver, Washington Territory, in 1856. Beneath the statue is the inscription, "She made monumental contributions to health care, education, and social works throughout the Northwest." If we substitute the word *country* for *Northwest,* we can say that this statue could represent all of the sisters who have pursued their lives of prayer and good works in America from the founding of the country until the present day.

Several chapters in this book refer to the ideal of "true womanhood," which was held up for the emulation of nineteenth-century American women. For Catholic women who did not wish to be wives and mothers, with all that those roles entailed, there was another option that conferred an even higher status: they could enter the convent. The story of the women who chose this path must play an important part in any chronicle of those who helped to form the Catholic community in America. Where did the Catholic women, who were supposed to be the moral centers of their homes, instructors of their children, and inspiration of their husbands, learn the lessons they were to teach? Often it was from sisters or from women who had learned them from sisters. But the influence of sisters on American

Catholic life extended far beyond the sacred precincts of the home—into every area where there was need or ignorance or suffering.

We speak of the Catholic church as a "pilgrim church," and this image resonates on several levels. Its pilgrim people are people on the way, passing through the nations and cultures and epochs of this world with no abiding city here, but headed for the eternal kingdom. The church should not be the captive of any one period or culture, but at home in all of them. However, for many centuries the church has been strongly influenced by Western European culture and the mores of certain historical periods. A portion of the story of American sisters is that of a struggle to develop a form of religious life that would be compatible with the church's expectations—tainted as they were by undue emphasis on particular periods and cultures—and with American life in the various epochs of its history.

This chapter will examine several stages in this struggle while also discussing the many ways in which sisters contributed to the building up of the American Catholic community. I estimate, based on the *Catholic Directory* figures of 1,344 sisters in 1850, 40,340 in 1900, and 177,354 in 1963, that possibly as many as 220,000 sisters have served the church in America since the foundation of the republic. Generalizations about trends and sketches of a few representative figures will have to serve to indicate what the experience and contribution of these sisters might have been. My discussion will begin with the period 1727–1829, continue through the nineteenth century, and end with an assessment of events that took place in the twentieth century.[1]

THE BEGINNINGS, 1727–1829

> It is scarcely possible to realize how contagious even to the clergy and to men otherwise well disposed are the principles of freedom and independence imbibed by all the pores in these United States. Hence, I have always been convinced that practically all the good to be hoped for must come from the congregations or religious Orders among which flourish strict discipline.
>
> > Bishop Louis William DuBourg
> > to Cardinal Peter Caprano
> > of the Congregation of the Propaganda, 1826.[2]

In his frustration in trying to cope with the American milieu, Archbishop DuBourg voiced the quintessential complaint that Europeans have continued to make about the American church. In looking to the discipline of religious orders and congregations as a countervailing force to pernicious American tendencies, he points up a basic misunderstanding that has plagued the American church from his day to ours. In the dichotomy that characterizes his worldview, American freedom and independence are dangerous tendencies and religious life, with its understanding of the "correct" Western European way to do things, is the only antidote. Implicit in his statement is the idea that religious life could never join forces with American freedom and independence to form a new, vital, and valid expression of that ancient institution. Yet, that is precisely the challenge that American sisters have faced from their first foundation until now.

John Carroll, the first American bishop, was well aware of the context of American values and the nuances that the establishment of a convent would have among the mostly Protestant and English citizenry of the new nation. Since the abolition of convents and monasteries in England by Henry VIII in the sixteenth century, convents had been "foreign" institutions associated with many of the evils attributed to the Catholic church. Carroll saw education as the great need of the church in America and realized that convents might be more palatable to Protestant America if they could be seen to be actively contributing to the common good.

Father John Thorpe wrote to him from Rome in 1788 noting that "a house of Ursuline nuns, or of any other who by institute make a profession of educating female youth, might be of singular advantage in the provinces contiguous to your own residence. If means can be procured for settling both Theresians and Ursulines, perhaps it would be admissible to bring in the latter before the others on account of their immediate visible utility."[3] If only Theresians came, he noted, they would have to become schoolmistresses. Ursulines had come to New Orleans in 1727, but they would not become a part of the United States until the Louisiana Purchase of 1803. In the meantime, American women who had joined a Belgian Theresian (Carmelite) community in Hoogstraeten, were alerted by an American relative that "now is your time to found in this country for peace is declared and Religion is free."[4] Impelled, no doubt, by fears generated by the French Revolution as well as a longing to minister in the new democracy, three members of the Matthews family and one English nun founded the first convent on American soil at Port Tobacco, Charles County, Maryland, in 1790.

They were the first of thousands of sisters who would make that journey across the Atlantic, and their experiences presaged those of all who would follow. Aware of the precarious state of religion in a continent ravaged by revolutionary fervor and hostility toward popish institutions, these women traveled incognito, or tried to. They used the names "Mrs. Matthews," "Miss Matthews," and "Miss Nellie." Mother Clare Joseph Dickinson noted in her diary that she looked extraordinarily fine in her silk petticoat and chintz jacket, but the women were ridiculed in the streets of Amsterdam, and their ship's captain reported that he had four escaped nuns on board, so their dress was not exactly *à la mode!*

John Carroll knew that Carmelites led a strictly cloistered life of contemplative prayer, but he was acutely aware of the need for schools in the young church of this vast republic, and wrote to Rome requesting permission for them to pursue this work. "Their convent would be a far greater benefit in the future if a school for the training of girls in piety and learning were begun by them," he wrote.[5] This is the first of many instances in which bishops—or the sisters themselves—would seek to modify constitutions to meet the needs of the American milieu. Very often it was the local bishop or pastor who tried to pressure sisters into adapting their rules, but Carroll went to the Roman Congregation of the Propaganda, which had jurisdiction over American church affairs until the early twentieth century.

Many assume that nuns would be powerless against an influential bishop in an encounter with Rome, but this was not the case in this instance or in many other differences of opinion between sisters and male clerics. The right—and obligation—of sisters to live according to their constitutions was generally upheld by Roman authorities. Cardinal Giacomo Antonelli wrote that they could be "exhorted not to refuse" to undertake the work of education, but were "not to be urged to undertake the care of young girls against their Rule."[6] The members of this first American religious community for women exercised their rights to continue in the lifestyle to which they had dedicated themselves, despite the powerful pressures which were exerted to get them to change it. Carroll must have been chagrined when he wrote of them to his friend, Father Charles Plowden,

> They have multiplied themselves considerably and give much edification by their retirement and total seclusion from the world, and I doubt not the efficacy of their prayers in drawing down blessings on us all; but they will not concern themselves in the business of female education, though the late Pope, soon after their arrival, recommended it earnestly to them by a letter sent to me by Cardinal Antonelli.[7]

This question of how best to live religious life in America is one that vexed most communities and many bishops and pastors. Sometimes clerics may have been right in urging changes, as were sisters when they sought dispensations from their European motherhouses. In other cases, there seems to have been undue interference in the internal affairs of a community in matters that only the sisters themselves could decide. Very often, the American sisters had to reluctantly withdraw from the jurisdiction of their European motherhouses, but in other instances, it was the motherhouse itself that cut the ties.

When we are dealing with over 200,000 sisters in 400 independent communities, simple generalizations will not suffice.

When Elizabeth Seton established the first indigenous community of American sisters at Emmitsburg, Maryland, in 1809, there were powerful pressures from the French émigré priests who advised her to adopt the rule of Saint Vincent de Paul's French Daughters of Charity, and even to affiliate with that community. This convert and mother of five children, who was living in Italy when her husband died, had some experience of European religious life. She realized when she studied the rule of these sisters that it could not be used successfully for her community unless it were adapted to American needs.

She and Bishop Carroll both realized from the very initiation of religious life for women in America that it had to be uniquely American if it was to serve the American church. He noted this very explicitly when he wrote:

> At the very institution of Emmitsburg, though it was strongly contended for its being entirely conformable to and the same with the Institute of St. Vincent de Paul, yet this proposal was soon and wisely abandoned for causes which arose out of distance, different manners, and habits of the two countries, France and the United States.[8]

This was a lesson that many other communities, whether founded in America or established from Canada or Europe, would learn only through slow and painful stages. Indeed, this question of the appropriate adaptation of religious life to various cultures and milieus is one that continues to concern the Congregation for Religious and Secular Institutes.

Both the Ursulines, whose New Orleans foundation of 1727 became a part of the United States, and the Emmitsburg Daughters of Charity established precedents for American sisterhoods that became normative for the communities that came after them. The Ursulines established a boarding school or select academy for the daughters of the upper classes, both Protestant and Catholic, and free schools for the poor. When necessity demanded it, they nursed in the military hospital; they even brought General Jackson's wounded troops into the convent precincts to nurse them after the Battle of New Orleans. They took in the orphans, rehabilitated girls and women of ill repute, and instructed blacks and Indians. The superior of their French motherhouse probably did not foresee such a wide scope of activity for her sisters when they first set out for the New World, but these pilgrims were obviously attuned to the need to adapt to new situations encountered along the way. These sisters sought, and received, assurances from President Jefferson that they would be allowed to practice their religion in peace before deciding to live on American soil. Mother Seton's sisters also opened "pay schools" and "free schools," cared for orphans, and nursed the sick.

This practice of running two kinds of schools represents a distinctly American development. In Europe, convents and monasteries usually received dowries from those who joined them, as well as endowments, gifts of land, etcetera, from wealthy patrons. Active sisters and cloistered nuns could be supported by the income from this endowment, and could thus serve the poor gratis. In America, there were few wealthy Catholics who could endow convents, so sisters had to find other ways of supporting themselves. Sisters often ran farms to provide food for themselves and their charges, spun cloth and sewed for themselves and others, and charged tuition in schools patronized by the wealthy. Several communities whose rules stipulated that they would work only for the poor had to change their rules in order to survive. A band of French Poor Clare nuns, who landed in Baltimore in 1793 but failed to adjust to the American milieu, tried an interesting way of supplementing their income, as is reflected in a Georgetown newspaper advertisement of March 8, 1799:

> MADAME DE LA MARCHE also informs the public that she has Excellent Waters for the care of almost all kinds of sore eyes. There are bottles at half a dollar; and others at three-quarters of a dollar according to the kinds of sores they are to be applied to. Directions will be given with bottles. She has also salves for the care of different sorts of sores, hurts, wounds, etc.[9]

How were these sisters able to run farms, make their own clothing, provide food for all in their care, and teach in the schools besides? All but one of the communities that survived in this period had the help of slaves brought as part of a dowry or given as an American form of endowment. When they did the farming and household tasks performed by lay sisters or servants in European convents, the burden placed on the teaching sisters was eased. The Ursulines' contract with the Company of the Indies, which arranged for their coming to New Orleans, stipulated that they would be given a plantation for their support and eight black slaves in each of the first five years. One of the pioneer sisters explained in a letter to her father, "Be not scandalized at it, for it is the fashion of the country; we are taking a Negro to wait on us."[10] In the South, this was a form of adaptation to American customs.

It would take some time before sisters and their advisers would achieve a healthy balance between manual labor, prayer, penance, and works of mercy. The Sisters of Loretto, under the guidance of their austere founder, Father Charles Nerinckx, observed silence except during the recreation hour, went barefoot from March 25 to November 1 and slept in their clothes on straw ticks spread on the bare floor. They never touched coffee, tea, or sugar.

The combination of this austere life, farming, caring for orphans, and running a school took its toll of the sisters, and other priests complained about Father Nerinckx's rule. On one mission, eleven sisters died in the first seven years. Bishop Benedict Flaget of Bardstown reported to Bishop Joseph Rosati, C. M., of Saint Louis on September 11, 1824, that,

> in the space of eleven years, we have lost twenty-four religious, and not one of them had yet reached the age of thirty years. Besides, of the eighty religious of the same family that we have in Kentucky, there are at present thirty-eight who have bad health and who are perhaps not yet four years in vows. I learn that in your convent you have five or six whose health is almost ruined. All these deaths and other illnesses so multiplied, do they not prove . . . that the rules are too . . . austere . . .?[11]

After the founder's death, the rule was revised and the ecclesiastical superior, in an effort to rid the sisters of the austere spirit Nerinckx had bequeathed to them, ordered all of his writings burned. Rome had also suggested modification of the rule, and after it had been accomplished, Cardinal Fesch wrote to Rosati from there: "Would to heaven it had been in your power to do so more speedily; perhaps the health and life of many sisters who died prematurely would have been preserved."[12]

The Dominican sisterhood, which was founded in Kentucky in 1822, experienced another kind of lack of balance that would characterize many American communities until well into the twentieth century. Dominican Father Samuel T. Wilson, their founder, definitely intended that this group should belong to the active "Third Order" branch of Dominican sisters, not the cloistered, strictly contemplative "Second Order" of nuns, and this is mentioned in a papal rescript, a letter to the master general of the Order, and a letter from the vicar general. Yet, they were given a rule intended for cloistered Second Order nuns. Besides regular hours of prayer during the day, they rose at midnight to pray. In addition, they taught school, worked in the fields, and spun cloth for additional income. When a Spanish Dominican who had no understanding of American life ordered them to disband, they refused. The gradual acquisition of slaves brought as dowry eased the physical burdens on the sisters, but the ambiguity of their situation would continue for many more decades.

Canon law recognized only one form of religious life for women, that of cloistered, contemplative nuns with solemn vows, as an authentic "state of perfection." Yet dozens of communities of sisters active in works of mercy and bound by simple vows came into being after the French Revolution. Very often these sisters themselves and the clerics who advised them looked to the "authentic" religious life of the solemnly professed nun as the ideal toward which they should strive. The result was the same mixture of monastic practices, long hours of prayer, etc., coupled with the charitable works of the active life that we have seen above. Not until 1900 would Rome recognize active communities that taught, nursed, and helped the needy outside their convent walls as authentic religious within the church.

Of twelve groups that attempted to establish religious communities for women in America between 1790 and 1830, all six started by Americans survived into the 1980s, but only one founded by Europeans did. Americans knew the culture into which they were inserting this age-old institution; for Europeans, the adjustment proved too difficult. They were pilgrims on the way who were unprepared or unable to enter fully into the new situations they encountered. The one community that succeeded did so, I think, because its foundress, who was still alive, took the broad view that religious life is not culture bound, but can and should find a way to acclimate itself anywhere.

The Congregation of the Religious of the Sacred Heart was only eighteen years old when Mother Philippine Duchesne led the first band of missionaries to Saint Louis in 1818. Concern over the extent to which they should or could adapt their French customs to the American milieu occupied this intrepid leader from the day of their arrival. The canon law requirement that sisters should remain always behind the walls of their convent precincts—the rule of cloister—was impossible to fulfill. "There is not a wall within a thousand miles of here," she wrote to the French motherhouse.[13]

Mother Madeleine Sophie Barat, the foundress, assured the sisters that adaptations to a new culture were to be expected. The imposition of a rigid French curriculum on American school children caused much dissatisfaction and gradually, after considerable discussion on both sides of the Atlantic, concessions were made. Unity with the French motherhouse was maintained and the community established solid foundations on both the upper and lower Mississippi.

In this early period of American history, when both the new republic and the Catholic church were struggling to establish themselves, women religious quickly developed patterns of adjustment to the American milieu that would characterize their lives for many decades. They also faced the major issues that would concern American religious and mark their history into the twentieth century.

NINETEENTH-CENTURY GROWTH AND DEVELOPMENT, 1830–1900

The period from 1830 to 1900 was one of great growth and development in American religious life for women. The number of sisters increased from 1,344 in 1850 to 40,340 by 1900. One hundred six new communities were established, twenty-three of them by Americans, eight from Canadian motherhouses, and seventy-five from European foundations. The latter figure speaks volumes. As millions of immigrants poured into the country seeking relief from Irish potato famines or refuge from the German *Kulturkampf*, and religious, economic, and political freedom, the church was hard-pressed to meet their needs and actively recruited help from Europe.

Each new community that arrived from there had to go through the cycle of bewilderment at American customs, efforts to cope with the language, and problems with clerics and motherhouse officials over adaptation of their rule to the new situations they were encountering. Sometimes a community could only succeed by severing all ties with the European motherhouse that refused to sanction an accommodationist posture to the New World. For some, the adjustment to America was eased by the fact that they worked among their compatriots and could retain their language and customs until an influx of postulants of other nationalities or the insistence of a local bishop or pastor forced them to reconsider their options.

Anti-Catholic sentiments flared in the 1830s when women like Maria Monk, who purported to be an ex-nun, took to the lecture platform and published best-sellers with titles such as *Awful Disclosures of the Hotel Dieu* or *Convent Life Exposed*. Sisters, who seemed to bigots to be the living embodiment of all that they despised and feared in Roman Catholicism, were the chief targets of these anti-Catholic tirades. Immoralities that supposedly went on in convents were described in graphic detail. It was said that sisters were held in them against their will, a curtailment of freedom that was particularly repugnant to Americans. Sisters were insulted and spat upon in the streets, and their convents were stoned and even burned to the ground, as happened in Charlestown, Massachusetts, in 1834. Sisters learned to don secular clothing when going out of their convents. When the Know-Nothing party united many who were uneasy with the influx of immigrants in the 1850s, accusing them of diluting and undermining American values, nunnery inspection laws were passed. These subjected convents to surprise visits from legislators, who searched for evidence of un-American practices.[14]

Communities that began with small numbers and few resources slowly grew and established firmer foundations as the century wore on by dint of their own hard work, the respect they won from those who could help them, and by the exercise of great ingenuity. Communities that grew quickly faced the constant need to expand and replace their motherhouses and other institutions. Fires and other disasters destroyed what had been painstakingly accumulated.

Private lessons in music (and sometimes in art) were a major source of income. Sisters worked in stores and factories (even making shot-bags for a penny apiece during the Mexican-American War), ran laundries, and opened dress and flower shops. Some printed and bound books. Begging trips were common, either in Europe or America, as were appeals to German, French, or Bavarian groups that funded missionary work, and even to the members of the European nobility.

The Civil War provided the occasion for sisters to completely reverse the general public's image of them and of the Catholic church. Recalling the excellent service rendered by the sisters who had nursed with Florence Nightingale in the military hospitals of the Crimea, and the good will that was generated by it, church leaders offered the services of the sisters as nurses in military hospitals. It is estimated that 640 of the 3,200 Civil War nurses were nuns. They came from twenty different communities and nursed in hospitals and camps, on battlefields and hospital boats in eighteen states and the District of Columbia. The Sisters of the Holy Cross earned the title of the first Navy nurses for their services on board the *Red Rover*.

The names of several sisters became bywords in American homes and newspapers. Sister Anthony O'Connell of the Cincinnati Sisters of Charity, for example, personally knew Generals Grant, Sherman, Sheridan, McClellan, and Rosecrans, as well as Jefferson Davis. One soldier wrote of her in his diary:

> Amid this sea of blood, she performed the most revolting duties for those poor soldiers. She seemed like a ministering angel and many a young soldier owes his life to her care and charity. Happy was the soldier who, wounded and bleeding, had her near him to whisper words of consolation and courage. She was reverenced by blue and gray, Protestant and Catholic alike, and we conferred on her the title of the "Florence Nightingale of America." Her name became a household word in every section of the North and South.[15]

Thousands of soldiers who had previously known only what bigots had told them of nuns now experienced their ministrations firsthand. Daily contact with these women, who came to be hailed everywhere as Angels of Mercy, convinced many of the value of Catholicism and the virtues and principles that it promoted. Sisters had single-handedly changed public opinion, and the religious habit, which had earlier evoked hatred and vituperation when worn in public, was now revered by all as a badge of honor.

It is easy to get caught up in generalizations and statistics when dealing with a period in which there was as much growth and activity as there was in the nineteenth-century church. These do not convey what individual lives were like, however, or the extent to which some of their sisters were trying to achieve "true womanhood" in their Victorian homes.

That the convent was a perfect place for Catholic women to develop and use all of their talents and abilities is evident when one examines the lives of individual sisters in detail. A number of remarkable women whose names we know, and thousands more whose identities will be discovered only upon a closer scrutiny of archival resources, peopled nineteenth century American convents: Mother Theodore Guérin, foundress of the Sisters of Providence in Indiana; Mother Caroline Friess, who got her German motherhouse to give her a free hand in planting the School Sisters of Notre Dame in America and who personally gave the veil to over two thousand American women; Mother Cornelia Connolly, who separated from her husband so that he could become a priest and then founded a community of her own; Mother Angela Gillespie of Notre Dame; Mother Katherine Drexel, whose fortune supported her community's work for blacks and Indians; Mother Theresa Maxis, who was one of the founding sisters of the first community for black women and then one peopled mostly by whites; Mother Catherine Sacred White Buffalo of the Congregation of American Sisters; Mother Joseph Periseau, whose skill in designing and building her community's institutions gained her the recognition of the American Institute of Architects; Saint Frances Xavier Cabrini who founded a community to provide for the needs of Italian immigrants. The list could go on and on.

Let me indicate the scope for personal experience, use of one's talents, and creative service to the church through a more detailed discussion of the life of just one of the thousands of sisters who worked in nineteenth-century America, Mother Austin Carroll, Sister of Mercy. Her story has its unique twists, as would that of any one of the forty thousand sisters of this period, but it is also representative of the kinds of experiences that were common to many. As Mother Joseph Periseau is honored for her monumental contributions to health care, education, and social works in the Northwest, Mother Austin Carroll should receive the same accolades for similar work in the South.

An outline of her accomplishments contains enough material to fill at least three very full lifetimes. A discussion of her work will show many of the ways in which sisters built up the Christian community and responded creatively to the needs of the people around them. In her person we see a religious lifestyle that seems well adapted to the American scene. John Carroll and others thought it was important that sisters be actively engaged in serving their fellow Americans—and be seen to be so engaged. The works of the Sisters of Mercy certainly fulfilled that requirement.

In the introduction to her translation of the life of Blessed Margaret Mary Alocoque (as she was then called), Mother Austin reflected on qualities found in sisters throughout history:

> Not only do we find the chronicle of religious congregations . . . [replete] with everything gentle and holy, we find, too, among these . . . exotics of the Church—when occasion requires—a patient endurance, an invincible energy, an unconquerable activity, which go far to prove that the term "weaker sex" is a definition that has nothing to do with the soul.[17]

She herself exemplified these qualities that she had noted in the lives of other sisters. Born in County Tipperary in 1835, she joined the Sisters of Mercy in Cork in 1853 after having qualified for the state teaching certificate. For three years she was under the tutelage of Mother Josephine Warde, a personal friend of Catherine McAuley, the Mercy foundress, and one who taught all to admire and love her.[18]

Austin Carroll preserved and passed on the spirit of the foundress to other Mercy sisters when she wrote a biography of her based on careful research and primary resources. She also collected the annals of Mercy convents all over the world and published them in four volumes, thus making known the ways in which Mercy sisters adapted Catherine McAuley's principles to diverse situations. It would be difficult to overestimate the importance of Carroll's work in fostering an authentic "Mercy spirit" among all of Catherine McAuley's daughters.[19]

During her formation years in Cork, Austin worked in various types of schools and gained experience in the broad variety of social works carried on by the Sisters of Mercy, whose policy was to help the needy to help themselves. In 1856, she was sent to the American mission in Providence, Rhode Island, and assigned to teach in academies, parochial schools, industrial schools, and Sunday schools in several branch convents. She also helped with a soup kitchen, a home for women, a day-care center for children of working women, and sodalities for girls and boys. A brief interlude in Chicago in 1864 gave her the opportunity to visit and nurse wounded Civil War veterans from both the North and the South.

In 1869, Mother Austin was assigned to join the pioneer group of Mercy sisters founding a convent in New Orleans, and thus began her work in the South, which would continue until her death in Mobile in 1909. Her "invincible energy" and "unconquerable activity" are reflected in the accomplishments of her first months there. In her first three months, she inaugurated regular visits to the sick, established a prison ministry in two penal institutions, opened a home for women and an employment bureau, set up a pantry with free food and clothing for the poor, and taught French in the parish school.

In her second three months, she and the other sisters gained their first experience in what would become a perennial and very costly work for them: the nursing of the victims of the periodic yellow fever epidemics. She took in girls orphaned by the epidemic, opened a dispensary with free medicine, and set up a chapel in the prison. The Mercy spirit, which stressed responsiveness to the needy in every situation, enabled her to move into action as soon as she had sized up a situation.

After three years in New Orleans, when several sisters had contracted yellow fever and died and the superior had succumbed to tuberculosis, Mother Austin was the only one of the original sisters left. Fortunately, her personality and the good works of the sisters had drawn many young women of New Orleans to join the Mercy community. Carroll instilled in them the spirit of Mother Catherine McAuley and they followed her own example as well, and together they made a tremendous contribution to the church and the people of the New Orleans area. By the time of Mother Austin's death in 1909, they had opened sixty-five schools, not only in Louisiana, but also in Florida, Alabama, Mississippi, and Belize (Central America). They had also established fourteen convents, thirty-eight libraries (one of Carroll's favorite projects), and nine residences for needy groups, such as orphans, the elderly, and working women.

Mother Austin always tried to respect local mores. In that era of segregation, this meant that she had to set up separate schools for blacks and mulattoes if she was going to educate them. This she did in Florida, Alabama, Mississippi, and Louisiana. (American sisters from the very beginning had tried to provide for blacks, slave or free, but often, local pressures forced these schools to close. As early as 1824, black women were received as postulants by the Sisters of Loretto. Later, three communities were founded specifically for blacks, three for Indians, and one for Eskimos).

Generally, the Sisters of Mercy worked with the poor, but they, like most other communities, needed the income from "pay schools" or "select schools," often elitist academies, to support their works for the indigent. Mother Austin made all of her schools as democratic as possible, stressing enrichment in the arts and other subjects for all, but she, too, had to follow the example of so many other sisters who had adjusted to the American economic situation by opening academies. Some sisters objected, but she pointed out that even the Mercy foundress had participated in this work among the upper classes.

Always on the lookout to spot new trends that would affect women,

Carroll planned a college for them long before most other communities had begun to consider this work. In 1887, she purchased land and put up a building for this purpose, but the local clergy, who were aghast at the idea of the church promoting higher education for women, succeeded in terminating the project. Carroll had much to suffer because she was ahead of the times and full of the Mercy spirit of responding immediately to local needs and always being alert, looking to the needs of the future. In this case, the ideal of "true womanhood" obviously dominated the thinking of the New Orleans clergy, and "true women" did not need higher education.

Prison work always held a special place in Carroll's heart; she was particularly effective in working with those on death row, many of whom asked to be baptized. She pressured officials to make separate provision for women prisoners and got them to hire female wardens for them. She taught religion and other Rs in evening classes at the newsboys' homes, thus providing for yet another group whose needs had not been met.

The House of Mercy for women was an extremely effective vehicle for meeting contemporary needs. Here immigrant women, widows, and others were taught job-related skills according to the needs of the marketplace. Jobs were then found for them through the home's employment bureau. The goal was training that would lead to self-sufficiency. The record of the New Orleans House of Mercy would compare favorably, I think, with contemporary programs of the 1980s. At the end of two years, 600 women had been placed in jobs, 240 of whom had lived at the home.

I have noted many ways in which sisters sought income that would support their works for the poor. Austin Carroll was a consummate expert on a way of earning income that was used by some other sisters as well: She was a tireless writer and translator of books, and supported her sisters' works of charity for forty years through her pen. Her life of Mother Catherine McAuley brought in more money than any of her other publications. She published some forty other books and wrote innumerable articles for newspapers and magazines. Children's stories, translations of spiritual works from French or Spanish, lives of the saints and historical essays all flowed from her pen. At the World's Exposition held in New Orleans in 1884–85, twenty-two of the forty-five works on display in the women's literary department were by her.

In a long dispute with some German priests and a bishop who lodged false charges against her in Rome, Mother Austin suffered much while trying to remain a true daughter of the church. Both she and her sisters spoke out with great vigor—too much, the clerics said—in defense of their rights. Some of the charges stemmed from differing

American and German expectations about the role of women and the way religious women should conduct themselves—the latter being a perennial topic for discussion in the American church and the European church as well. Though we cannot examine the details of the dispute here, we can admire the sisters' spunk and learn something about the clashes that did occur from time to time.

Carroll's pride in her Irish heritage was a cause for antipathy among the German priests in the parish in which she was serving. So were the customs of the Sisters of Mercy, which differed markedly from those of the German School Sisters of Notre Dame, who were required to ask permission of their Redemptorist director every time they stepped outside their convent walls. First, the Redemptorists tried to change the Mercy rule, and then they cut the sisters' salaries. When they eliminated them all together, the sisters protested vigorously. The Redemptorists complained that the sisters were too forthright and lacked proper respect for priests. In the eyes of some, it seems, "true womanhood" carried certain connotations for sisters' conduct, or should we call it "true sisterhood"?

When Bishop Francis Xavier Leray, who sided with the Germans, told the sisters in a talk in their chapel that his predecessor had made incorrect decisions in their regard, Mother Austin was incensed. She reported to her friend, Bishop James O'Connor of Omaha, what happened afterward:

> I went up and he heard me, but wouldn't give in. I said I couldn't allow Archbishop Perché to be so spoken of in our chapel, that he had always been a Friend and a father to us, that he was a gentleman and a scholar, thoroughly versed in everything related to religious life. "Now," said I, "if such a man gave us wrong directions, what guarantee have we that Your Grace will give us the right ones?" It would take a volume to describe the scene—all the sisters were crying and sobbing. His Grace abused them soundly, not a kind word or even a courteous word. Yet they had done all that Rome had asked.[20]

When Austin Carroll was under attack, her sisters defended her in letters to the bishop and even sent a petition to Pope Leo XIII. They pointed up the importance of fair play, the right to confront one's accusers, and other basic rights deemed sacred by Americans, as can be seen, for example, in a letter to the Irish Bishop Kirby, their agent in Rome:

> For the thirty-two years of her religious life, she has devoted her best energies to the spread of our holy religion, especially in providing education for the poorest and most abandoned classes. . . . You will understand, my Lord, how strange it will seem to Americans accustomed to "fair play" that . . . [anyone] would condemn unheard the Mother and Foundress of our eight convents. . . . It is for us, her spiritual children,

to demand that justice which we have heard Rome always shows to the weak and persecuted.[21]

There is a very modern tone in several of the letters exchanged during this period in Austin Carroll's life. They tell us, however, that the struggle to gain Vatican acknowledgment of, and acquiescence to, values that Americans hold dear is an old one. After years of investigations carried on by various groups and individuals, Rome exonerated Austin Carroll; some of the decisions in her favor were shared with others, but not with her. The original documents have only come to light recently, thanks to the indefatigable efforts of her biographer, Sister Mary Hermenia Muldrey, R.S.M.

THE TWENTIETH CENTURY—MATURITY AND RENEWAL

When we consider major events in twentieth-century American history, developments in the American church, and what has transpired in religious life, we find a plethora of material to deal with: two world wars, a depression in between, and a controversial undeclared war afterward, plus a battle for civil rights that had profound effects on American life. The church came of age with the election of John Fitzgerald Kennedy as president in 1960, and it began to recognize and support new roles for the laity as a result of the Second Vatican Council.

I think the changes in the lives of sisters in the twentieth century have been more drastic than those in the lives of married women. The latter have gone from a fairly restricted life in the home to membership in women's groups, to the suffragette movement, to the lay apostolate, the Christian Family Movement, cursillos and lay ministry as directors of religious education, teachers in Catholic schools, and various parish ministries.

Catholic sisters with an active apostolate were finally recognized by the church as "real religious" (even though they lack the qualities previously considered indispensable for this approbation—solemn vows and papal cloister) in 1900 with the promulgation of the bull *Conditae a Christo*. Anthropologists tell us that basic changes in a culture take a long time to take effect, and if pursued precipitously, they take an inordinate human toll.

History has shown that it can take centuries for the church to assimilate profound cultural change. This is exemplified in the Dominican Order and its understanding of its charism and life-style. Saint Dominic founded the Order for preaching, a role previously restricted only to bishops. Dominic wanted all aspects of Dominican life to support this preaching mission and moved his friars out of monasteries and into "convents," where they would come together after having been out preaching. Observances, such as those in monasteries that professed stability and had liturgical prayer as their major work, were not important to him if they did not support the life of preaching. Yet, in every reform of the Order since Dominic's death in 1221, monastic observances rather than the preaching of the friars have been stressed. It is only since the Second Vatican Council that the founder's charism has come to be understood in a new way. Active Dominican sisterhoods in America also stressed monastic observances even though they might interfere with their major work of teaching.[22]

A similar thing has happened with the church's understanding of the charism of active congregations of sisters with simple vows. *Conditae a Christo* approved a partial cloister for them, though this concept was really part of the monastic life of cloistered sisters and had no place in the newer type of community. Practices related to cloister, such as not going out alone, control of all contact with the outside world, etc., continued to be held up as norms for active sisters. After the promulgation of the New Code of Canon Law in 1918, such a "cloister mentality" became even more pronounced. In the 1920s, 1930s, and 1940s, sisters were warned to restrict contact with the outside world as much as possible. Newspapers, radios, libraries, and so on, were seen as dangerous distractions, as were various kinds of public events and meetings. The eyes of the sisters were turned inward and the world outside convent walls was full of snares.[23]

The idea of sisterhoods that would be actively engaged in works of charity outside the convent had been around for several centuries, and Mary Warde, Nano Nagle, and Angela Merici all tried to found communities with this kind of mission. But the church was not ready to assimilate this idea, and they were not successful. Vincent de Paul warned his Daughters of Charity not to call themselves religious, for he knew they, too, would be forced behind cloister walls and kept from doing their proper work if they were so identified. The church is still trying to assimilate the true role of active religious congregations.

A major theme in the twentieth-century history of American sisterhoods is that of the shift of the locus of religious life from the cloister to the contemporary world. An important force in the development of a clearer understanding of the mission of active sisters has been that of education. Sisters needed to be educated themselves if they were to educate others, so continuing education has been a constant thrust in their lives. Often civil regulations have required certification and there was constant concern about and provision for courses on Saturdays and in the summers so that the sisters' schools would not be found lacking.

As previously noted, Mother Austin Carroll envisioned the establishment of a Catholic college for women in New Orleans in the 1880s. The members of other congregations involved in education were also reading the signs of the times and making plans to provide Catholic equivalents of the colleges for women that had been begun at Mount Holyoke, Bryn Mawr, and elsewhere. The establishment of the colleges of Trinity in Washington, D.C. and Notre Dame of Baltimore spearheaded the move of American sisters into the ministry of higher education. Today they sponsor over 125 institutions in this field, a phenomenon unique to America. They share ideas and other resources through the Neylan Conference and are planning to join forces in order to better serve the needs of their own constituencies and those of women of the Third World.

As congregations planned to open colleges, they prepared for entry into this new apostolate at the beginning of the twentieth century by providing, first of all, for the education of the sisters who would staff them. It seemed natural at the time to send sisters to study at the leading universities of Europe and America. (Later, many bishops would object to the attendance of sisters at "secular" institutions.) Sisters involved in advanced study became aware of the latest developments in many fields of knowledge and frequently surprised their professors with their intellectual and scholarly abilities.

To listen to or read the accounts of the experiences of these sisters is to gain a new insight into the special contributions of the American sisterhoods, as well as some understanding of the growing gap between their spiritual development and that of European sisterhoods. Sister Edward Blackwell, for example, studied musical composition under Nadia Boulanger in Paris in the 1930s, was a friend of Stravinsky, and had to carry a special papal bull with her when she studied at the St. Cecilia Conservatory in Rome because the Vatican had decreed that any Catholic crossing its threshold would be excommunicated. Sister Mary Madeleva's autobiography, *My First Seventy Years*, gives a delightful picture of the many contacts made by this president of St. Mary's College at Notre Dame. The Dominican Sisters, who in 1947 established a graduate school of fine arts in the Florentine villa given to Pius XII by Myron Taylor, experienced the hardships of postwar Europe, but formed warm friendships to counter the bitter cold. They regularly entertained diplomats, members of the hierarchy, the mayor of Florence, and ex-Queen Helen of Romania; Harry Truman played on their piano and Giovanni Montini signed the guest book. Sisters who received intellectual stimulation in experiences like these passed that spark along to their students, their sisters, and their congregations.

In the meantime, the kind of clerical resistance to higher education for Catholic women that Carroll had experienced continued. No doubt some of it was based on the oft-repeated notion that women's brains were inferior to men's and their proper roles concerned childrearing. The Catholic University of America, whose problems intrude so on late nineteenth-century American Catholic history, had no place for sisters. A few professors deigned to meet with them at Trinity College on weekends to share their lecture notes, but it was an uphill struggle to get this university, sponsored by the American hierarchy, to admit sisters to regular classes. When no Catholic institution would allow women into its theology classes, Saint Mary's of Notre Dame offered undergraduate and graduate courses to serve their needs. Today the Vatican is still concerned about the attendance of women at seminary theology classes and their roles in staffing seminary courses. The mindset that is ever suspicious of American ideas and innovations persists despite the impressive record of almost a century of service by American sisters in higher education.

Sisters who pursued advanced study in such fields as economics, sociology, or political science gained new insights into social problems that they had been encountering for decades on an experiential level. Their personal experience of the trauma of war, the sufferings caused by economic depressions, the struggle of the poor, and the evils of racism was supplemented by a knowledge of historical trends, the national and international extent of social ills, and various theories about ways to correct or alleviate them.

Those who came under the influence of that powerful proponent of the popes' social encyclicals, Monsignor John A. Ryan of the Social Action Department of the National Catholic Welfare Conference, were inspired to combine theory with practice. Thus did colleges sponsored by sisters emphasize responsible action for the betterment of society as an obligation of women who had the advantage of higher education. They planned lectures and conferences designed to increase the awareness of national and international problems, and attendance at them was required of all students. In the days when most students lived at the college and the sisters conversed with them over dinner, lectures and the ideas they generated sparked lively discussions. Numerous opportunities to volunteer in settlement houses, work in poor parishes, join Catholic Action cells, or explain the Catholic faith were available to Catholic college students and alumni in the 1920s, 1930s, and 1940s. The emphasis of Pius XI on Catholic Action and the Bishops' Program of Social Reconstruction provided the impetus for activities of many kinds in these decades.

I use as an example what happened at Rosary College in Chicago, but I feel certain that similar events were taking place at other Catholic colleges. Rosary students were exposed to contemporary problems in a number of ways. Faculty members took the lead in living according to the principles which they espoused. Sister Mary Ellen O'Hanlon wrote and lectured on race relations long before most people were aware of the problem. Sister Vincent Ferrer Bradford, economics and political science teacher, was in demand around the country to explain the church's teachings on the rights of labor, and began working with international peace groups in the 1920s. Indeed, the speaker at the first regional conference of the Catholic Association for International Peace, held at Rosary in 1937, was Eleanor Roosevelt.[24] Sister Thomas Aquinas O'Neill, the college president, cosponsored with Sister Madeleva a lecture series by Dorothy Day and Peter Maurin in 1933, when they were just beginning the Catholic Worker Movement. Students did street preaching in the rural South in the summer and helped in settlement houses in the winter.[25]

When sisters who were inspired by the church's social teachings and who studied the application of gospel principles to the solution of human and societal problems looked outward towards a needy world, they ran into the same basic contradiction that had plagued American sisters for centuries. The church had not come to a mature understanding of the essential character of active sisterhoods or the implications of the papal encyclicals. It continued to espouse a cloistral mentality that stressed separation from the world as the norm for sisters. It pitted a theology of transcendence against one that was incarnational and hearkened back to the old distinctions between the realms of the sacred and secular.

This created obvious tensions for sisters whose ministry and insights encouraged them to look outward toward a world that canon law said they must shun. There was confusion as to which was the "real world," that to which papal encyclicals and the bishops' social action agenda called them, or that of canon law. The same contradictions faced sisters in other ministries. Elementary and high school teachers were not encouraged to visit their students' homes and learn about factors that might impinge on school achievement or offer counsel and aid where there were problems. Sister nurses were not supposed to have anything to do with cases involving babies or obstetrics. (Indeed, there was still living in the 1960s an American Daughter of Charity who was refused admittance to both the English and French—but not the American—provinces of her community because she had been a midwife!) The monastic silence that was enjoined on so many religious for much of the day restricted the kinds of healthy interchange that give support or contribute to the deepening of a friendship.

Canon law for religious, which was the source of this contradiction and tension, was enforced rather rigidly by many superiors in the decades following its promulgation in 1918. They felt a heavy responsibility to obey the mind of the church, and had to report to Rome on the extent of their compliance every five years.

How could independent young American women fit themselves into a mold that was based on a European mindset and social conditions that dated back to the thirteenth century? It was accomplished through a whole system of control that began in the novitiate and was maintained afterwards through complex strategies. Sociologists Erving Goffman (in *Asylums*) and Helen Ebaugh (in *Out of the Cloister*) have studied techniques used to encourage the putting off of the "old self" and the taking on of a new mode of life in such institutions as prisons, mental hospitals, and communist "reeducation" camps. They have found similarities between the techniques used in these institutions and those used in convents, particularly novitiates. Removal from one's former world and support system, total dependence on those in charge, and control of all communication—including those nonverbal and verbal messages that help us to define who we are—are part of the complicated process they describe. Maintenance is achieved by restricting association to those who are a part of the system so that no questioning or contradictory voices are heard and group values are constantly reinforced. This process is similar to that popularly known as "brainwashing."

Many published accounts of novitiate experiences and personal reflections by those skilled at analyzing what happened during this period of their lives support this contention.[26] (Stories of the stages of "putting on" the new personality of one's chosen religious community while in the novitiate form an important early chapter in the genre of nuns' autobiographies.) However, the human spirit is infinitely resilient, and many young women came through this period virtually unscathed. They had chosen to enter a religious community in order to dedicate themselves to a life of prayer and good works in conformity with God's will for them. An authentic spirituality, common sense, and a sense of humor enabled them to separate the essential from the nonessential. Practices that were anachronistic or silly were looked on as part of God's will for religious. That was reason enough to carry them out, however unreasonable they might have seemed to an outsider. When women who have shared the same novitiate experiences gather for reunions, they talk about the harmful effects of what they went through, but they also regale one another with stories of subversion of the system and the triumph of high spirits and common sense. Many accepted the contradictions as part of the life and went on to develop deep spiritual lives and do excellent work for the church.

There is one group of American sisters in the early decades of the twentieth century that was able to develop a lifestyle that supported their ministry without the encumbrance of obsolete customs from other times and places. This group, the Maryknoll Sisters, members of the Catholic Foreign Mission Society of America, was founded shortly after America ceased to be mission territory in 1908. Mary Josephine Rogers, Thomas Price, and James Walsh founded this first American Catholic missionary society with branches for men and women, and chose China as their first mission territory.

The sisters began their work in South China in 1922. Unlike missionaries who establish in foreign lands the same kinds of institutions they have at home, Maryknoll studied the situation in China and pondered the best methods to use. They were aware that the church should be at home in any culture and sought appropriate ways to promote Catholicism without the trappings of Western European culture. The sisters decided to go into the villages and live among the people, explaining the Catholic faith to any who showed interest. The church was to be one of people, not buildings. The development of a native clergy would be an important priority so that the church would be seen to be compatible with Chinese culture. Gradually sodalities and Catholic Action groups would be formed to bring gospel principles to bear on contemporary problems.

The sisters could never have carried on the work that they did if they had allowed their lives to be circumscribed by the rigid rules and cloistral practices that characterized Western European religious life. It would be interesting to study archival documents and talk with survivors to discover whether the establishment of this policy in China was preceded by lengthy discussions and disagreements about the proper role of religious in China vis-à-vis canon law prescriptions.

The Maryknoll practice of going out to the people, studying their culture, and offering an appropriate response (not very different from the methods used by Austin Carroll) had a tremendous appeal to and influence on the Belgian Cardinal Leon Joseph Suenens. He saw Belgian sisters living behind their convent walls and being oblivious to the problems of the world around them. Yet there were innumerable suffering people who could have been helped by them. The Maryknoll idea gave him the impetus in the 1950s to propose a new model for the sisters of his diocese, one that he would later disseminate to sisters everywhere through his influential book, *The Nun in the World*.[27]

I have described several inward and outward thrusts that characterized American religious life for women in the twentieth century. These "pushes" toward the outer world had to be balanced by a "pull" into the safety of the cloister if the stability of the forms of religious life practiced in most convents was to be preserved. The precarious balance is just as delicate as it is in that feat of engineering skill that is a medieval cathedral. Remove the buttresses and the whole thing might collapse.

That balance was disturbed when there were pressures from two sides to remove the walls that buttressed the whole "convent culture" of the 1930s, 1940s, and 1950s. As noted above, the perpetuation of a way of life that promotes adherence to outmoded customs was dependent on a closed system in which one's contacts were carefully restricted to those who held similar values. This whole system was severely shaken by pressures from two sources that opened convents up to new ideas and critical questioning that sometimes challenged the status quo: The pope himself exerted some of the pressure; the rest came from the realization of the weaknesses in the methods used in many congregations to prepare sisters for ministry.

In 1949, Sister Madeleva presented a paper at the annual meeting of the National Catholic Education Association that questioned the way sisters were educated. It sparked widespread discussion and was reprinted under the title *The Education of Sister Lucy*. Subsequent conferences continued to search for the best way to prepare a sister for her ministry, and ultimately the Sister Formation Movement grew out of this inquiry. This questioning of the quality of the education given to sisters occurred just when Pius XII was stepping up his own campaign to get sisters and other Catholic women to become aware of the problems that afflicted the world around them. The effects of a worldwide depression followed by a cataclysmic war must surely have brought home to him the need for people of good will to bring their best efforts to bear on the search for the solution to pressing world problems.

Aware of the common problems facing religious communities and the need for a fresh impetus if age-old attitudes and customs were going to be changed, Pius XII called major superiors of religious congregations all over the world to Rome for international conferences in 1950 and 1952. Along with urgings to adapt their lives to meet contemporary needs were exhortations to provide professional education for sisters that would put them on a par with their secular counterparts. In 1952, the Conference of Major Superiors of Women was established to enable sisters to discuss together problems that individual congregations had hitherto faced alone. This organization was to become a major force in the continuing search for authentically American modes of religious life for women.

In the meantime, the discussions regarding the best ways to prepare sisters for their ministries continued. There was a tremendous influx of new members into religious communities in the years following World War II, which gave increased urgency to these discussions. Vocations to the religious life seem to increase in those places where the church has special need of them (witness the burgeoning of vocations in Africa today).

In a 1953 master's thesis done at Marquette University, Sister Mary Richardine Quirk, B.V.M., used questionnaires to elicit information from women's communities regarding current practices and problems in the education of sisters. She found that there were three crucial problems: time, lack of resources, and inadequate understanding of the problem being discussed.[28] In 1954, the Sister Formation Conference was formed under the aegis of the National Catholic Education Association. Its leader, Sister Mary Emil Penet, worked tirelessly to promote the idea that young sisters should be fully prepared for their work before they embark on it. A newsletter and annual conference provided for the sharing of ideas and expertise. There was much discussion of ways to integrate a sister's learning and lifestyle so as to eliminate the dichotomy that some experienced between the intellectual and the spiritual life.

The deep-seated mistrust of "worldly education" and "intellectual pride" that marked much of the theology and spiritual writing to which sisters were exposed had to be pointed out and dealt with. Meetings in the mid-1950s, therefore, discussed the question, Is there and should there be a tension, opposition, or dichotomy in the sister's life between her spiritual and intellectual formation, between her personal religious life and her active apostolate? Open discussion of the tension between the traditional "convent culture" and that of the intellectual milieu in which sisters prepared for their ministries opened the way for a questioning of irrelevant practices, whereupon the whole system was thrown open to critical examination and the buttresses began to crack. The effort to achieve an integration of all aspects of a sister's life certainly exposed areas of disharmony.

Sisters trained in the liberal arts with critical thinking skills and a solid historical and theological base were prepared to look at religious life and separate the essentials from the nonessentials. They could make allowances for historical circumstances, different schools of theology, and the various ideologies that have dominated the thinking of various epochs. A knowledge of developmental psychology would alert one to elements of religious life that did or did not promote a healthy personality.

It was not only the young sisters who studied the latest trends. Superiors and formation personnel had opportunities for updating in the various workshops and courses that were offered by the Sister Formation Conference, the Conference of Major Superiors of Women (CMSW), and other organizations. Thus, there existed in most congregations by the early 1960s a group of sisters who were prepared to respond to the new ideas that came out of the Second Vatican

Council (Vatican II). An awareness of the need to cleanse religious life of obsolete practices already existed. All that was needed was the willingness of the church to bring its practice into line with contemporary needs.

Few groups in the church responded to the decrees of the Second Vatican Council with the alacrity shown by American sisters. They eagerly studied each document as it was released, particularly those affecting religious. Many of them were trained to understand the theological and scriptural nuances, and they had a broad base of experience in working with the people of God. When they were asked to renew their lives by returning to the charisms of their founders, studying the signs of the times, and reflecting on ways of living gospel values in the contemporary world, they set about the task with great seriousness of purpose. The energies of whole congregations were engaged for years in the study of historical sources, the careful revision of constitutions, and consultation with experts from many fields. Finally, the struggle of sisters to reconcile religious life with American culture would be over. No longer would American freedom and independence be suspect.

While the young people were reaching out towards the sunlight of new ideas, their elders were also expanding their horizons. CMSW, Sister Formation, and other groups sponsored workshops for superiors, formation personnel, and others where contemporary theologies were explained and basic problems discussed. The whole system of convent culture that required unquestioning acceptance and reinforcement to continue in existence began to crumble. Dissatisfaction with outmoded customs and contradictory messages that made an honest living of religious life difficult led to deep questioning even before the Second Vatican Council.

When John XXIII convoked the Second Vatican Council, many sisters were ready for it. As the various Council documents appeared, they read them eagerly and discussed their implications with growing excitement. Sisters were told to return to the spirit and charism of their founders, to study the application of gospel principles to contemporary problems, and to be aware of the signs of the times. They were to experiment with constitutions that would embody these ideas and eliminate those that did not.

When American sisters, following the directives of the Council, looked around them at the contemporary world, they saw problems of racism, domestic abuse, the threat of nuclear war, the plight of migrant workers, and many others. Individual sisters responded to these problems according to their circumstances. They participated in civil rights marches, protested the Vietnam War, organized tenant groups, brought health care to the indigent, and made the option to serve the poor a top priority. The renewal of their religious lives meant that time and energy could be spent where they were most needed, and sisters were freer to respond to calls for help. Sister Mary Luke Tobin, president of the Sisters of Loretto, who was one of the fifteen auditors at the Council, describes her experience in responding to the call of the gospel as the opening of successive doors, all of which lead to Christ. In a collection of accounts of sisters' experiences in the pre- and post-Vatican II eras, one notices a sense of freedom as religious life is made more compatible with American life, and an enhancement of the self through new relationships, broader experience with the people of God, etc.[29]

Such a rapid change from a closed society to an open response to needs on all sides was not achieved easily or without pain, however, as can be learned from any sister who lived through those years. People assimilated the new understandings of the Council documents at different rates, and there were naturally differences of opinion over methods of implementing their directives. Those trained in theology disagreed with others who were not.

Most communities went through a period of tension as the Council documents were studied and new constitutions experimented with. Valuable lessons in trust, tolerance of differing opinions, and concern for each sister no matter what her viewpoint were learned by those who followed the process of study and discussion through to the end. Many sisters decided to leave religious life for a variety of reasons. For some, their communities were moving too slowly; for others, too quickly; in still other cases, there was a dissatisfaction with community life or a realization that they really had a vocation to marriage.[30]

One unfortunate feature of this period in the renewal of religious life is the fact that sisters were so involved in their own soul-searching study and discussion that they did not have the time, opportunity, or energy to share their insights with priests, bishops, or laypeople. Because of their education, sisters may have been far more aware of current theological thinking than most when the Council began. Others were shocked when those things that had always been popularly associated with religious life—the all-encompassing religious habit, confinement within convent walls, and a myriad of petty regulations— began to change.

Bishops and others were sometimes angry and indignant over decisions made by sisterhoods within their dioceses, and determined to do something about them. The whole process of study and consultation mentioned above was short-circuited in some communities by bishops and others who stopped it in mid-course. In such cases, the tensions, which mitigated at a later stage of the process for most communities, were frozen in place, and dichotomies magnified, with tragic consequences for all.

This happened in 1965 when Archbishop Karl Alter legislated for the lives of the Glenmary Sisters and caused half of them to leave their community and form a lay group. It occurred again in 1968 when 400 of the 450 Sisters of the Immaculate Heart of Mary chose the same alternative rather than allow Cardinal McIntyre to overrule their chapter decisions. Needless to say, these clerical interventions had a chilling effect on sisters everywhere. They seemed to contradict the Council's directives and to undercut the trust in sisters' abilities to solve their own problems that was at the heart of the Council documents. No doubt the patriarchal attitude that women are immature, emotional creatures with underdeveloped brains, incapable of running their own lives has had something to do with this. Such a lack of trust and support from the administrators of the very church whose decrees sisters had been following with great sincerity was painful and bewildering. With Mother Austin Carroll and her sisters, their twentieth-century counterparts might complain, "We have done all that Rome has asked of us. If we were misled when we followed the bishops' directives before, how can we be certain that we are not being misguided now?"

There were movements in some communities to lessen the tensions of this period and sidestep the consultation process by appealing to the hierarchy for solutions. Thus were the Franciscan Sisters of Christian Charity of Manitowoc assigned an Italian visitator who guided them in the rewriting of their constitutions (and the alienation of several of their members, who left to form a new community). The Boston Sisters of Notre Dame de Namur were not forced to laicize, but were divided into two provinces representing two irreconcilable points of view.

The Leadership Conference of Women Religious (or LCWR, the new name adopted by the Conference of Major Superiors of Women as a result of a deeper understanding of its role) has been very concerned about misunderstandings between congregations and members of the hierarchy and their destructive effects on individuals and whole communities of sisters. They have tried to find channels of communication and mediation with the hierarchy and the Congregation for Religious and Secular Institutes (CRIS) so as to save from destruction that form of religious life for women that has served the American church so well in the past and deserves to continue to do so into the future.

In an effort to explain the insights from Council documents that have brought American sisters to their present state of development, the LCWR in 1978 prepared a report on "U.S. Religious Orders Today" for CRIS. It documents the kind of mentality that has developed among American religious as a result of their commitment to the values espoused in documents of Vatican II and other Vatican statements. Careful study of it could help those who have been mystified by the actions of American sisters to understand the sentiments that motivate them. It could be particularly useful for members of CRIS, most of whom belong to other cultures.

Theirs is a life of gospel holiness, the document states, not apart from the other people of God but in solidarity with them. This leads to an understanding of the poverty of a large percentage of the world's people and efforts to change the structures that cause it. Their model is Jesus, who "dared to liberate from sin and death" but also "from unjust structures—from a Torah that only burdened, from a priesthood that bound people in darkness." He "identified with the poor and the powerless. He took sides and acted politically. And it was this that brought Him to His trial and death."[31]

LCWR was trying to explain how a commitment to gospel values led some religious working within American systems to come very naturally to a decision to work within the political structures that are so much a part of the fabric of American life. It is through various kinds of political activity—voting, lobbying, applying pressure, or becoming a legislator or government official oneself—that American citizens shape their country's policies and laws.

In 1971, an organization called Network was formed in Washington, D.C. as a social justice lobby through which sisters and others could influence legislation. It also attempted to raise the consciousness of sisters regarding the political process and mobilize their energies and numbers to support key issues. Those who became involved in this important ministry came to see that it was possible to accomplish much more from within the government than could ever be achieved from the outside. The Sisters of Mercy were especially drawn to this work. If we recall Austin Carroll's shrewd assessment of the most practical ways to serve the needy, this should not surprise us.

Elizabeth Morancy, a Mercy sister who has served several terms in the Rhode Island House of Representatives, notes that her interest in this work flowed from Vatican II:

> When American women's congregations started to struggle with the Vatican II mandate for renewal, nuns began to search for the roots of their orders. We Sisters of Mercy again claimed a heritage which recalled that Catherine McAuley and her co-workers in nineteenth-century Ireland sought to address unmet needs and in so doing challenged both Church and government on behalf of working women in Dublin.[32]

Morancy and others were inspired by Paul VI's *Call to Action*, in which he notes, "Politics is a demanding manner of living out the Christian meaning of service to others." She thought of this option when searching for possible solutions for the problems of the lower-class neighborhood in which she lived. She realized that elected officials were the ones with the power to implement change and determined to become part of the decision-making process herself if she could. She writes of her inspiration to do this:

> Given the complexities of our time and the power centered in our social structures, it seemed so natural to seek to influence the government processes that often determine the quality of people's lives. . . . Pope Paul VI encouraged Christians to penetrate the economic and political centers where decisions made were having enormous impact on the way people could live.[33]

During her tenure in the Rhode Island General Assembly, she has been able to help the needy by working on such issues as fair housing, emergency shelter appropriations, handicapped rights, sexual assault, and criminal justice.

Though Morancy and others in political ministry went through all of the appropriate channels of obtaining permission from congregation and diocesan administrators, their work was challenged on several fronts. Let us examine the context. Canon law allows for the participation of religious in politics as an exception, in special circumstances and with the proper permissions.[34] In 1983, the Congregation for Religious and Secular Institutes issued a document called "Religious Life and Human Promotion," which gave its views on the appropriate involvement of religious in the solution of human and social problems. Though this document is "reserved about religious in politics," it does "not prohibit such activity absolutely," according to several experts.[35]

In the early 1980s, CRIS began to question administrators of the Sisters of Mercy regarding the participation of their members in political life. One of those administrators, Emily George, has given an account of the methods used in this intervention—which led ultimately to the laicization of Elizabeth Morancy, Arlene Violet (who was running for attorney general of Rhode Island), and Agnes Mary Mansour, director of social services for the state of Michigan.[36]

These cases of involvement in political life underscore the controversy surrounding contemporary issues of renewal in the religious life. The liberal interpretation stresses the particularism of the American experience and the sanctity of an individual's conscience in the discernment of the Spirit and in deciding the proper spheres of social action. Conservatives do not oppose the call to struggle against social evils, but rather stress the traditional notion of the vowed life and the role of authority in setting the boundaries of social action.

CONCLUSION

We have looked at some of the trends that have marked the lives of the more than 200,000 sisters who have worked to build up the Catholic community in America since the establishment of the hierarchy in 1789. Bishop John Carroll gave the theme for our study when he noted that European concepts of religious life were impractical in America because of this country's very different habits and customs. The story of American sisters is the story of their struggle to develop a form of religious life that would be compatible with American customs and in conformity with the expectations of the Vatican.

Though the church is a pilgrim people, and as such should be able to be "at home" in any culture, it has actually for many centuries been very much under the influence of European manners and morals. The same has been true of its conception of religious life. Unless concepts of ethnocentricity and an awareness of one's own cultural biases and the willingness to set them aside can become a part of the ecclesiastical mind-set, there will continue to be a struggle to accommodate religious life and American values. Until the concepts inherent in patriarchal attitudes can be brought to the hierarchical consciousness and exorcised, churchmen will continue to oppress churchwomen.[37]

And so, we are still debating today, as did John Carroll with the first American Carmelites, what works are or are not proper for American sisters. But today women can work in church ministry without belonging to a religious community, and this has undoubtedly played a part in the decline in vocations. Further curtailment of sisters' response to the Spirit could accelerate that trend. It may again be true in the future, as it was in the days of Saint Vincent de Paul, that lay groups will be formed to do the work that the church prohibits for religious. Indeed, the fastest growing group of "religious" women in America today is a lay organization composed mostly of former sisters called Sisters for Christian Community.

Perhaps the church is at a point now similar to that which it had reached in 1800, when the old cloistered forms of religious life had been suppressed in Europe and a flowering of new active communities was just about to begin. The new concept of the church as all of the people of God has implications for the religious life of women that are just beginning to be plumbed.[38]

Contemporary development in religious life, dedication to prayer, gospel values, mutual support, and service to God's people, are such that they can offer a deeply fulfilling life in every age and culture. In America, they have enabled women to achieve many of the goals that their feminist sisters are still reaching toward. Whether American women will still find in the convent, in future years, a place where they can lead an authentic religious life remains to be seen.

CHAPTER
3
Catholic Domesticity, 1860–1960

Colleen McDannell

$\mathcal{M}$aternity, sweet sound!" exclaimed the *Catholic Home Journal* in 1887. "Nature has put the mother upon such a pinnacle, that our infant eyes and arms are, first uplifted to it; we cling to it in manhood; we almost worship it in old age."[1] By the end of the nineteenth century, middle-class American Catholics possessed a domestic ideology as colorful and sentimental as any proper Victorian. Advice books written by Irish priests, popular novels penned by laywomen, and anonymous articles in popular newspapers sang the praise of home and motherhood. Angelic smiles, tender looks, and sacrificial courage demonstrated the irresistible love of mothers. Cloistered in their home, the domestic ideology explained, mothers devoted their energies to their little ones and modeled their homes on the Holy Family. Catholic writers fully agreed with their Protestant counterparts that without good mothers, there could be no family, no religion, and no nation.

Catholic domestic ideology firmly placed the mother at home surrounded by devoted children and husband. Woman's place, it emphasized, was in the home. For many Catholic American women, their place historically *has* been in the home. From the frontier Catholic who let the traveling priest say mass in her house, to the Irish serving girl who cleaned and polished, to the suburban mother baking Easter bread, home life has been the center of many women's lives. That home life, however, has often reflected little of the prevailing domestic ideology. While some Catholic women wrote books on the ideal woman, others struggled to support their families, maintain their own ethnic domestic traditions, and carve out a measure of independence in their households.

To discuss the role of Catholic women within the home is a complicated and far-reaching task. We cannot merely survey the rhetoric used to praise home and mother, nor can we assume that those ideals did not influence the behavior and feelings of real mothers. While the model mother and wife are painted with vivid colors, real Catholic wives and mothers have left to us few statements of their inner feelings. We cannot limit our study to the middle class, since that eliminates a large portion of America's Catholics. Since each ethnic group expresses unique domestic customs, we cannot assume a unified Catholic culture. We cannot even assume that the mother was the chief caretaker of the children, the organizer of home celebrations, and the focus of domestic piety. While a woman's place may indeed have been in the home, her role within that family varied by class, ethnic group, educational level, and age.

To understand the religious role of Catholic women in the home, we have divided the time between 1860 and 1960 into three overlapping periods. From 1860 to 1920 domestic ideology hailed the mother as the center of the home and the perfect family as the foundation of Catholicism. This ideology, created by the arbiters of Catholic culture—middle-class laymen and -women, Irish priests and bishops, and the Roman hierarchy—remained for many women too idealistic. Out of necessity it was frequently modified or ignored. Concurrent with the establishment of this "mainstream" Catholic ideology was the influx of new immigrants to America. In the second period, from 1880 to 1940, American Catholicism underwent rapid growth and diversification. Since we cannot describe the domestic religious activities of all the immigrant communities, we will focus on the domestic piety of Italian, Mexican, and Polish women. Although their religiosity differs from Irish and American Catholics, they share two themes: the tendency to imbue everyday home life with a sense of the sacred and the attempt to tame supernatural characters by associating them with the family. Finally, in the period between 1940 and 1960, the principal focus of mainstream Catholic culture with regard to domesticity has been to describe how the values of modern, secular society conflict with family values and how women should respond to such threats. The domestic ideology created in the nineteenth century is still present but less richly articulated. The praising of mothers subsides as Catholic writers begin to encourage men to take over the religious leadership of their families. Women continue to serve a primary role in their family's religious activities, but during the 1940s and 1950s Catholic culture reasserts the patriarchal nature of Catholicism as a balance to suburban domestic life.

A difficult task is thus set before us. We must try to find order and meaning in a domestic ideology that for a modern reader may be hopelessly sentimental. Underneath or around that ideology we must discover what values and behaviors women incorporated into their lives. How did the views of priests, novelists, and critics—both men and women—penetrate into the homes of American women? In this study we can only begin to ferret out the actual behavior of Catholic women within the home. By looking at the development of domestic ideals and the activities of real women at home, a private American Catholicism emerges.

CREATING DOMESTIC IDEOLOGY, 1860–1920

The Catholic ideology that served as a standard measure of womanhood until the Second Vatican Council was a combination of the unique social characteristics of Irish-Americans, the efforts of a Catholic literary elite, traditional European views on women, and a strongly articulated Protestant (*qua* secular) cult of domesticity. Catholic domesticity presented an ideal picture of the behavior and values of women within the home. Spanish-speaking women in the western parts of the United States, newly arrived immigrants from south and central Europe, and rural Catholics contributed little to the creation of domestic ideals. These women carried their domestic values and customs with them from their homelands and maintained them in small, cohesive communities. Either geographically or culturally far from the urban centers of publishing, the seminaries, and the ladies' academies, these women had little contact with emerging Catholic domestic culture. It would be educated Irish and Irish-American Catholics, well acquainted with acceptable European and American standards, who created norms for home life and described women's place within it.

From 1830 to 1920, approximately 4.7 million Irish immigrated to the United States. The vast majority of those men and women felt themselves to be Catholic, although many were unchurched and religiously ill-educated. In spite of the immigrant's dream of a better life in America, life in the New World held little joy for most of the arriving Irish. Those who stayed in the major East Coast cities faced lives riddled with discrimination, Protestant hostility, slum housing, and poverty. Their infant mortality rate was higher than that of any other early immigrant group; Irish crime in New York City at mid-century exceeded by five times that of the American-born and German populations; and their occupational mobility appeared to be as low as that of American blacks. Fleeing poverty and oppression in Ireland, many confronted a similar fate in the United States.

The Irish immigrants who flocked to New York, Boston, Philadelphia, and other industrial cities were unprepared for urban living. Eighty percent of the Irish who emigrated between 1850 and 1920 were unskilled farmers. Few had ever worked in a city or even visited one. Family patterns in Ireland conformed to this social reality: because of the scarcity of land, people married late, if at all. Most of the immigrants arrived in America unmarried and hoped to send money back to their families. Many men and women remained single in America, but those who did marry and bear children did so with enthusiasm. By 1910, the Irish were second only to the French Canadians in their rate of reproduction.

The prevalence of permanent celibacy in Ireland encouraged the development of a sex-segregated social structure. Men who waited for marriage in Ireland met together in pubs, at fairs, or in the fields to drink and share stories. Women gathered in their homes, chatting with relatives and friends while working and watching children. Both men and women felt most comfortable with others of the same sex. In most cases, this same-sex bonding continued after marriage. While the marriage rate increased for the Irish in America, same-sex bonding remained strong. Life in urban America did not make it any easier for men and women to socialize freely. Irish men, whose occupational opportunities were initially limited to laboring, found little opportunity to meet or converse with women. Single Irish women, who arrived in America at the same rate as men (coming in even greater numbers during several years), worked primarily as domestic servants or in the needle trades. As servants, their associations with men were severely limited; as seamstresses, their interactions were primarily with other women.

The American Catholic church struggled to minister to the arriving immigrants. With little knowledge of Catholic doctrine and a history of British religious persecution, the Irish were infrequent church-goers and practiced a folk religion their clergy condemned. In New York City during the 1840s the priest-to-people ratio was 1 to 4,500 and in the western territories it grew to 1 to 7,000. After the great potato famine, however, the bishops in Ireland and America conducted a major effort to increase the number of clergy and religious, to teach the people the basics of religion, and to cement their loyalty to the church. In a remarkably short period of time, the Irish in America came to dominate the Catholic church. By the closing decades of the century, the vast majority of priests were Irish and about half of the bishops were of Irish background. Since the appointment of the first U.S. cardinal in 1875, only four out of seventeen cardinals have *not* been Irish. Although the clergy still complained about sporadic mass attendance by men, by the end of the century the Irish had become devoted to the parish and its priest.

The social situation for most of the Irish in America up until the late nineteenth century was not conducive to the establishment of a domestic ideology that promoted the nuclear family, the isolation of women in their homes, and the Christian rearing of children. The importance of the extended family in Ireland, the continuation of same-sex bonding, high rates of permanent celibacy, child labor, and slum living provided an inhospitable environment for the growth of domestic sentiments. There were, however, some Irish Americans who felt that proper home sentiments needed to be articulated and developed among their countrymen. Before the Civil War, Catholic novelists played a crucial role in the development of Catholic domesticity. While the majority of Irish Catholics lived in poverty, these writers detailed what they believed to be a proper home life. They fabricated their images from the ideal of an aristocratic Catholic upper class—Europeans who lived in Old World charm in America—and nostalgic memories of an old-fashioned Irish working class one step out of the bog. While some were priests, the majority were laymen and -women who used their writing skills to detail an appropriate Catholic lifestyle and provide strategies for coping with the difficulties of life in the New World.

Mary Ann Madden Sadlier best represents those middle-class novelists who worked to create a Catholic domestic culture in the New World. She was born in 1820, in County Cavan, Ireland. Her father was a prosperous merchant who eventually suffered financial problems in the 1840s. After her father's death in 1844, Mary Ann Madden emigrated to the United States. In 1846, she married James Sadlier, the manager of the Canadian branch of a Catholic publishing house founded by his brother. Moving to Montreal, the family settled down to a comfortable life. Mrs. Sadlier began to write professionally, continuing an interest begun in Ireland. She eventually gave birth to six children. After moving to New York in 1860, the family maintained a summer home and commanded the attention of Catholic notables like Orestes Brownson. In her almost fifty novels, Sadlier commented on life on both sides of the Atlantic with humor and sensitivity. Through her own prism of upward mobility, she created domestic situations that were descriptive of Irish-American life and prescriptive for appropriate Catholic behavior.

Sadlier's novels were a part of a general trend in Catholic publishing during the second half of the nineteenth century that articulated the meaning of a good home. In 1850, when Sadlier published *Willy Burke; or, the Irish Orphan in America*, a remarkable seven thousand copies were sold in the first week. Many of Sadlier's stories were serialized in Catholic newspapers, thus reaching a larger audience. Her novels were kept in print for more than fifty years and, when the Sadlier publishing house was purchased in 1895 by P. J. Kenedy and Sons, the new press reprinted her books throughout the early twentieth century. According to one report, Sadlier's books were "evidently read to pieces."[2]

Catholic domestic advice books, either written by Irish priests or translated from the original French, German, and Italian were also published. American presses eagerly translated and distributed European books on proper Catholic behavior, from Jean François Landriot's *The Valiant Woman . . . Intended for the Use of Women Living in the World* (1874) to Wilhelm Cramer's *The Christian Father: What He Should Be and What He Should Do* (1883). These books reflected European middle- and upper-class concerns about the state of the family. American advice books were more popular because they exhibited a slightly more realistic appraisal of family life. Father Bernard O'Reilly's *Mirror of True Womanhood* published in 1876, had gone through seventeen editions by 1892. Two years later, the Irish-born priest published *True Men as We Need Them*. As the Irish slowly entered the middle class, publishers tried to keep up with their demands for reading materials and the Catholic church's demand that suitable books be available.

Catholics, who prior to 1880 could claim no successful family or women's magazine, could boast by century's end that Boston's *Sacred Heart Review* had a circulation of over 40,000. Before the Civil War, Catholic newspapers focused on reporting news of Ireland and local U.S. politics; they showed no interest in describing the "ideal home." By the 1870s, however, practical household columns appeared, and by 1890, Catholic family newspapers contained a virtually unlimited supply of paeans to family life. The *Sacred Heart Review*'s stated purpose was not to present "news of the world in general, not the occurrences of every-day life in the parish," but rather to "enter the Christian home" with "cheering, hopeful words, and words of counsel and instruction."[3] With almost twice the circulation of the popular devotional journal *Ave Maria* (22,000 in 1892) and far surpassing the meager numbers of the erudite *Catholic World* (2,250 in 1897), the *Sacred Heart Review* helped create a Catholic domestic ideology where there had been none.

By the turn of the century, Catholic women could learn about proper home life by reading novels, advice books, or Catholic newspapers or by listening to the sermons of their parish priests. Through-

out the century, though, some women learned a domestic ideology
not from Catholic sources but from working as servants in Protestant
Victorian households. Irish women who emigrated to America found
ready employment in the homes of middle-class and upper-class
Americans. They were asked to help create a "proper" home through
their housekeeping, cleaning, and childrearing activities. Their urban
Protestant mistresses taught them how to keep an orderly, efficient
home that reflected the values of upwardly mobile Americans. Irish
women, many of whom had had no contact with Victorian domestic
ideology before leaving Ireland, learned from their Protestant mistresses how a "good" woman acted and what a "good" family looked
like. Even after most Protestants gave up rigid nineteenth-century
domestic values, Irish Americans clung to those virtues as signs of
their social status.

Mid-nineteenth-century novelists, late-century family newspapers,
and translated European advice books echoed a central theme regarding Catholic domesticity. Without a strong family, they exclaimed, religion, the nation, and the economic structure would
crumble. The family served as the "nursery of the nation," and the
nation was nothing "save a large family."[4] In spite of the economic
and social problems that the Irish found in the New World, Catholic
culture told them that social, spiritual, and personal ills could be
averted if the family coped with hardship and maintained its integrity.
The family performed this function not because it was merely a natural or economic unit but because it was an institution founded by
God. Writers compared the "true home" to the joys of heaven and
the perfect harmony found in Eden. Just as Jesus had lived in a family
and followed the dictates of his parents, so the Catholic family was
blessed by God.

Some writers went as far as to say that nothing was more sacred
than the family—even the church—and that the church was actually
created for families. A Miss Barry wrote in 1890 that "all institutions
and ordinances which God has created in civil society, and bestowed
upon his Church, have for their main purpose to secure the existence,
the honor, and the happiness of every home."[5] Laywomen saw their
domestic roles as increasingly important as they were told that their
homes were sacred schools for the production of good Catholics. In
1877, the editor of *Catholic World* specifically sought to counter the
overestimation of home life by reasserting the superiority of celibacy.
In an article on French home life, a translation of *La Vie domestique*
by Charles de Ribbe, a certain Madame de Lamartine had compared
her married life to that of a Sister of Mercy. In a footnote, the editor
clearly pointed out that "in regard to the heroic virtue that can be
practised in the married state there can be no question. As little can

there be any question that in the scale of perfection the religious is the higher state."[6] Catholics encountered a long-standing tradition that accorded the life of the celibate religious the highest merit, while maintaining that the home was "the spot where angels find a resting place / When bearing blessings, they descend to earth."[7]

What was the ideal Catholic home supposed to look like? Since the earthly home was asked to imitate the celestial realms of Eden and paradise, as well as the divine home of Nazareth, it was crucial that it be well ordered. Order in heaven dictated order on earth. To have control over one's environment demonstrated control over personal passions and societal flux. Catholic writers used a theory of correspondence to assert that a well-ordered home created well-ordered citizens, which created a well-ordered nation. The home should always be neat and tidy. Cleanliness and order went hand in hand as the guiding principles by which families controlled their domestic space and thus their personal and political space.

Cleanliness could not be taken too seriously. The "true family" realized that cleanliness was "proved by sense of smell, rather than by the sense of sight." Even if the outside appeared tidy, the "rat and roach could tell of hidden drawers and undisturbed nooks where the straightening-out process is culpably neglected."[8] Poverty was no excuse for disorder and filth. The nostalgic image of the neat and tidy Irish cottage stood as a perpetual symbol of the righteousness of Old World homes. Mrs. Keane, a fictitious washerwoman in a short story by Sister Mary Teresa Carroll, lived in a very small cottage that was "so exquisitely neat, and so attractive in appearance, that the beholder readily attributes to its presiding genius a superior mind."[9] In an 1890 article entitled, "A Peasant Home," the Sylvie Kiely family lived in a detached cottage near an orchard. Their peasant house had uncarpeted floor boards "white as a hound's tooth," a book case with a "nice collection of books," wallpapered walls, and a "not expensive but pretty" tea service sitting on a table cloth "white as snow."[10] While contemporary photographs taken in Ireland show dilapidated one-room cottages overrun with animals and children, the creators of Catholic domesticity ignored the reality of their past lives and envisioned an orderly and controlled domestic environment.

The brunt of demonstrating domestic virtues was borne by women, although good Catholic men were also to manifest orderliness in their lifestyles. Irish women were assumed to possess a high level of purity and simplicity, no matter how refined they became. Their scrupulous neatness and cleanliness would produce a cheerful and restful home for their families. Novelists created pictures of families in their parlors or sitting rooms, enjoying each other's company, but not directly interacting. Father might be reading, mother sewing, and the children playing or studying. The overall effect was one of harmony, peace, and love. Brawls, bickering, noise, and disorder were eliminated from the scenario. No one demanded too much attention from the others nor sat apart in isolation.

This cheerful home provided a source of recreation and relaxation for the working men of the family. In an 1894 sermon, Cardinal James Gibbons colorfully described the model home. "Christian women, when your husbands and sons return to you in the evening after buffeting with the waves of the world," he pleaded, "let them find in your homes a haven of rest. Do not pour into the bleeding wounds of their hearts the gall of bitter words, but rather the oil of gladness and consolation."[11] Note that Gibbons included sons as laborers, referring to male children, but he ignored working daughters. The male world was perceived as being chaotic, threatening, and exhausting—only the ordered space of the home could truly restore the men. Women, understood by the cardinal as naturally more domestic, could somehow cope better with work-related stress. The reality of women's home activities, which frequently included taking in laundry, doing piecemeal finishing work, or coping with boarders, did not fit well into the pattern outlined by the cardinal.

The purpose of keeping a clean, cheerful house was to keep the wandering members of the family—the men and boys—close at home. The logic inherent in the idea was that if the father was happy and relaxed, he would stay in his cheery house and not go out to the cheery pub. Even middle-class women confronted the masculine habit of preferring male companionship to home delights. Many women coped with the reality of caring for large families because their husbands either had deserted, gone west to find employment, or become chronic alcoholics. The creators of domestic ideals pressured women to strive to keep their men at home. Wives and mothers, who saw what happened when men became disenchanted with their families and shirked their responsibilities, must have felt they shouldered a tremendous responsibility. From the pulpit, the popular novel, and the Catholic newspaper, women were told that a poor home life—not poverty, slums, or social disorder—made men forget their families' needs.

Nicolas Walsh, author of the 1903 publication *Woman*, asserted that not even piety should get in the way of domestic responsibilities. Religious duties must not interfere with the convenience, comfort, or happiness of the family. If a woman went to morning mass, she should make sure that she had a good breakfast prepared for her husband and sons. Not only should she fix the breakfast, she should also preside over it in order to make the meal more pleasant and familylike. If mass conflicted with this, she must find a different service or skip it altogether. Walsh believed that not only should women provide the meals and housekeeping, they should engage the family members in entertainment in order to solidify the family bonds. "No one, I think," he wrote, "need fear to say that the female members would do better by staying with the others, enjoying with them music or some pleasant game, than by leaving them in order to spend the time before the blessed Sacrament."[12] The message was quite clear: a woman's spiritual concerns should never conflict with her commitments to her family.

Although Catholic domestic ideology assumed that women did not work outside of the home, it did not promote a life of leisure. While the home functioned as a place of rest and repose for men, women were supposed to reflect the work ethic of the family. Catholic writers insisted that increased financial stability did not mean that women became idle objects. Women in the home had to be busy producers. "If half the time and money wasted on music, dancing and embroidery," chided the *Baltimore Mirror,* "were employed in teaching daughters the useful art of making shirts, and mending stockings and managing household affairs, then . . . the number of happy homes would be multiplied."[13] Catholic writers did not subscribe to the notion articulated by Thorstein Veblen that idle women symbolized male attainment and status. Catholic women were told to occupy themselves with the practical tasks of housekeeping. Mary Sadlier particularly liked ridiculing in her fiction those seminary-educated daughters who could only play the piano, make wax flowers, and speak a few words of French.

On the other hand, Irish and Irish Americans much admired French culture and the leisured, aristocratic, but Catholic, life it symbolized. Rather than imitating upper-class America, which was decidedly Protestant, Catholics found that French style and customs provided the refinement through which they sought to separate themselves from the "bog Irish." Many advice books were translated from the French. Families sent their daughters to French-language boarding schools where they learned not housekeeping, but the useless embroidery and piano. French religious articles were advertised in Catholic newspapers. Even the French language was considered to be more polite and elegant than English and refined ladies were believed to say their prayers and do their daily devotions in French.

The fascination with French Catholicism also brought a reassertion of the patriarchal household. European advice-book writers were especially rigid in their description of the hierarchical organization of the family. Catholic domestic ideology emphasized traditional lines of authority within the home. Authority in the household permitted the continued assertion of order. The domestic hierarchy reflected the relationship between God and his people and also the church where a pope headed a procession of cardinals, bishops, and clergy. In the introduction to *The Christian Father: What He Should Be and What He Should Do*, Stephen Vincent Ryan, C.M., the bishop of Buffalo stated that "the father actually holds the place of God, and exercises an authority subordinate only to that of God, over his children." In return, he should receive respect and honor "approximating the honor paid to God himself."[14] Children, and wives to some extent, were under the natural and God-given authority of the father (husband). Breaking away from the family—by men or women—was looked upon as a fundamental domestic sin.

The belief that women were to be under the patriarchal authority of either their father or husband was balanced in Catholic novels by matriarchal trends. In many novels, powerful female characters emerged who were quite independent. These women were always unmarried—either being single or widowed. They ran large households, managed inherited money, traveled, and had adventures. Although the single ones usually ended up married at the end of the story, there was a strong trend to subvert the domestic message by presenting women who were not under the rule of men and yet appeared to be quite independent and happy. Although still within the acceptable realm of the home, as widows or servants, these women were freed from male control. The novelists acknowledged the rule of men over women, but when they wanted to create interesting female characters, they eliminated the authority problem by eliminating the men.

Another way that writers subverted male authority was to emphasize the woman's capacity to "save" her family. This trend had become very popular in Protestant America where women were seen to be more religious and virtuous than men. While Protestants had limited the influence of Mary and the female saints, they had discovered female saving power in mothers, daughters, and wives. Although Catholic literature had a strong streak of the "Eve" character— the seductive, evil woman—popular writing heralded women's redemptive character. Countless stories recalled how sons, remembering their mothers, are saved from evil influence. In 1890, a Philadelphia newspaper carried a story where a mother's "dumb look from her death-bed" motivated the "wretched youth" to become a Jesuit missionary.[15] Likewise, the *Sacred Heart Review* explained in "A Mother's Influence" that the kiss "my mother gave me, has often proved the password to purity and honor in a young man's career and a shield against the many temptations in a young girl's life."[16] The wife or mother not only provided for the physical and psychological well-being of the husband or son, she also shouldered much of the responsibility for his spiritual life.

Catholic culture permitted women such great responsibilities because their everyday lives were perceived as intrinsically religious. Although wives and mothers had chosen the lesser path to heaven, their married life could in many ways duplicate that of a celibate religious. The *Catholic Home Journal* called mothers "home heroes" because they were modestly secluded from "men's praises" and devoted their energies to their children which the "outer world does not know."[17] The mother, like the nun, was retired and secluded, cloistered in her home. Like a saint, her sacrifices went unknown and unacknowledged. The conviction that married women could imitate the life of the nun has a long tradition beginning with François de Sales's advice to French women. Following this trend, French priest Paul Lejeune created a "rule" for women that imitated the life of the religious without its precision and severity. Translated in 1913 and published by a major Catholic press, the *Counsels of Perfection for Christian Mothers* encouraged mothers to rise and retire early, to say their morning and evening prayers kneeling, to spend fifteen minutes per day with spiritual reading, to meditate, attend daily mass, and to receive Holy Communion frequently. Although women were encouraged not to let a day pass without reading a page from the Bible, they were warned against reading the mystical writings of John of the Cross and Teresa of Ávila because women's imaginations were too sensitive to the "extraordinary phenomena recorded in the works."[18]

Even novelists like Mary Sadlier, who included many independent women in her novels, saw the true Catholic woman as one who retired from the world. Servant girls might be virtuous, but eventually they would marry and step out of the working world. There were no Sadlier women who worked outside of the home for reasons other than poverty. Another writer, Eleanor Donnelly, recalled the life of "Marguerite" who sought fame on the stage as a singer. After a professional tragedy she settled down to housekeeping, telling her new husband "my pride is justly punished."[19] The nun's life of poverty, chastity, and obedience was to be replicated in the Catholic home.

Mary Sadlier acknowledged that this Catholic view of women differed from the Protestant perspective. In 1855, she described a Catholic teaching sister who "had she been a Protestant she would have been 'a strong-minded woman'; beyond all doubt; she might have taken the lead at public meetings, edited a daily newspaper in some of our great cities, delivered public lectures, and written huge volumes on metaphysics or philosophy." This woman, however, "being a Catholic . . . and born in Ireland" chose the better path of feminine modesty and Christian humility. She was "taught to consider human learning as a mere accessory to the grand science of salvation." The true woman chose the higher calling, "the unworldly step of retiring from the world . . . to live a life of seclusion and of mortification."[20] In the convent or in the home, the woman was to direct her attention not to worldly activities, but to the higher cause of God and family. To say that a woman's place was in the home was similar to saying a woman's place was in the cloister—both assumed an otherworldly mentality that isolated women from the public sphere.

Catholic women who for economic or personal reasons sought paid labor were encouraged not to seek careers that took them too far away from the home. In 1886, "Hannah" wrote a letter to "Aunt Bride" that appeared in the *Sacred Heart Review*. Hannah was currently doing domestic work, but she wanted to learn "typewriting" and to become a secretary. "It is not that I am above domestic work," she wrote the newspaper, "but would like to try something different."[21] Aunt Bride spent the bulk of her response telling Hannah how difficult such jobs were—you must learn two languages and have perfect grammar and spelling. Encouraging Hannah to go back to housekeeping, Aunt Bride suggested she learn specialty cooking, become a trained attendant for the sick, or a nursery maid. For Aunt Bride—a good representative of Catholic attitudes toward women and the family—if a woman needed to work, let her work in the confines of the home, even if it was a Protestant family who paid her for her labors. Domestic work was approved because it meant that women stayed in the home. Many Irish women, however, well-versed in the difficulties of domestic labor rejected this advice and moved into factory and clerical work, teaching, and other nondomestic positions as quickly as they could get the proper education. While domestic work was presented as an acceptable way for women to earn money if they must, the realities of being a servant—poor pay, no independence, and cranky mistresses—drove Irish working women away from such jobs.

The activities of the Catholic mother were also compared to the role the Virgin Mary played within the Holy Family. The association of women with Mary presented certain problems for domestic writers. The Virgin Mary enjoyed in Catholic tradition a long history that emphasized her powerful and royal characteristics. Mary was the queen of heaven who was often portrayed in medieval and Renaissance art as the "fourth member of the Trinity." Her connection to Christ was more direct than that of her husband Joseph. In order to reduce the feminine power of the Virgin Mary, writers placed her within the domestic structure of life in Nazareth. No longer the queen of the universe, Mary became a Hebrew housewife who looked after the needs of husband and child. "The Blessed Virgin," explained an 1887 article in the *Catholic Home*, "was beyond all measure superior in dignity to St. Joseph, but it is not she who guides and rules in this model family." The author summarized this perspective by finishing with the Pauline quote, "Let women be subject to their husbands as to the Lord."[22] In the *Catholic Girl's Guide* of 1905, Mary made her home inviting and comfortable for St. Joseph when he came home from work. Joseph was pleased to see "his evening meal ready and everything as orderly as possible."[23] Advice book writers stripped Mary of her supernatural powers and presented her in the peaceful house of Nazareth industriously pursuing the vocation of a poor artisan's wife. Mary, seen from this perspective, was the ideal model for women—an ever-virgin mother, obedient, suffering, unselfish, and pious.

If women followed the model of Mary and maintained the spirituality of a nun, they were considered worthy to become priestesses of the domestic shrine. Although they were not real priests, they could officiate at the sanctuary of the home by directing their domestic sacrifices to God. Women were asked to cultivate religious sentiments in their family through their personal religious activities. In 1868, Sister Mary Carroll described a scene from *Pleasant Homes* in which a mother listened to her children recite the catechism and helped them "to ask questions about anything they did not understand, that she might be able to instruct them correctly." She also read from a book for twenty minutes, explaining the evening chapter [from the Bible?], told stories about the saints to "enliven the lesson," and corrected the children's pronunciation of theological terms. The evening ended with prayers.[24] Mothers were to teach their young children how to make the sign of the cross and say the sacred name of Jesus and the holy name of Mary. "What is the Christian mother?" queried a French priest whose advice book circulated in America. She was the one who has chosen "the slavery of home duties" and made "maternity a priesthood" by pouring the "faith of Christ into the very veins of her child as she nurses him at her breast."[25]

The informal religious tasks such as helping children with their catechism or hearing evening prayers were activities that easily fell to the mother to perform. Mothers did this not only because they were close to their children, but because such religious activities were not considered to be the duties of the father. Unlike the Protestant family where the father presided over formal family prayers, family worship was not traditionally promoted among Catholics, who rather were told to say morning and evening prayers as individual, private devotions. Beginning in the late nineteenth century, however, American and international sources began to encourage families to pray together. Papal encyclicals *Supremi apostolatus officio* (1883) and *Fidentem piumque animum* (1896) asked families to pray the rosary together. In 1891, Cardinal Gibbons pleaded for family prayers. In none of these cases was the father asked to direct these activities, although Gibbons specifically called on both the mother and the father to gather their children in the evening for devotions. While some European sources tried to insist that father act as priest to his household, American writers appeared willing to assign this task to both parents or to the mother alone.

Catholic newspapers described a variety of religious activities that women supposedly did at home. A mother and daughter made charity boxes and brought them out every Sunday to be passed around for contributions. Another pair of ladies wrote Catholic hymns to be played on the family piano or organ. Advertisers encouraged the purchase of medals, statues, holy water fonts, and religious calendars. Religious engravings and lithographs, crucifixes, family blessings, and even Catholic Bibles were marketed to families who could afford to buy them. Holy Communion certificates and samplers with Catholic images could be framed and hung on the walls. The *Boston Pilot* in 1876 advertised an "Angelus clock," which did not chime the hours of the day but the times for reciting the Angelus. Women who purchased and displayed such objects helped create the proper environment for the production of good Catholic families.

When describing the ideal Catholic home, few writers neglected to mention the display of domestic altars. While novelists described how the "better" Catholic families had chapels or oratories, popular newspapers recommended every family to set aside at least a corner for God. Since most Catholic devotions were private and not done by the family as a whole, bedrooms often were described as containing impromptu altars. When the door to the Kielys' "peasant" bedroom stood ajar, one could see "a statue of the Sacred Heart on a little altar with gauze curtains and a red lamp lighting [it]."[26] Lit candles, statues, holy pictures, flowers, as well as the articles advertised by Catholic religious goods stores made the home into a sacred space. After the turn of the century, the cult of the Sacred Heart became popular among Irish Americans, and in 1915 Benedict XV granted special indulgences to those who consecrated their homes to the Sacred Heart. Although house blessings by priests had a long Catholic tradition, house blessings connected with a picture of the Sacred Heart became a symbol of the Irish Catholic home.

The proliferation of religious articles in the home accompanied the rise in Catholic attention toward the family. Homes in rural Ireland during the early and mid-nineteenth century did not display a vast number of religious handicrafts. Poverty limited the expenditures of the family, the lack of mass-produced religious articles restricted the number of goods available, and a lack of interest in religious matters curbed the display of Catholic sentiments. The traditional St. Bridget's cross of blessed palms was often the cottage's only religious adornment. By the end of the century, however, the situation had greatly changed. A coordinated effort by bishops and clergy to re-awaken Irish Catholicism had succeeded and sparked a new interest in displaying religious articles in the home. As more Irish recovered from the great famine of the 1850s and entered into the middle class, they found a plethora of mass-produced religious articles to buy, a change that may be seen in the home exhibits at the Glencolumbkille Folk Museum in County Donegal. The prefamine cottage has no religious art except a crucifix; the 1850s cottier's cabin has a crucifix and a statue of Mary (as well as a misplaced 1893 house blessing); and the 1900 home has house blessings, holy pictures, statues, and a crucifix.

A similar development occurred in America. As Irish American Catholics moved into the middle class, they possessed the resources and the proper domestic sentiments to motivate the purchase and display of religious articles. Late-nineteenth-century Catholics readily combined their religion's penchant for sensuality with the Victorian trend for display and surrounded themselves with symbols of their religion and culture. Although few homes could live up to the ideals set before them by the Catholic press and the pulpits, the message was too loud to be ignored. For those Catholics who aspired to religious, economic, and social respectability, striving to present the proper home became an important goal.

It is difficult to evaluate to what extent the message of Catholic domesticity influenced those Irish who were not in the middle class. Photographs of the period show that even in poor families religious prints and statues could be found. In 1903, social workers from Barnard College interviewed working-class Irish families from the West Side of New York City. Although their descriptions reveal a considerable middle-class bias, their observations depict typical conditions that many Irish families experienced throughout the nineteenth century. From one of the interviews, we can get a glimpse of the interaction between Catholicism and home in the life of one Irish woman. It provides us with a brief, if provocative, indication of how domestic Catholicism appeared in the working classes.

Bridget Donelly came by herself to America in 1876. Her father and brother had died in Ireland and her mother had gone mad with grief over their deaths. Upon arrival, she went to work in a silk and wool factory, lived in factory housing, sent money home to her mother, and paid for the passage to America of her two elder sisters. After her mother's death and the accumulation of some savings, Bridget felt free to quit her job and marry Martin O'Brien, a friend who had followed her over from Ireland. The next year, at the age of twenty eight Bridget had her first child, who died fourteen months later. Another son was born a year later, who also died in infancy, and a third son was delivered stillborn. Other children came in rapid succession, and by her fifty-third birthday, Bridget O'Brien had six living children all of whom had had bouts of scarlet fever, chronic bronchitis, stomach trouble, and pneumonia.

Bridget O'Brien saw to the religious education of her children. Those children who did not work attended parochial school, but one son refused to learn his catechism well enough to be confirmed. Daughter Ellen, however, learned so well that she received a new white dress and veil for her confirmation. Bridget told her interviewer that she heard her children's prayers every morning and evening, and she and her husband attended their parish church regularly. Her husband, Martin, was strong willed, often drunk, and sporadically employed. Bridget rarely discussed domestic matters with him because he angered easily. Although he stayed home nights, during the day, when he was not working or drunk, he hung out at the local saloon. Bridget insisted that she would stay with Martin even if he drank continuously, but her children ignored him in their nightly prayers. Bridget explained to the interviewer that poor people ought to stay single because their lives are so difficult. If she had known about married life, she would have never married. Nine children were too many to bear; six too many to clothe and feed. But, Bridget summarized, "it is God's will if he wants them to come or to go from us."[27]

Irish women in America, like Bridget Donelly O'Brien, had mixed feelings about marriage and family. Many had come from Ireland to escape family problems, the lack of suitable marriage mates, and domestic poverty. In America, they experienced for the first time a semi-independent status by earning their own wages. While some squandered their earnings on clothing, most sent money back to Ireland and gained respectability in their extended family. To marry meant to lose whatever hard-earned freedom they had won, to be subject to frequent childbearing, and to cope with the family instability that chronic poverty produced. Although the prospects of being a spinster domestic servant looked bleak, the alternative of marriage also held little promise of happiness. The realities of everyday life left little room for a sentimental picture of motherhood and family life.

On the other hand, Bridget's efforts to send her children to parochial school, to see that they learn their catechism, and to find the money to purchase a confirmation dress point to a strong commitment to Catholic principles. The Barnard sociologists also reported that in a three-room tenement that held two parents and six children they found a family shrine containing an image of the Virgin, a rosary, a family Bible, a picture of Saint Anthony, several brightly colored vases filled with artificial flowers, two glass crucifixes, a china image of the Virgin, a plaster image of Mary with the infant Jesus, colored pictures of Saint Benedict and other saints, a newspaper print of Leo XIII and of Pius X, photographs of a relative's tombstone in Ireland, and family photographs in a gilt frame decorated by palm leaves. While Bridget and the other Irish of New York's middle West Side might have no use for the sentimental idealization of the home, they did respond to reform efforts in both Ireland and America to involve the poor and working class in Catholic life. The availability of inexpensive mass-produced religious prints and articles made it possible for even the poor to show their piety while infusing color and individuality into their drab surroundings. Although the middle-class social workers might have considered the profusion of religion and color overdone and tacky, this type of religious expression was encouraged by the prevailing Catholic domestic ideology. Women, poor or wealthy, were expected to maintain a visibly Catholic home.

ETHNIC DIVERSITY, 1880–1940

Irish Americans, through their monopoly of the hierarchy and lay leadership, set the standards for Catholic life in the United States. But while they dominated the community, they were not the only Catholic ethnic group in America. At the same time that Irish Americans—with help from European advice books—articulated a domestic ideology, new immigrants were arriving from southern and eastern Europe. Each brought with them customs and traditions that varied both from the Irish and from the accepted traditions of Counter Reformation Catholicism. The religious activities of women from other ethnic groups provide a rich picture of an active religious life, even if not always approved by Catholic leaders. In their homes, women preserved and modified traditions from the Old World that had been passed down in their families for generations. While many of their husbands and fathers would find little of comfort or spiritual uplift in Catholicism, immigrant women maintained their associations with the church—on their own terms. We cannot describe the full religious life of ethnic women, but we can give a flavor of their piety by focusing on a few of the domestic activities of Italian, Mexican, and Polish mothers and wives.

Between 1880 and 1920, approximately four million Italians emigrated to the United States. Increases in population, decreases in available arable land, and changes from the "old way of life" threatened the stability of the southern Italian peasant farmer. Although many Mexicans had resided in what was to be the southwestern United States for generations, the social situations of Mexicans and Italians present certain structural similarities. The annexation of

Mexican lands to the United States after the Mexican-American War (1846–1848) caused many Mexicans to lose control over their land. Like the Italians, many Mexicans became unskilled laborers and, because of their location in the rich agricultural areas of the west, migrant farm workers. Although emigration from Italy radically decreased after the 1920s, Mexican immigration into California, Texas, New Mexico, Colorado, and Arizona continued to grow.

Both southern Italian and Mexican immigrants exhibited a cautious relationship with institutional Catholicism. In both cases, Catholicism in the homeland was associated with the landowning upper classes and the status quo. Immigrants who arrived from Sicily and other regions of southern Italy brought with them anticlericalism, religious indifference, and a folk Catholicism frequently labeled as superstitious. After Mexico claimed its independence from Spain, the recruiting of clergy from Europe stopped and the number of priests decreased. For a few Mexicans, this meant that the father of the family replaced the priest and that home devotions increased, but for most it meant that being Catholic became a biological fact that had little to do with conviction or practice. Like the Italians, the Mexicans felt alienated from a religious tradition perceived to be the support of the rich and powerful. These two immigrant groups differed significantly from the Irish who had found support for their claims against their English rulers and landlords among the Catholic clergy.

Furthermore, the Italian and Mexican immigrants found an American Catholicism thoroughly steeped in Irish ways. The state of one's Catholicism was measured by attendance at mass, respect for the priest, and participation in parish activities. The Italian and Mexican preference for communal religious celebrations (the *festa* or *fiesta*), their elaborate rites of passage (baptisms, weddings, funerals), and their emotional devotion to the saints had little in common with the more restrained Irish. While the Irish were willing to follow their educated clergy and lay leaders, Italian and Mexican immigrants chose to continue the religious traditions brought from their villages. The public space of the streets and the private domain of the home served as the places for religious expression, so that parish life held little importance.

The family was the most important element in Italian and Mexican life—not merely the nuclear family of mother, father, and child, but also the extended family of aunts, uncles, grandparents, and cousins. More important than the Catholic church, American culture, or the individual aspirations of its members, domestic values superseded all others. Men were expected to assume the responsibility for the extended family's economic and general well-being. They were to be aware of the political forces and organizations that could either challenge or support the family's integrity. Jobs, politics, the institutional church—these were the domain of men. Women were responsible for the day-to-day well-being of the family. They maintained lines of communications between relatives, saw to the balancing of the family budget, and coped with daily problems. While the men criticized the institutional church, women developed a private relationship with Christ, the Virgin Mary, and the saints. In Mexican and Italian families a division of outlook separated the men's world from the women's world.

Since women were responsible for the everyday well-being of their families, their religious activities within the home centered around family needs and personal concerns. In spite of Mexican or Italian men joking about their wives' attendance at mass, the women found a source of uplift and comfort in their religious activities. In Italian and Mexican families, mothers passed down to their daughters a religious attitude that included church attendance, private prayer, and the knowledge of folklore. Although men probably had more respect for domestic Catholicism than for parish Catholicism, they still tended to leave the creation of a religious home environment to their wives and mothers.

The most visible expression of a woman's piety was the maintenance of domestic shrines. In Mexican families, women often maintained shrines in a corner of their bedrooms. Frequently, the largest statue would be of the Virgin of Guadalupe (the protectress of Mexico), but she would be surrounded by other statues—the miraculous child Santo Niño de Atocha, his mother Santa Maria de Atocha, a Nuestra Señora de San Juan de Los Lagos, and Saint Anthony of Padua. Candles, fresh or paper flowers, and important documents from the family such as a marriage certificate or letters might be placed with the statues. One or two candles would be lit signifying the continual devotion of the woman to the saints. A rosary, novena cards, special medals, and crucifixes were often placed on the altar and pictures of the saints and family members hung on the wall. Souvenirs from old Mexico added to the eclectic nature of the shrine.

The placement of both religious and family objects together at the shrine emphasized the close association of the family and the supernatural world. The altar was not a separate religious space, but a place where family and religion were brought together. The religious characters were understood as a family and the family was understood as being the source of ultimate meaning. The family itself had a sacred quality. With its sensual, tactile, and colorful aspects, the family shrine underscored the lively character of home religion. Catholicism practiced at home by women was not abstract and intellectual, but immediate, practical, and earthy.

Similar altars were constructed by Italian women. In each room a shrine would contain statues, favorite pictures of the saints, religious candles, and dried palms from several Palm Sundays. The saints most frequently depicted in statues and in engravings were the sacred figures who expressed the relationships of the extended family: The Madonna who held the infant in her arms connected the mother of the family with the divine; the saints Cosmos and Damian were brothers who died together; and the Holy Family of Nazareth reminded the earthly family of the biblical model. For many Italians, the Holy Family itself became the Trinity—mother, father, and child—but always with grandmother St. Ann standing in the background. The Holy Family, like the extended Italian family, had to be multigenerational. Since the saints themselves were understood as being a part of the extended family, if they did not respond to the petitions of their earthly children, they could be chided or ignored like any other family member. Italian women, like Mexican women, saw Catholicism as tightly connected to the well-being of the family. Praying in front of statues or at home was not merely supplementary to church prayers, but in many cases replaced church activities.

Italian and Mexican immigrants who settled in America brought with them fears that could only be controlled by careful behavior and ritual precaution. The world in which they lived was not only filled with saints but also with demons, the evil eye, and ghosts. In Italian homes animal horns were placed in doorways as protection against the evil eye. Amulets were worn, especially by women and children, to ward off evil. Teeth, claws, and replicas of animal horns were sewn on clothing, held in pockets, or included on necklaces or bracelets. Medals were placed in the swaddling clothes of babies, and mothers taught their daughters how to cope with the power of witches. Richard Gambino recalled how his grandmother did not feel that the gold crucifix he wore was sufficient protection; when he was ill, she sewed little sacks filled with an unknown substance to his clothes.

In 1954, a sociologist studying Mexican American families living in public housing in San Antonio, Texas, reported a similar concern of women for protecting their family against the evil eye (ojo). To detect whether or not a person was suffering from ojo a woman would rub the body of the suspect with an unbroken egg while repeating the Our Father and Hail Mary, finishing at the feet with the Apostle's Creed. The egg would eventually be broken into a glass of water. If, after a number of hours, a round spot resembling an eye appeared on the egg, the conclusion was that the person had been inflicted with the evil eye. Holy water was also valued for its power to help families avoid misfortune and calamity. While present-day readers might scoff at the odd mixture of folklore and standard Catholicism, these rites stress the connection between a woman's concern for her family and her belief in supernatural forces. The orthodox Catholic promotion of the grand scheme of salvation, with its doctrines of sin, atonement, and heavenly reward, held little meaning for immigrants tightly rooted in the here-and-now.

Catholicism for Mexican or Italian women had to "work" for them and their families. Perhaps one of the most important ways that women used religion within their homes was in healing rituals. In 1947, Beatrice Griffith published an account of growing up in a Mexican-American community. Her younger brother Jesusito had been quite ill and nothing the doctors did improved his condition. Each Holy Saturday *(Sábado de Gloria)* before Easter, her mother organized a healing rite performed by her grandfather. While in Mexico the rite was performed by the grandfather outdoors, in the United States he had to go inside the private space of the home to do the healing. Only old men and young boys—those outside of the mainstream male world—were involved in such rituals in America. The house was prepared by the mother and daughters by sprinkling holy water and arranging white carnations and roses. A son held a baby chick. The grandfather began the rite by praying in Spanish and touching the children present with the white carnations. He touched Jesusito's useless legs and prayed *"Creo Dios Padre."* Finally he took the baby chick and tried to make it drink water from the mouth of the sick child. "For my mother," Griffith wrote, "it was a good time. Every year it was a good time at *Sábado de Gloria*, it was a new beginning for everyone, a new chance for good living—a prayer for God's blessings."[28] It was a time when a mother could try to heal her sick child.

Richard Gambino reported that when he was sick, his grandmother tried to cure him by placing cups over his body to draw out the illness by suction. Gambino made it quite clear that his grandmother believed in modern medicine because she had seen it work. She also, however, believed in the power of Jesus and the saints. By petitioning the holy figures and promising to give them special worship, she believed she could enlist their help healing the sick. Women like Gambino's grandmother and Griffith's mother were not interested in parish societies, charitable organizations, or Catholic novels. They developed a strong domestic religion that centered on providing cures for incurable illnesses, receiving comfort from the saints, Christ, and his mother, and creating a sacred space in their homes. It was not important that children learn the doctrines of the institutional church by memorizing the catechism. What was essential was that they respect the extended family and its traditions.

While the first generation of immigrants insisted on the maintenance of Old World customs, the second and third generations often resented the ways of their parents. The resentment did not stem from the younger generation's involvement with institutional Catholicism, but rather with the desire to become Americanized. Children ridiculed folk Catholicism not because of its unorthodox nature, but because it was old-fashioned and unscientific. In Griffith's account of the *Sábado de Gloria* ritual, her oldest sister, Carmen, rejected the efforts of her mother to get her involved with the preparations for the healing ceremony. "I'm not going to get cleaned with those flowers and prayers," she yelled from the kitchen, "it's just black magic. I don't want any of that stuff. The kids at school make fun of you if you do that. They think we're dumb anyway."[29] Likewise, Gambino's mother removed the little amulets his grandmother sewed onto his clothes as soon as she discovered them. While the second and third generations of Italian Americans did not become more involved in parish life, they did show some skepticism about the traditions their parents brought from the old country. Private healing rituals in particular appeared to contradict the American preference for a scientific and impersonal medical system. Italian and Mexican women experienced intergenerational conflicts as they tried to negotiate between tight-knit families whose values were based on generations of rural life and the individualistic and work-oriented expectations of urban American society.

A third new immigrant group, the Poles, provide a contrast to the Italians and Mexicans. Between the 1880s and the 1920s, over 2 million immigrants came to America from the dismembered ancient kingdom of Poland, which had been divided between Germany, Austria, and Russia. Like most immigrants, they came because the economic and social situation in their homeland made it impossible for them to own land. More men came than women, and those who decided to stay permanently sent for wives. Polish women in America did not stay single for long. Polish Catholic men worked primarily as unskilled laborers in the meat packing industry and the steel mills of Chicago, the car manufacturing plants of Detroit, and the coal industry of western Pennsylvania.

Unlike the Mexicans and the Italians, the Poles who came to America accepted the parish as the center of Catholic religious life. In their villages in the Old World, the parish was the focus of both religious and community life. Once in America, the Poles associated themselves so closely with the parish that they defined where they lived not by street designations, but by their parish names. They also respected the clergy: "Who has a priest in the family," according to a Polish saying, "will not be butted by poverty."[30] Polish priests and nuns, familiar with the cultural traditions and expectations as well as the language, ran the parishes and parochial schools. Unlike the

Italians, there was no cultural split between the Catholic leaders and their people. Polish values and traditions flourished in mutual benefit societies, women's rosary groups, and church devotions.

As with most immigrants who could not own land in the Old World, home ownership became an important goal; it was an end in itself and not a sign of upward mobility. Polish women, like Irish women, were charged with keeping their homes in absolute order and cleanliness. The Polish home, according to anthropologist Paul Wrobel, "is considered sacred, almost like a shrine, and cleanliness is a sign of respect."[31] Floors were scrubbed, dishes polished until they shone, and yards were kept immaculately trimmed. Once a home was purchased, it was considered to be a treasure not to be misused. To symbolize the importance of the home and to protect it from evil, the priest came with blessed chalk once a year at Epiphany and inscribed "K + M + B" (Kaspar, Melchior, and Balthasar) on all the doors. Before entering or leaving the rooms, guests and family crossed themselves with holy water found in small fonts inside the doors. As late as 1910 in America, Polish women on Whitsuntide decorated their houses and doorways with branches of birch, willow, lilac, and syringa to give their homes a special festive appearance for commemorating Pentecost. This custom was a variation of the Polish rural tradition of women and girls weaving garlands with crosses on them and placing them on the walls of their houses.

Women also maintained family shrines in Polish households. In a Polish home at the turn of the century, there were holy pictures on the walls, often in thick gilded frames, hanging high up near the ceiling. Our Lady of Czestochowa and large oleographs of Jesus and Mary were particularly popular. Candles burned in front of the pictures or statues and pussy willows and a herb bouquet were stuck in the frame. On the feast of the Assumption (known in Poland as *Matka Boska Zielna*, Our Lady of the Herbs), women bought from the markets bouquets made of field flowers and herbs. They took the bouquets to church to be blessed and then placed them with other holy objects in their homes. Prior to the 1930s, pussy willows were used instead of Easter palms on Palm Sunday. Sometimes children were given some of the catkin to swallow to cure or ward off sore throats. When pussy willows were replaced by palms, children received sips of holy water brought from the church on Holy Saturday to help prevent throat ailments.

An important religious role of Polish immigrant women was to manage the elaborate seasonal dinners that gave the family a vivid reminder of the sacred calendar. For Easter, women spent all Holy Week scrubbing the house, decking it with flowers and flowering plants, and making traditional food. Colored eggs, sausages, ham, veal, pig's feet jelly, horseradish, butter shaped like lambs, and babas were prepared by mother and daughters. The mother brought the Easter food in baskets to the church to be blessed or else it was blessed by the priest who came to the home. Blessed Easter eggs were broken and shared at the meal. Easter celebrations were not only conducted in the church, but each family participated in the drama of Holy Week and Easter at home.

Likewise, for the Christmas Eve dinner *(wigilia)* the women prepared cheese and sauerkraut pastries *(pierogi)*, fish in various forms, mushroom soup with noodles, herring and boiled potatoes, dumplings with plums or poppy seeds, stewed prunes with lemon peel, and poppy seed cake. Mothers taught their daughters that the meal symbolized the source of the family's food—the grains from the field, the vegetables from the gardens, the mushrooms from the forest, the fruit from the orchards, and the fish from the water. Such meals were not merely elaborate feasts but confirmed that the family recognized its dependence on each other, the natural world, and the divine world of God. This dependence was symbolized in the breaking of the Christmas wafer *(oplatki)*. The wafer, made by the nuns or the parish organist, was brought to the homes of the parishioners by altar boys or purchased at the rectory or convent. At the Christmas Eve dinner, the wafer was broken and given to the family and guests. Pieces of the wafer were sent to relatives living out of town as a token of the connectedness of the whole family—including those far away.

Because Polish men were not as estranged from Catholicism as Italian and Mexican men, they participated to a larger extent in domestic religion. Where it was left up to Italian and Mexican women to organize religious rituals, create domestic shrines, and say their private devotions, in the Polish family these activities might be shared by the men. In 1910, the father in a second-generation Polish family took the bread prepared for the evening meal by his wife and ceremoniously made the sign of the cross with a knife over the bread explaining that this bread symbolized the Eucharist. Although women prepared the meal, gathered the family, and passed on detailed knowledge of the customs, men, as the heads of their families, officiated at the family religious rites.

Generational conflicts and the demise of domestic religious traditions also occurred in Polish families. Helen Stankiewicz Zand reports that by 1949 the marking of the doors of Polish homes was rapidly passing away. An aunt of Zand who had come to America at the age of two confessed that she wrote the "K + M + B" on the narrow, top edge of the door facing the ceiling where God would see it, but not scoffers. By 1942, it was no longer the women who carried the heavy baskets of Easter food into the church to be blessed. Zand reports that the children of St. Stanislaus's parish in Buffalo carried small bright colored baskets arranged with token quantities of ham, eggs, sausage, bread, horseradish, salt, and vinegar to church. Children performed a watered-down version of a ritual once carried out by women. The tendency among many ethnic groups, including the Poles, was to simplify ethnic domestic traditions and to have children do what had once been done by adults, especially by women. As home life became more and more geared to children and the succeeding generations became more detached from the traditions of the old country, ethnic domestic traditions became something suitable only for children and old people.

AMERICAN CATHOLIC DOMESTICITY 1920–1960

While ethnic domestic traditions still remained strong in the twentieth century, some Catholics married out of their ethnic group, moved to the suburbs, and left Old World ties in the cities. While grandmothers continued the ways of the old country, granddaughters were attaining more education, going out to work after bearing children, and even divorcing. Catholic leaders, especially the clergy, became hypersensitive to the changes in American life. Their addresses to the family became more impassioned. In 1928, James Gillis, the Paulist editor of *Catholic World*, exclaimed, "there exists today, in all civilized countries, a considerable movement for the abolition of marriage and the disintegration of the family."[32] *The Homiletic and Pastoral Review* of 1935, which provided food for pastors' sermons warned that "Bolshevism appeals directly to young girls. Each dictator sets up his program to win the women, young and old."[33] The situation had not improved by the 1940s. A writer in *America* feared that the "American scene [has begun] to resemble slightly the Soviet one in which public nurseries, birth control clinics and loose marriage arrangements weakened long established ideals of family life and parenthood."[34] Wartime morals, the priest feared, threatened the sanctity of the family.

Even the postwar suburbs of America were not safe. Andrew M. Greeley worried in 1958 that the Americanization of the immigrants might be a mixed blessing and that the suburban Catholic could become *too* American. "Catholics can accept much of the American way of life with little hesitation," he wrote in the family magazine *The Sign*, "but in certain matters—birth control, divorce, and premarital sex experience, for example—we must part company with the average American. We simply cannot accept his ideas." While Catholics in national parishes and old neighborhoods "were somewhat insulated from the infection of pagan influences," Greeley observed, "in the suburbs they are in the main line of the enemy's fire."[35] Suburban Catholics, writers agreed, although free from the economic and social ills of the urban ethnic slum, now faced the spiritual problems of modern life.

Clerical and lay fiction writers also warned Catholics about the modern world. In Joseph McShane's survey of short stories published by Catholic magazines between 1930 and 1950, he found that readers were told that the world was a dangerous place that sought to destroy their faith, morals, and true happiness. Business, education, and the modern notion of marriage were particularly seductive. Women lured into the business world, the stories warned, found their lives empty, their feelings selfish, and their families slowly disintegrating. Educated, but devoid of proper Catholic values, such women were doomed to languish in pain and superficiality. The good Catholic woman, like the proper woman of the nineteenth century, regularly communed with God, protected her family from physical harm, reformed her errant husband or child with her prayers, and saved her home from the corrosive influences of the world. With her individuality and ambitions surrendered, the Catholic woman submitted joyfully and fully to the will of her husband. Housekeeping and childrearing, the fiction concluded, gave the woman the highest sense of fulfillment imaginable. McShane justifiably concludes that "the wife/mother becomes the icon of the community's highest value: selfless service to others, service which is motivated by faith. Moreover, in her daily performance of her duties, she becomes a visible model for all the members of the family to follow."[36]

Catholic fiction reiterated on a popular level the same beliefs that priests preached to families. "Your Catholic family," wrote Father George Kelly, a New York parish priest, in *The Catholic Family Handbook* (1959), "symbolizes in miniature the Mystical Body of Christ. The husband and father is the head of the body and represents Christ. The wife represents the Church, and the children, as members of the body, represent the faithful."[37] According to Father Kelly's handbook, the family worked along with Christ to secure the redemption of its members and the world. It was through the family that God channeled grace—the husband and wife exchanged grace between each other as well as with their children. Emphasizing paternal leadership, Kelly insisted that men who have "mentally divorced themselves" from the family left their homes "in a state of anarchy or matriarchy."[38] More than ever, writers and clergy presented the family as a sacred entity like the church, which could save its members through an exchange of grace. The notion that somehow the celibate life was superior to the married life totally fell by the wayside. Catholic families were told that the home best represented the Trinity, the Holy Family, and the Mystical Body of Christ.

In 1948 and 1949, two pastoral letters from the American bishops summarized the pre-Vatican II Catholic attitude toward the family. The family, the bishops explained, was a divine institution that human will cannot alter or nullify. A growing tendency to ignore God and his rights in society provided a "lethal danger" to the family—"more fearsome than the atom bomb." Consequently, every Christian "must make his home holy"; allowing the whole atmosphere to be "impregnated with genuine Christian living." A secularized home was "at the root of so many of our greatest social evils." As the child's first school, the family taught responsibility to God and to others. Family life provided dignity, peace, and security for the mother and exercised an ennobling and steadying influence on the father. For both parents, it awakened and developed a sense of responsibility while fostering their growth in selflessness, sacrifice, and patience. While the government should not interfere with parental authority, it should make provisions for adequate housing and schooling. The family must demonstrate a "staunch loyalty" to God, his commandments, the church, and Catholic doctrine. Daily family prayer, the dedication of the home to the Sacred Heart, group recitation of the rosary, and frequent reception of the sacraments were the means through which pure family life could be established. The bishops concluded by asking Catholics to make their family life "a mirror of the Holy Family of Nazareth" and a "shrine of fidelity, a place where God is the unseen Host."[39]

Catholics responded to the plea to maintain good families by founding organizations dedicated to domestic virtues. During the nineteenth century, countless advice books, novels, newspapers, and sermons explained to women what a Catholic home was and how they could create one. During the twentieth century, Catholic organizations also became involved in promoting Catholic family life. In 1920, the National Council of Catholic Women set up committees on family life and domestic education. A decade later, a group committed to the scholarly and scientific study of family and parent education organized the Catholic Conference on Family Life. Much of this interest in family life by Catholic organizations was stimulated by Pius XI's encyclical letter on Christian marriage, *Casti connubii* (1930). The response to the pope's call for a strengthened Christian family included the rise of popular movements for the promotion of Catholicism in the home. The Christian Family Movement (1940s), Cana Conferences for married couples (1944), Marianist Family Sodality (1950), and the Family Rosary Crusade (1960) were organized efforts to focus attention on the well-being of the family.

The liturgical movement, launched in the 1930s, also helped Catholics create a religious foundation for home life. Through revitalizing the liturgy, the reformers hoped to instill in Catholics a spiritual alternative to the materialism of American society. One of the main American proponents of the movement, Dom Virgil Michel, O.S.B., believed that the family was the "Mystical Body's spiritual miniature." According to his biographer, Michel felt that home devotions were a preparation for, or continuation of, corporate worship in the parish church. "Christian homes," Michel believed, "would be citadels of Christian culture radiating light into their neighborhoods, a kind of sanctuary of God."[40]

The liturgical movement promoted a series of family liturgies that were detached from ethnic ties. By the 1950s, suburban Catholics were reading the numerous books and pamphlets on appropriate family religion published by Liturgical Press out of St. John's Abbey in Collegeville, Minnesota. In exchange for giving up "superstitious" folk customs, the liturgical movement offered families a series of approved Catholic seasonal liturgies. Ethnic traditions were not ignored, but liturgists purified them of any magical or pagan connotations. In the spirit of America as "melting pot," the *Catholic Family Handbook* encouraged families to try the Dutch traditions of St. Nicholas, the Mexican celebration of *Los Posadas*, the German custom of baking lenten pretzels, and the French Canadian Emmaus walk with grandparents on Easter Monday.

The twentieth century brought about a loud cry from clergy and lay leaders that formal family prayer be instituted in every Catholic family. Although late-nineteenth-century critics were satisfied with traditional prayers and the recitation of the rosary, twentieth-century writers insisted that family worship include Bible study and perhaps a reading selection from the day's gospel or epistle. The recitation of Hail Marys and Our Fathers gave way to more varied family worship. Although Bible reading, either individually or in family groups, was not a traditional Catholic practice, the papal promotion of family Bible reading in 1893 and again in 1943 strengthened the use of the Bible within family worship. European writers, notably Marie-Louise and Jacques Defossa, described their regular Bible reading within their family as including commentary, prayer, and singing. They concluded that such readings changed the atmosphere of their family by allowing them to be more conscious of the presence of God and more "relaxed" and detached from events since they knew that "everything which happens to us comes from the hand of the Father." "Little by little," they wrote, "we are passing from a too uniquely moral conception of religion to a more fundamental and more personal one."[41]

What were women asked to do in order to promote their well-being and develop Catholic consciousness in their families? Although it was still assumed that the woman's place was in the home training her children, providing a peaceful environment for her husband, and developing her own spirituality, the rhetoric praising women's piety was gone. By the end of World War I and the demise of Victorian sentimentality, Catholic women were discussed with less ornate prose. As middle-class women in American society stepped down from the pedestal to vote, acquire higher education, and take their place in the work world, Catholic writing responded by toning down its maternal rhetoric. Catholic writers turned away from equating the home with mother and began to point out the importance of the father as the head of the household.

The Defossas and others who wrote on formal family prayer in the fifties assumed that the father, and not the mother, should lead family devotions. They cited Pius XII's encyclical *Summi pontificatus* (1939), which emphasized that the father should fill the position of priest in his own house. While it was crucial that the mother attend these sessions, they made it quite clear that the father should read from the Bible, pray for his family, and improvise commentaries on the readings. Likewise when the journal *Worship* included an article on blessing children, it described how the father extended his hands over the child's head in benediction. When a 1957 article in *The Sign* showed a mother blessing her son before he went to bed with the sign of the cross on his forehead, Timothy Heffernan, a reader, wrote an irate letter to the editors complaining about "the total neglect of the role played by the father."[42] Heffernan reminded the readers that it was a common teaching of the Catholic church with reference to family life that the husband was the head of the wife and the leader of the family. He echoed the same sentiments contained in the *Worship* article when it stipulated that men should refuse to be "victims of petticoat tyranny" and instead assume their "sacred position of being God's representative in the home."[43]

Suburban living in the forties and fifties had placed men in a precarious position with regard to the family. On the one hand, suburban life allowed for a radically improved standard of living over immigrant life in the city. In the suburbs, children could play in their yards instead of in the streets, the air was free from urban pollution, and educational opportunities provided a means of economic improvement. On the other hand, fathers drove long distances to work and frequently juggled two jobs while mothers spent their whole days minding children. While in the city paternal authority could be exerted by an extended network of male relatives even if the father was absent, in the suburbs only women were left to watch over their children. What many Catholics resented was the assumption that women were the head of the home and men the head of the workplace. They insisted that men serve as both the head of the home and the workplace. Andrew Greeley had correctly predicted that Catholics would face important challenges in the suburbs.

To reinstate the paternal authority over the family, Catholic writers tried to minimize the mother's role in domestic religion and empha-size the father's. It was, however, a losing battle. Unlike Protestants who had a long history of family worship with the father substituting for the male minister, Catholics did not have such a tradition. Prayer within the home, until the late nineteenth century had been an individual matter. There was no strong tradition of male leadership in family worship. Because of women's traditional role in informal religious activities—heightened by their isolation in the suburban home—the duty to organize family worship most often fell to them. While fathers might lead the prayers or read from the Bible, it was most likely the mother who would bring the family prayer book, pick out the reading from the Bible, assemble her children, and explain the process to her husband. The enthusiasm with which the advice literature of the 1940s and 1950s insisted that the father organize and lead family prayer only confirms the reality that domestic religion still was the domain of women.

What made it even more difficult to convince men to take over family worship was the stress Catholic writers laid on celebrating seasonal devotions in the family. Catholics traditionally may not have had evening and morning family prayer, but they did have family celebrations oriented to the liturgical year. During the 1950s, Catholic writers made a great attempt at encouraging families to bring Catholicism into their families by conducting seasonal religious rituals. These domestic liturgies had little to do with ethnic traditions and were based on approved church worship styles. Saying the family rosary, reading from the Bible, and having group prayer were considered important for the promotion of home life, but seasonal domestic rituals captured the Catholic preference for the connection of sensuality and the sacred: the everyday with the divine.

Advent, Lent, and Holy Week provided ample occasions for families to become involved in religious activities. The construction and lighting of the advent wreath (an activity invented by the liturgical movement with only vague ethnic origins) became standard in good Catholic families. Sociologists Ernest and Johanna Winter suggested in a 1957 article that on Ash Wednesday parents and children assemble in front of the home altar in the living room and proceed in procession through the house reciting antiphons, gathering up the old palms and ceremoniously burning them. On Holy Thursday, according to Emerson and Areleen Hynes, select family and friends could be invited to participate in a paschal meal of lamb or a roast, with "a lamb cake baked and frosted white" surmounted by a small white banner for a centerpiece and dessert.[44] The *Catholic Family Handbook* suggested that matzos be served at dinner on Holy Thursday, that the home altar be stripped on Good Friday and a very plain meal be eaten during which the whole family would stand. Although the articles urged that the father be actively involved, there can be no question that it would be mother who baked the cake, bought the matzos, stripped the altar, and made the Friday meal. Even the Hyneses admitted that Holy Saturday would be the only day that father would be home and then he should have the day in silence and meditation "appropriately [mixing] this with working outdoors on the lawn or garden or at manual labor of some kind."[45]

The trend to ask both parents, not just the mother, to create a Christian home was not a universal phenomenon. In 1952, Newman Press published "a treatise on the mental hygiene of the home" by "A Carthusian of Miraflores," which asserted that the mother ultimately created a well-organized and religious home. It was the mother who was the main channel for the transmission of religious ideas to her children. When they see her kneel and pray in front of the family altar or before a crucifix her children "will soon do as you do." Mothers should consider it their duty to beautify their home and to keep it clean and orderly. "And last but not least," the book explained, "you should always be neatly though inexpensively dressed, wearing a pretty apron when doing the housework." The ideal Christian mother lived for God and worked for her husband and children. In true nineteenth-century spirit, the author summarized that the mother abided in the divine presence throughout the day's duties and sought "Eternal Wisdom by holy reading and mental prayer." The Catholic mother picked up her cross and followed Christ "joyfully," leading her children to everlasting life.[46]

The development of a domestic ideology that centered on the love of mothers and the authority of fathers helped create a lay-oriented American Catholicism. By expressing the belief that women, or at least the family, could be a means for the salvation of souls, it weakened the preference for the celibate life promoted by traditional Catholicism. Women were allowed the privilege of "saving souls" because they fully embraced an otherworldly outlook—they were selfless, obedient, charitable, modest, and cloistered in their homes. Women who rejected these otherworldly values and attempted to cultivate a life *in* the world through careers, elaborate social life, or extensive charity obligations relinquished their ability to save their families. Even immigrant women, who may have had no understanding of mainstream Catholic domestic values, perceived that their religious activities in the home could "save" their families. Mothers and grandmothers conducted healing rituals, rites to ward off the evil eye, and petitions to the saints for the good of the family. The home, and the woman as its caretaker, was understood as a sacred space marked by St. Bridget's crosses, Angelus clocks, statues of Our Lady of Guadalupe, or the chalked initials of the three Magi.

Catholic culture, which hailed the importance of the woman in the home, created a fundamental problem for traditional, patriarchal Catholicism. If the home and family reflected the order of heaven and if the home were a miniature church, then women must *not* enjoy such a powerful position within the household. If the mother acted as the main strength of the household, which reflected the cosmic order, then what of the importance of the male deity, the male savior, and the all-male priesthood? Traditional, hierarchical Catholicism demanded that the father serve as the head of his home. Thus, Catholicism fought throughout the nineteenth century to preserve male authority within the home, only to be faced in America with a growing separation of spheres that placed women in control of the home. This same American culture assumed women were more pious, more selfless, more charitable, and thus more religious than men. As Catholic culture encouraged families to worship together at home, and liturgists created formal devotions that duplicated church services, the father was asked to take his position as domestic priest. By the 1940s and 1950s, while women continued to be the domestic priestesses for informal religious instruction, once that instruction became formalized and blessed by the church men were asked to direct family religion. Only the radical rethinking of the mission of Catholicism and the meaning of God beginning after the Second Vatican Council would cause a shift in the understanding of women's religious role within the home.

CHAPTER
4
Catholic Laywomen in the Labor Force, 1850–1950

Mary J. Oates

Given the high representation of immigrants in the American Catholic community after 1840, its female work force has been depicted by historians as initially unskilled or semiskilled, heavily confined to domestic service and factory work, advancing slowly by late nineteenth century to such female-dominated occupations as school teaching, nursing, and clerical work. Women in the labor market have been largely ignored by church historians who, with a few recent exceptions, do not even mention their contributions to the progress of Catholics into the American mainstream. Women who do appear are nearly always linked to the institutional church as nuns or to leading laymen as mothers, wives, or daughters. Since normal lay female activity was identified as the private, domestic sphere, which for wealthy women was defined to include various church charities, it is hardly surprising that laywomen considered noteworthy in their own right have remained wealthy philanthropists and officers of women's auxiliaries. With the exception of a few converts, career women are rarely mentioned in discussions of Catholic leaders.

Despite significant and, in some cases, unprecedented achievements of women in diverse occupations and professions, their story remains largely untold. Yet pioneer working women challenged conventional attitudes and social standards by their work choices and accomplishments. Through their example, they widened the vision of the young of their day and fostered professional ambition in future generations of women. Within the constraints imposed by traditional perceptions of what women could legitimately accomplish, the collective advance of employed laywomen in the century after 1850 represents an impressive chapter in the history of the church in America.

Catholic churchmen, like their Protestant counterparts, strongly discouraged women from public activity throughout the nineteenth and for much of the twentieth century. Females who abandoned domestic tasks designated for their sex in favor of careers represented a clear danger to social order and to the welfare of future generations. Atypical behavior elicited stern rhetoric and reminders that exceptions only proved the rule. Even in the 1930s, when many Catholic women were attending college, ecclesiastics were unwilling to concede that a long-term professional career might be a legitimate option. Rev. Karl Alter (later archbishop of Cincinnati, 1950–1969) typically defined a brief female career horizon, ending at marriage:

> With the greater opportunities which are being presented to women nowadays, it is no longer necessary for the young woman with a college degree to consider the alternative of returning to private life in her own home or entering the field of teaching. . . . Marriage, of course and home-making still remain the great vocation and career of womanhood, but it is not possible, as a rule, to step immediately from the stage on graduation day to the altar of matrimony.[1]

It is difficult to exaggerate the paucity of data on Catholic working women. While essays and biographies exist for a number of outstanding individuals, no analysis of the professional progress of laywomen as a group exists. In this study, we draw upon several major directory sources to identify nearly five hundred women born before 1930 who participated in the labor force. Their professional histories provide the basic data for this chapter.[2] By focusing on representative women among them in various fields and historical periods we are able to determine how female work choices and accomplishments were affected by the social environment of their day. We find that Catholic women gradually moved into all the major professions, some achieving national prominence and large numbers gaining regional recognition. They were not a homogeneous group. In fact, their diversity was notable, as were their professional and personal backgrounds. Yet certain patterns can be identified in their movement into the labor force that challenge the pervasive stereotype of Catholic working women as relatively lacking in professional motivation, content with traditionally female occupations, and more accepting than other American women of socially circumscribed spheres of female activity.

At the very time that the cult of domesticity was beginning to narrow work options for early-nineteenth-century American women, manufacturers were aggressively seeking workers for New England factories. They identified in young, single Protestant girls a plentiful supply and attracted them to mill towns at increasing rates after 1815. The primary collective interest of these native operatives understandably focused on wages, hours, and working conditions and they readily joined male workers in protesting wage reductions or unfair treatment. When Irish Catholic women replaced native workers by the 1840s, female participation in strikes and protests diminished. Unlike their Yankee counterparts, Catholic women lacked male figures—whether husbands, fathers, or brothers—who could support them should they lose their jobs. Although Irish women received significantly less pay than native women and did the least desirable work, by 1870 they accounted for 58 percent of all Lowell, Massachusetts textile operatives and two decades later comprised the largest group of immigrant women workers in the state, representing 17 percent of all women in industrial occupations.[3] After 1890, French-Canadian Catholics moved in large numbers into the textile workforce. From the standpoint of occupational status, the position of both groups was unenviable and native response to their unpopular religion only reinforced their isolation from middle-class America.

Not all Catholic working women flocked to manufacturing establishments. Thousands of single Irish women found employment as live-in domestic servants. By 1876, for example, 76 percent of Irish women working in New Jersey were domestic servants. Polish women resembled the Irish in this work choice, as did women in ethnic groups arriving in the 1880s and 1890s. In sharp contrast, Italian and French-Canadian women shunned domestic service for employment in textile and garment mills. In all ethnic groups, married women worked outside the home only when necessary, preferring to supplement the family income by taking in boarders or by doing piecework at home.[4]

Working-class women had little success in moving out of low-skill, sex-segregated occupations, especially if they were immigrants, but they encouraged their own daughters, whose educational opportunities surpassed their own, to avoid domestic work and factories in favor of teaching and clerical positions. While 60 percent of Irish-born women in the labor force nationally were in domestic service in 1900, only 19 percent of second-generation Irish were thus employed.[5] By the late nineteenth century, a significant number of factory women had acquired an acute social consciousness from their experiences as operatives, and they more readily identified with efforts to organize women workers. One of the pioneers was Irish-born Winifred O'Reilly, who arrived in New York in the 1840s and was forced by family circumstances to go to work as a stitcher at the age of eleven. She developed into a vigorous union organizer, effectively opposing speedups and other employer tactics exploiting women workers. Her more famous daughter, Leonora (b. 1870), caught her mother's enthusiasm, joined the Knights of Labor at sixteen, and in time became, as union men testified, "the best labor man among them all."[6]

Leonora Barry (b. 1849) also emigrated from Ireland as a child. Her situation as a young widowed mother laboring in a New York hosiery mill led her to join the Knights of Labor in 1884 and, despite severe criticism from Catholic clergy, to champion publicly the cause of the working woman.[7] She drafted the Pennsylvania State Factory Inspection Act, and played a pivotal role in its passage in 1889. Barry shared the conventional view that only economic necessity justified a woman's work outside the home and retired upon her second marriage in 1890.

Family reverses occasioned the entry of convent-educated teenager Augusta L. Troup (b. 1848) into the labor market. Her experiences as a typesetter at the New York *Sun* catalyzed her interest in organized labor. She began by assisting Elizabeth Cady Stanton and Susan B. Anthony in founding the New York Working Women's Association in 1868 and in publishing its paper, *Revolution*. Her election as the first female officer of the International Typographical Union in 1870 provided further opportunity to encourage women in all industries to unionize. After her marriage in 1874 she, like Barry, retired from the labor force, engaging mainly in Chatauqua and lyceum activities thereafter.

Irish-born Elizabeth F. Rodgers (b. 1847) stood in sharp contrast to her two contemporaries. Rather than confine herself to the domestic duties entailed in raising her ten children, she entered wholeheartedly into labor work. Without doubt, the presence of a supportive husband facilitated her decision. In 1876 Rodgers was the first Chicago woman to join the Knights of Labor and the first to hold leadership positions in that organization. By 1887 she had emerged as a national leader in the struggle for workers' rights.

A generation later, the young Mary Kenney (b. 1864) was prompted by her work experience in printing and binding to take up the cause of the working woman. With the help of Jane Addams she held union meetings at Hull House and established the Jane Club, a cooperative housing agency that provided apartments where Chicago working women could reside and share food and companionship at nominal cost. This innovative and beneficial arrangement was widely imitated. In 1891 she became the first female organizer in the American Federation of Labor. At her marriage in 1894 to Jack O'Sullivan she moved to Boston where she continued her organizing efforts, helping in 1903 to found the National Women's Trade Union League. The last employment of this remarkable woman before her retirement was as a Massachusetts factory inspector from 1914 until 1934.

A contemporary of O'Sullivan was Connecticut-born Katherine Williamson, whose work experience as a proofreader on the *Denver Post* introduced her to the cause of labor reform. Marriage did not impede her efforts, and, as a prominent member of the Typographical Union and the Women's Trade Union League and as Colorado's first female factory and pure food inspector, she lobbied for child labor legislation, the minimum wage, and equal pay for equal work.

Early factory toil similarly mobilized Agnes Nestor (b. 1880) to collective action. The daughter of Irish immigrants, Nestor worked in Michigan glove factories where she witnessed unremitting exploitation of women and children. Shy as a young woman, she appeared an unlikely organizer. A group planning to file a grievance was warned by her sister Mary, "Don't take Aggie, she can't talk."[8] But Nestor soon became an orator to contend with, known for her calmness and incisive, logical arguments. Beginning as shop steward, she had advanced by 1907 to secretary-treasurer of the Glove Workers Union and member of the American Federation of Labor's Committee on Industrial Education. With Elizabeth Maloney of the Waitresses Union, she fought for protective legislation, especially for the eight-hour workday.

Thanks in part to determined efforts of such women, the late nineteenth century witnessed the emergence of the labor movement as a "good Catholic cause." More rank-and-file women felt comfortable in joining unions and assuming leadership roles in them. By 1900 the Women's Trade Union League had a large Catholic membership and, by 1913, a Catholic president in Agnes Nestor.[9]

As industrialization in the early decades of the nineteenth century lured men from farming to wage work, the home increasingly became exalted as a safe refuge in a troubled and secular society. Woman's particular duty was to cultivate in herself the peculiarly female virtues of purity and self-sacrifice and to develop within her family circle a climate of peace and devotion. The model American woman became the lady at home. By the 1840s, when Catholics in greater numbers began to move into the middle-class, the extremely narrow definition of women's place was being modified by Protestant women. Although Catholic sermons continued to emphasize the critical role of motherhood and its moral priority for women, gradual adaptation by Protestant women of their appropriate sphere to encompass social concerns soon affected Catholic women. Middle-class women wishing to be "socially useful" had long established a growing number of religious benevolent societies. These preserved a conservative image of limited extradomestic female interests, especially by married women, while allowing women to extend their activities beyond the confines of home.

Religious discrimination had already encouraged the Catholic community to develop separate schools and social agencies to serve its members. Their staffs, typically members of sisterhoods, welcomed the financial support and volunteer services of laywomen in the burgeoning female charitable societies. The unusually warm liaison that marked middle-class laywomen and religious sisters in this era had its roots in the many convent schools for girls that had existed from the early years of the nineteenth century and that by 1850 were educating substantial numbers of daughters of well-to-do families throughout the country. While the administrative experience acquired in charity endeavors did not impel Catholic women to political action to the same extent as it did their Protestant counterparts, participation in the numerous associations and auxiliaries legitimated their advance from the confines of the home and eased the transition to wider spheres of female labor.

Rigid differentiation of work by sex characterized the American labor market by the time Catholic women began to have the education and means to enjoy work options beyond factory or domestic work. Nonetheless, despite the constraints of occupational segregation, by the 1890s unprecedented numbers of single women were undertaking full-time careers and, in the process, intimidating the hierarchy who deplored their independence and their rejection of traditional exhortations that they find identity in home or convent. Many married women shared clerical apprehensions and society matron Alice Timmons Toomy ably voiced their sentiments;

> They dress like men, they talk like men, they force themselves into the manliest avocations of men, and strive to fill them, loud-voiced and aggressive, to the criminal neglect of their own bounden duties.[10]

Toomy concluded that these women were simply oddities. "Exceptional women have been born to exceptional vocations. . . . But the average woman can have but one mission, one kingdom—that of home."[11]

By 1900, however, more working women were finding such conservative attitudes intolerable. In 1904, aged forty-nine and contentedly single, essayist Agnes Repplier minced few words in her defense of the working woman:

> It is not the rich and presumably self-indulgent woman alone who is admonished to mend her ways and marry. . . . Even the factory girl, toiling for her daily bread, has been made the subject of censure as unjust as it is severe. . . . What if she does enjoy her independence, and the power to

spend as she pleases the money for which she works so hard? These things are her inalienable rights. To limit them is tyranny. To denounce them is injustice. . . . She does not owe matrimony to the world.[12]

Despite the progress of Catholic laywomen in advancing into the professions, they differed in several key respects from mainstream professional women in 1914. First, as a group, they were not as well educated as their Protestant counterparts. While 64 percent of prominent Protestant professional women had some schooling beyond high school, the Catholic figure was only 38 percent. Second, they were disproportionately single. Hierarchical opposition to the employment of married women is reflected in a lower marriage rate of 37 percent among these career women, in sharp contrast to the 55 percent recorded for Protestants. Finally, the fact that 42 percent of Catholic professionals but only 32 percent of Protestants were concentrated in the arts, on the stage, and as writers, reflects not only fewer educational opportunities but also the effects of Catholic disapproval of female participation in male-dominated professions.[13]

Although opportunities in the American work force were limited and their status in the home subordinate, women, including Catholic women, had never been discouraged from expressing ideas in written form. Before 1900, their writings tended heavily toward prescriptive literature, pious autobiography, sentimental romance, and pieces for women's magazines. The reassuring tone of these publications apparently comforted a heavily female audience attempting to embody in their own persons the virtues of the ideal wife and mother.

Early writers were frequently convent school graduates who typically came from more affluent backgrounds than the average Catholic. Writing was viewed as an ideal enterprise for them since it was fairly easy to find a publisher and they were not competing with male writers, who, for the most part, did not favor light fiction or juvenile literature. Then, too, no specific credentials were needed for entry into the field and women could pursue careers without leaving their homes. These positive features led Agnes Repplier to comment that "fiction is the only field in which women have started abreast with men and have not lagged far behind."[14]

Given the relative poverty of the early Catholic population, it is not surprising that many of the best known women writers born before 1850 were converts. Their interests were remarkably varied. For example, the influential Elizabeth Ellet (b. 1812) of New York, a convert late in her life, was the first to give explicit consideration in her work to the role of women in American society. Historians also remain indebted to amateur anthologist and convert Abby Hemenway (b. 1828) for her prodigious five-volume treatise on Vermont history. Another convert-author and pioneer, Julia A. Wood (b. 1825), migrated from New Hampshire to become in 1859 editor of *The New Era*, a Minnesota Territory newspaper, a dramatic achievement for a woman of her day. And Boston poet, artist, and lecturer Eliza Allen Starr (b. 1824) opened a Chicago studio in 1856, two years after her conversion to Catholicism. Under her dynamic leadership it remained an important force in the city's intellectual life for nearly five decades.[15] Starr was especially supportive of efforts of religious sisters to advance women's education and gave generously of her time and talent to the development of the art department at St. Mary's Academy, Notre Dame, Indiana.

Philadelphia convert Caroline Earle White (b. 1833), founder of the Pennsylvania Society for the Prevention of Cruelty to Animals, wielded her powerful pen for that cause. Lighter fare was produced by prolific convert Frances C. Tiernan (b. 1846) of North Carolina, writing under the name Christian Reid, whose early novels were immensely popular with a national audience. Her later fiction lost its broad appeal as she used it increasingly as a proselytizing forum for Catholic doctrine.

As Catholic families acquired resources to provide better educations for their daughters after 1850, more born-and-raised Catholics joined the ranks of authors. Agnes Repplier, for example, gained early and sustained recognition from the literary establishment for her finely crafted work. A Philadelphia native, she began to write at twenty-one to help support her family, publishing pieces in the *Catholic World* and the *Young Catholic*. By 1886 her essays in the *Atlantic Monthly* were attracting high praise. She had the distinction of becoming in 1928 the second female member of the American Philosophical Society, and over the years received honorary degrees from Yale, Columbia, and the University of Pennsylvania. Her convent school classmate Elizabeth R. Pennell (b. 1855) won fame as a historian, biographer, and art critic for *The Press* and *The American*.

Another convent school graduate was Massachusetts native Louise Imogen Guiney (b. 1861), a daughter of Irish immigrants, who gained national attention as a poet, essayist, and literary scholar. Her striking talent ensured her acceptance in Boston literary circles and her presence did much to dissipate the prejudice against Catholics still prevalent in late nineteenth century New England. A contemporary, Elizabeth Jordan (b. 1867) of Wisconsin, commenced her writing career as an investigative journalist for the *New York World*, and soon was known for her report, "The Submerged Tenth," which graphically described living conditions in New York tenements. She was named editor of *Harper's Bazaar* in 1900 and remained a powerful role model for aspiring young women journalists. After 1900 she turned to writing exceptionally fine novels, giving credit for her distinctively disciplined style to a favorite teacher, Sister Ethelbert, who had encouraged her to write with polished reserve, letting readers "shed their own tears."[16] Her considerable talent is reflected in her participation with such fellow authors as Henry James, Elizabeth Stuart Phelps, William Dean Howells, and Henry Van Dyke in writing *The Whole Family*. Although convert Molly Elliot Seawell (b. 1860) of Virginia gained wide readership for her nautical tales, drawn from reminiscences of a navy officer uncle, she was probably best known for "Maid Marion." In 1895 she won a major literary prize from the *New York Herald* for one of her novels.

Other nineteenth-century women wrote for more specialized audiences or edited journals in their fields. Georgina Pell Curtis (b. 1859), a convert and New York native, was a writer familiar to Catholics, especially through her work as editor of the first edition of *The American Catholic Who's Who* (1911). Californian Laura A. Calhoun (b. 1847) penned biological treatises, developing also several useful inventions, including a fruit harvester and a nonrefillable bottle. In 1846 Prussian-born writer and journalist Josephine McCrackin initiated a crusade to save the California redwoods and wrote also on behalf of more humane treatment of animals, becoming the first woman member of the California Game and Fish Protective Association. Margaret Halvey, born in Ireland in the 1860s, followed in this tradition by publishing pieces opposing vivisection while serving as managing editor of the *Journal of Zoophily*. Writings on astronomy by her contemporary and fellow native of Ireland, Rose O'Halloran, appeared in such journals as *Scientific American* and *Popular Astronomy*.

The number of Catholic authors expanded rapidly after 1900. Kathleen Norris (b. 1880) of California worked for nine years as a reporter for the *San Francisco Call* until her marriage in 1909. At that point she commenced writing the romantic novels that brought her fame. Totalling nearly one hundred, they gave readers vivid descriptions of early twentieth century Irish-American life. Like most Catholic women of her day, Norris was staunchly conservative about women's place and she depicted her female characters as firmly rooted and contented in the home. While she never received major literary recognition, her novels had national circulation and were among the most widely read of the era. More highly praised for literary merit was the juvenile fiction of Pennsylvania-born Margery Bianco (b. 1881) whose twenty published volumes made her America's leading children's author. Although black Catholic authors were always few, Ellen Tarry (b. 1906) continued the tradition of fine writing for young readers. Convert Justine C. Ward (b. 1879) achieved international approval for her music books for children. Her interest in church music motivated her in 1928 to establish a fund to promote the study and singing of Gregorian chant.

In contrast to the limited number of exceptionally talented authors who appealed to a wide spectrum of readers, the majority were mediocre writers who served religion more than literature. The post-1850 years saw a virtual outpouring of "Catholic" novels from women, short stories and poems aimed at counteracting the virulent anti-Catholic sentiment so frequently reflected in popular writing of the period. Typical of the many authors in this genre are Irish-born Mary A. Sadlier (b. 1820) who came to the United States in 1844 and Eleanor C. Donnelly (b. 1838) of Pennsylvania. Sadlier's sixty novels and her many short stories bolstered the faith of Catholics within a Protestant milieu and introduced young Irish immigrants to American ways. Donnelly, a popular poet and children's author, explained why she focused on young Catholics: "I have felt impelled to this work because I love their precious souls; because I am convinced that a good storybook is for them the next best thing to the Catechism."[17]

While these Catholic novels and magazine articles aimed to reinforce church teaching and women's domestic obligations within their female and youthful audiences, they also instilled in readers a much-needed sense of pride in their religious heritage and helped to unify an immigrant church still divided by heterogeneous ethnic cultures. Without doubt, also, they provided some Protestant readers with an introduction to Catholic beliefs and values. In these senses, they can be considered important molders of the American Catholic character.

Converts consistently comprised a sizable proportion in this category of writers. Susan L. Emery (b. 1846) of Massachusetts, for example, after her conversion at the age of twenty-nine, brought her experience as editor of an Episcopal youth magazine to a similar post with the *Sacred Heart Review* in the 1890s. Contributions of twentieth century converts like Katherine Burton and Anne Fremantle demonstrated considerably more technical skill. Ohio-born Burton (b. 1890) worked on the staff of *The Sign* and became the preeminent biographer of famous Catholics, while Fremantle (b. 1909), who was also known for her popular stories about church heroes, joined the editorial team of *Commonweal* in the late 1940s.

The acceptance of Catholic women writing independently at home was central to the emergence by the late nineteenth century of impressive numbers of career editors and journalists. That this was not yet a conventional path is aptly illustrated in a contemporary description of the eminently private lifestyle of one leading writer: "Except for a brief tenure of the post office at Auburndale, Louise Guiney's life was friendships and a library in Boston, and friendships and a library in England."[18]

By the 1870s women were beginning to redefine such professional boundaries on writers in critical ways. Since social approbation already existed for women to produce literature for children and for their own sex, pioneer journalists tended to focus on "women's issues," narrowly defined. But affected by the feminist movement and by their own rising aspirations, they soon abandoned these boundaries by broadening the definition of women's literary concerns to encompass burning social issues of the day. Inspired by social reformers and labor organizers fighting for justice for women and the poor, some journalists shifted their energies from simply writing about social problems to a more direct and public engagement in their resolution. One such was journalist Anne E. Murphy (b. 1866) who was appointed ward superintendent for the Chicago street cleaning department in 1910, the only woman in the country to hold such a public works post.

The Catholic press provided many opportunities for female journalists, although initially they were restricted to writing about traditionally female concerns. Irish-born Honor O. Walsh (b. 1870s), for example, was by 1895 an associate editor, responsible for the "Home and School Page" of the Philadelphia *Catholic Standard and Times*. While steady, if slow, progress continued in dioceses across the country, it was certainly hindered in a few quarters. The experience of Katherine E. Conway (b. 1853) of Rochester, New York, a writer of popular Catholic fiction and an influential, if conservative, essayist illustrates the tenuous nature of the "careers" of women employed by Catholic newspapers. Conway had had two decades of staff experience with the widely circulated Boston Irish newspaper, the *Pilot*, before she was named its editor in 1905. But her tenure at its helm was brief. Upon its transformation in 1908 into the official journal of the Boston diocese, Cardinal William O'Connell removed Conway as editor. While not unusual, such arbitrary treatment became less frequent. Although more subtle tactics limiting women's advance persisted, the number of female editors and journalists grew. In 1909, for example, at the time of Conway's dismissal in Boston, convert Alice J. Stevens (b. 1860), who had written for *Harper's* and for the *Los Angeles Times Magazine*, was editing the Los Angeles diocesan paper, *The Tidings*.

The Catholic press served as a training ground for other outstanding journalists like Anne O'Hare McCormick. Born in the 1880s in England and educated in an Ohio convent school, she began her career as associate editor of the *Catholic Universe Bulletin* in Cleveland and by 1922 was European correspondent for the *New York Times*. The first woman appointed to its editorial board in 1936, McCormick won a Pulitzer Prize for the paper the following year, again the first woman to win for foreign correspondence reporting. In 1940 she received the Outstanding Catholic Woman Award.

Other journalists were moving directly to the secular press by 1900. Florence H. Bork (b. 1869) of New York pursued a successful career under the name Alice Benedict, writing for the *Chicago Tribune*, the *Chicago Herald*, and the *Cincinnati Post*. And Winifred Black (b. 1863) of Wisconsin, writing under the name Annie Laurie, achieved dubious national distinction as "the greatest sob sister of them all"[19] for her sensational columns in the *San Francisco Examiner* and the *Denver Post*.

A few independent women joined male journalists in covering national news. Described at her death in 1903 as "the ablest woman journalist in America,"[20] Irish-born Margaret B. Sullivan wrote for the Chicago *Times* and *Tribune* and contributed pieces to the *Encyclopaedia Britannica* and major magazines. Kentuckian Marie M. Meloney (b. 1878), already chief of the Washington Bureau of the *Denver Post* at eighteen, became an outstanding journalist and effective magazine editor, writing for the *Washington Post* and the New York *Sun*. By the 1930s she was well established in a male domain, gaining national recognition for organizing such creative and pathbreaking ventures as the "Forum on Current Problems" of the New York *Herald Tribune*.

Another writer for the *New York Times* was Kathleen McLoughlin (b. 1898) of Kansas who began her career as a reporter for the *Atchison Globe* and the Chicago *Tribune*. Moving to the *New York Times* in 1935, she became successively its women's, foreign, and Washington correspondent. From 1951 until her retirement in 1967 she effectively represented the paper at the United Nations.

Women born at the turn of the century like McLoughlin were still able to advance to successful careers in journalism without benefit of postsecondary education. Convert Clare Boothe Luce (1903–1987), for example, worked until 1934 as associate and managing editor at *Vogue* and *Vanity Fair*, going on to a rewarding career as a playwright and essayist, a member of Congress (1942–46), and eventually United States Ambassador to Italy. Despite her frequent protestations about the primacy of the home for married women, her example served to establish her as a model for many ambitious laywomen. Nonetheless, it became increasingly common for women born after 1890 to prepare for careers in journalism by attending college. Montana native Helen Walker Homan had even acquired a law degree from New York University in 1919 before she took up the editorship of the *Pelham* (New York) *Sun* and *The Forum*. And Ellen V. McLoughlin (b. 1893) of New York, a graduate of Smith College (1915), studied for an additional year at Radcliffe before commencing her editorial career at Grolier

Press in 1924. By 1940 she was editor in chief there as well as managing editor of the *Book of Knowledge,* and at her retirement in 1964 she was a Grolier vice president and member of its board of trustees.

As theaters and music halls gained in popularity by 1850, we find Catholic women well represented among performers, both serious and light. Yet considerable ambivalence persisted about the propriety of Catholic women appearing on public stages and in music halls. In 1890 the great actress Helena Modjeska defended the legitimacy of her profession for women: "It certainly must develop in us a sense of independence and therefore of responsibility. . . . As for morals, I can only state that there are as many good women on the dramatic stage as in any other walk of life."[21] The Polish-born actress (b. 1840) commenced her unparalleled thirty-year American career in 1876 in San Francisco. Indisputably the finest Shakespearean actress of her day, Modjeska was known also as a generous contributor to Catholic causes, frequently braving threats from the American Protective Association to give performances to benefit Catholic charities.[22] Her devotion to her church inspired the popular actress Georgianna Drew Barrymore (b. 1854) to seek membership. Barrymore's career was bright but brief (1875–1892), and she is remembered today as the mother of noted actress Ethel Barrymore (b. 1879).

A career on the stage appealed to growing numbers of young Catholic women who disregarded social condescension and ecclesiastical scowls in the hope that good salaries would bring financial independence and more control over their own lives. While some, like leading actress Mary Anderson of Kentucky (b. 1859), abandoned their stage careers upon marriage, not all did so. Convert Laura Keene (b. 1820) turned to the American stage (under the name Mary Moss) to earn her living after her husband's prison exile to Australia. Already recognized as an actress of high standard in her native England, she made her American debut in 1852. In 1856 she founded "Laura Keene's Theatre" where she directed excellent comedies. Her production of "Our American Cousin" was playing in Ford's Theatre on the evening of President Abraham Lincoln's assassination. With the support of her husband, nationally hailed actress Minnie Madden (b. 1865) also continued her career after marriage. When he became manager of New York's Manhattan Theatre at the turn of the century, Madden was a star performer and the director of most of the plays produced.

Catholic women were prominent among the best vaudeville and comic actresses of the nineteenth century. An especially popular figure was Malvina Florence (b. 1830) who in the 1850s performed with her husband in "Yankee Girl and Irish Boy" farces. Massachusetts native Maggie Cline (b. 1857), a daughter of Irish immigrants, fled at seventeen from the shoe factory in which she had worked for five years to undertake a stage career. During the 1880s she was a particular favorite in New York vaudeville, known for her Irish comedy tunes. Another Irish-American musical comedian, the young Marie Cahill (b. 1870), was enthralling large audiences by the 1880s. At the height of her fame she prescribed marriage for all career women since "without marriage the professional woman is likely to become 'aggressive' and lose 'her higher sensibilities'."[23] While neatly justifying her own lifestyle, the intriguing argument pleased neither church leaders nor feminists.

A diversity of ethnic backgrounds characterized early twentieth-century actresses. Polish-born Anna Held (b. 1865) made her name in the United States as a musical comedy actress under the direction of Florenz Ziegfeld. Mary L. "Texas" Guinan (b. 1884), of Irish parentage, delighted audiences as she traveled from town to town in vaudeville and rodeos, eventually appearing on the silent screen. Mabel E. Normand (b. 1893), of French origin, an artist's model at fifteen, was the best known female comedian of the silent screen era, while convert Pearl White (b. 1889), of Scottish-English ancestry, was the favorite heroine of the silent screen serial thrillers, most notably "The Perils of Pauline."

Catholic women held a prominent place among more recent film actresses as well. Jane Wyatt (b. 1912) of New Jersey, Loretta Young (b. 1914) of Utah, and Jeanne Crain (b. 1925) of California provide representative examples. A perennial favorite of stage, screen, and television from her convent school graduation in 1917 has been Helen Hayes (b. 1900) of Washington, who, in the course of her long career, was voted best actress by the Motion Pictures Academy of Arts and Sciences (in 1932) and was awarded an Emmy (in 1954). Hayes has held major offices in many professional organizations, including the presidency of the American National Theatre and Academy.

In the fields of classical music and dance, Catholic laywomen have long been among American performers of the first rank. A significant number of these were born and educated in Europe, while most of the others studied abroad. For example, Augusta Maywood (b. 1825) attended the Philadelphia Ballet School before continuing her education in Europe to prepare for her exceptional American ballet career. Nationally acclaimed ballerina Giuseppina Morlacchi, born in 1836 in Italy, was fully educated for her career in Europe, arriving in America at the age of thirty-one.

Despite extensive and expensive training and unusual professional success, nineteenth century woman artists generally conformed to social norms and ceased to perform in public after marriage. The successful operatic soprano Sybil Sanderson (b. 1865), for example, retired from the stage in 1897 upon her conversion and marriage, returning to a public career only after her husband's death. And pianist Olga Samaroff (b. 1882) of Texas, by 1909 acknowledged by critics to be in the "first rank of the world's pianists,"[24] pursued a serious public career only after her brief 1904 marriage failed.

Poland was the birthplace of operatic soprano Selma Kronold (b. 1861) and pianist Antoinette Szumowska (b. 1872). Kronold was born of Jewish parents and became a Catholic at forty-one. An exceptional artist, she performed in the United States after 1885. Her deep interest in improving the quality of church music found expression in the Catholic Oratorio Society, which she founded and supported after her retirement from the concert stage. At twenty-two, the gifted pianist Szumowska emigrated to the United States and in time became one of the few women to join the Boston Symphony Orchestra. Her talents inspired appreciative audiences until her retirement in 1920. Thereafter she taught at the New England Conservatory of Music. One of her contemporaries was Tennessee-born Marie Louise Bailey (b. 1876) who, after musical training in Germany and Austria, achieved renown as one of the most distinguished pianists of her day. In 1902 she and actress Helena Modjeska remained the only women to have received the Persian medal for art and science.

Violin virtuoso Camilla Urso (b. 1842), daughter of Italian parents, was raised in France and had the distinction of being the first girl admitted to the Paris Conservatory. Her premier American tour, undertaken at the age of ten, was wildly popular; she became the first woman violinist to perform in concert in this country. Considered "one of the outstanding violinists of her day of either sex,"[25] she was also an ardent proponent of equal treatment for women performers, promoting the cause in her position as honorary president of the Women's String Orchestra. Remarking on the countless comediennes on the public stage and the acceptance of a female harpist by most orchestras, she pressed the cause of other female instrumentalists: "Let my sisters agitate this question and assert their rights."[26] After retiring from public concerts in 1895, Urso joined the faculty of the National Conservatory in New York.

In contrast to their substantial representation among noted musicians, fewer Catholic women are found among the nation's best visual artists. New York native Edmonia Lewis (b. 1845), a convert of Indian and black parentage, took up sculpture at the age of nineteen in order to support herself. Although she worked mainly in Rome, her pieces reflected American social themes. In 1868, she executed her most honored sculpture, "Forever Free," a depiction of two ex-slaves. Such sensitivity to the situation of black Americans was appreciated and her work continued to be significantly funded by the black community over Lewis's long and distinguished career. Another convert of the same era was the ceramist Maria Longworth Storer (b. 1849), whose art studio, "Rookwood," established in 1879, was the first art pottery in Ohio. Rookwood pottery was made from native clays and was marked by a patented yellow glaze. It earned Storer a gold medal at the 1889 Paris Exposition.

The earliest works of another late-nineteenth-century Ohio artist, Elizabeth Nourse (b. 1870s), were murals in the homes of affluent citizens, which she undertook in order to meet living expenses while attending the Cincinnati School of Design. Hailed as the "Millet of America" for such works as "A Breton Mother and Child," now in the collection of the Art Institute of Chicago, she was elected *associée* and *sociétaire* in the Société Nationale des Beaux Arts in Paris (1895, 1901).

The ranks of twentieth-century Catholic artists include two converts, Julia Lauren Ford (b. 1891) of New York and Irene Pereira (b. 1907) of Massachusetts. Ford was a highly regarded painter whose works are found in the Metropolitan Museum of Art, the Corcoran Gallery, and the Art Institute of Chicago. Pereira financed her night school art classes by working as a secretary and in time gained recognition as a major painter of geometric and abstract works. Muralists and illustrators are well represented in Hildreth Meiere (b. 1892) and Ada de Bethune (b. 1914). Meiere has been honored for her paintings in public buildings and churches including the University of Chicago, the National Academy of Science in Washington, D.C., and the Nebraska State Capitol. Religious art was the forte of the Belgian-born de Bethune, a graduate of the National Academy of Design. She continues to be especially appreciated by the Catholic community for her striking illustrations in the *Catholic Worker*.

Although Catholic women artists were not numerous, Catholic laywomen throughout the nineteenth and early twentieth centuries strongly supported women artists and the arts. Convert Sarah A. Peter (b. 1800) of Ohio, for example, founded the Philadelphia School of Design which in 1850 became affiliated with the Franklin Institute. This institution, described as "the pioneer school for industrial art in America,"[27] gave women the chance to prepare for paid employment in the field of commercial art. Although Peter reflected the attitudes of her day in her remark that "the arts can be practiced at home, without materially interfering with the routine of domestic duty," she nonetheless strongly championed educational opportunities for her sex, maintaining spiritedly that "it is among the stupid follies of our countrymen to exclude women as much as possible from all that may really tend to strengthen their intellects."[28] Esteem for art and the artist also characterized Mary J. Quinn Sullivan (b. 1877), art supervisor in New York schools and faculty member at Pratt Institute until her marriage in 1917, who became a respected connoisseur of fine art and one of the founders of the Museum of Modern Art.

The achievements and high representation of Catholic women among the nation's writers, actors, musicians, and artists occurred, in part at least, because neither church nor society vehemently objected to any female enterprise strictly limited to entertainment or cultural pursuits. In fact, at Mary Anderson's convent school in Louisville, Kentucky, traditional lessons were supplemented by "private lessons in music, dancing, and literature with a view to training her for her dramatic career."[29] In the 1890s Mary A. Dowd summarized succinctly and with some bitterness the perceptions of women whose professional aspirations lay beyond these confines:

> Women have gone into all kinds of mock transports on the stage, representing the different passions, and displayed their physical charms to the very best advantage with the aid of jewels and fine apparel. They have enchanted all classes without protest from the very ones who most vigorously oppose women lecturers, lawyers, and legislators. Women are encouraged to delight the senses, if they have musical talent, beauty, or the ability to impersonate, but not the mind, if they possess wealth of intellect. They are never to shock the respectable world by appearing in the character of human beings endowed by God with minds to reason, and souls to execute noble deeds.[30]

While the critical importance of education to women's advance into a wider range of occupations was evident to thoughtful Catholics by the early nineteenth century, opportunities for daughters of a disliked immigrant group were limited. In 1825 a one-room public school for girls was opened in Boston, with nearly 300 girls applying for a place. Enthusiasm ran high, but the school closed within eighteen months. Expense to the taxpayers was the stated reason, but it appears more likely that prejudice against educating Catholic girls was the precipitating factor. "Many young Irish girls had entered the school and had proved fine scholars; and an outcry was raised against education for the poorer classes, as unfitting them for domestic service."[31]

It was not long, however, before the expansion of public education throughout the country occasioned a rising demand for teachers, and by 1850 women outnumbered men in the work. Catholic women soon seized the opportunity to enter the profession and in a relatively brief period they comprised a substantial proportion of teachers in major cities across the country. By 1900, for example, over half the public school teachers in Chicago and Albany were Catholic women, mainly of Irish background.[32] Although upward mobility for female teachers was not common in most school systems before 1920, the number of

Catholic school administrators continued to expand, with single women generally more successful than married women in reaching positions of authority.

Before 1860 a majority of the nation's female teachers were still receiving little formal education, their natural instincts for child care presumably compensating for this deficiency. Accounts of the far-reaching concern of some teachers for the welfare of their young pupils remain extant. Two such women were Texas native Susan Blanchard Elder (b. 1835), a high school mathematics teacher in New Orleans, and the legendary Mary L. Schoolfield (b. 1839), who taught for sixty years in Maryland public and private schools. Others endeavored to work with adults as well as children. Over her long career in Saint Paul, Minnesota schools, Mary J. Cramsie (b. 1844) combated alcohol abuse as president of the Sacred Thirst Total Abstinence Society and founded and directed a special abstinence club for teenagers. Katherine O. O'Mahoney, with only a parochial school education, began her teaching career in Lawrence (Massachusetts) High School in 1873. By 1885 she was stepping well beyond the schoolroom to lecture to large adult audiences on history and literature, "one of the first Catholic women in New England . . . to speak in public from a platform."[33]

Despite uncommon commitment and genuine good will reflected in the lives of many nineteenth century teachers, the need for formal educational preparation for their work was widely acknowledged after 1860, and more states opened normal schools and teacher's colleges. These institutions were financially accessible to young people from working-class families and Catholic women flocked to them. Restricted in curriculum and design, the normal schools nonetheless paved the way for a regular college education for women. As publicly financed institutions, they represented the first social recognition that women, like men, ought to undertake formal study in preparation for a serious profession.

Although in 1870 women were admitted to state universities in California, Indiana, Iowa, Kansas, Michigan, Minnesota, Missouri, and Wisconsin, most of them were clustered, as in the normal schools, in traditionally female departments like home economics and education. Thus some scholars have concluded that higher education in this era may actually have "discouraged them from challenging accepted ideas about women, developing strong motives for pursuing independent careers, or trying to break into 'masculine' fields."[34]

As long as liberal arts programs were closed to them, ambitious Catholic women were necessarily excluded from, or limited to subordinate roles within, most professions. The high tuitions of the private coeducational colleges and of the new eastern women's colleges, which appeared after 1865, effectively precluded attendance by most Catholic women until about 1900. By that time, daughters of middle-class families were applying for admission, to the dismay of bishops who feared that their faith would be compromised in these Protestant settings. A number of early Catholic graduates of these colleges enjoyed success as educators. Representative were two Massachusetts natives, Katherine E. Cufflin (b. 1883), a 1904 Radcliffe graduate who had a distinguished career at Boston's Girls' High School and Victoria A. Larmour (b. 1887) who graduated from Smith College in 1908 and went on to head the English Department of the Goessmann School in Amherst, Massachusetts. By the turn of the century, however, graduates of the "Seven Sisters" colleges were moving away from public school teaching in favor of less traditional professional fields. While four-fifths of Wellesley graduates of 1880 who were in the labor force worked as teachers, the corresponding figure for 1889–1893 graduates had fallen to one-third.[35] Since the first Catholic women's colleges did not graduate their pioneer classes until after 1900, and were small in size for some years thereafter, the role of their graduates in public education was not evident until after 1920.[36]

Eastern school districts and school systems in the nation's larger cities tended to demand more formal education of prospective teachers than did school boards in more remote locations, which frequently faced teacher shortages. In these areas, Catholic women enjoyed unique opportunities. Amelia H. Garcia (b. 1876), for example, commenced her thirty-year career in Arizona at the age of fifteen. Despite a limited formal education, her teaching experience and fine reputation led to her appointment as county superintendent of schools in 1922 and later as member of the State Board of Education. Similarly, Adelina Otero-Warren (b. 1882) of New Mexico, a convent school graduate, became, in the course of her career, superintendent of schools for Santa Fe County and inspector-at-large for the Indian Division of the Department of the Interior. Pearmeal J. French (b. 1869) also had only a convent school education when she began to teach. She was State Superintendent of Public Instruction in Idaho by her early thirties and in 1908 became the first and most memorable dean of women at the University of Idaho.[37]

Even after normal schools had become more common, women continued to find relatively more numerous and varied advancement opportunities in western states. After attending the state normal school and graduating from the University of Wyoming in 1904, Rose B. Maley (b. 1884) "homesteaded under the old Homestead Act, living on a ranch for five years and teaching in schools within riding distances."[38] She was state superintendent of instruction at the age of twenty-six. And Mary E. Stannard, a 1920 graduate of the Minot (South Dakota) Normal School, was, a year later, not only a teacher but also superintendent of schools in Burke County, North Dakota.

Catholic women in time gained prominence as teachers and administrators in major school systems as well. Perhaps the most influential schoolteacher was Margaret Haley (b. 1861), a daughter of Irish immigrants, whose experience in Chicago public school classrooms led her to join the Chicago Federation of Teachers in 1897 and to become its full-time business agent from 1901 until her death in 1939. An outspoken feminist and suffragist, she was in 1901 the first female elementary school teacher ever to speak from the floor at a meeting of the National Education Association. Called the "Lady Labor Sluger," Haley brought national attention to the deplorable working conditions of thousands of women teachers and fought for substantive reforms in the areas of tenure, salaries, retirement benefits, and class size. By skillfully mobilizing the largely female membership of the N.E.A., she ensured the election of a woman, Ella Flagg Young, as its president in 1910.[39]

Given the traditional role of sisters in parochial education, few laywomen found employment as teachers or administrators in the Catholic school systems that were expanding rapidly throughout the country by late nineteenth century. An exception was Helena T. Goessmann, a New York native and Ohio University graduate (M.Ph., 1895) who headed the department of Catholic higher (high school) education in New York from 1904 to 1907. She also established and administered the Women's Auxiliary Catholic Summer School in Cliff Haven, New York, and lectured at other Catholic summer schools as well. In 1910 she moved to Massachusetts State College, Amherst, as professor of English.

B. Ellen Burke (b. 1850), a graduate of the New York Normal School at Oswego and by the 1890s a leading New York educator, generously employed her considerable organizational talents to assist sister-teachers in the parochial schools. In 1896 she introduced Teachers' Institutes, long popular among public school teachers, in several large dioceses, drawing faculty from among the best Catholic teachers in public schools across the country. These were very well received by sisters and were widely imitated, doing much to improve both teaching standards and curriculum in Catholic schools. Another New Yorker, Grace C. Strachan, attended the Buffalo State Normal School and by 1900 was a superintendent of public schools in New York City. Her long-standing interest in the advance of women was reflected in her support of the "equal pay for equal work" cause and of the Young Women's Catholic Association of Brooklyn.

In the late nineteenth century, educational requirements for women seeking high school teaching positions usually included simply a normal school diploma. Mary H. Dowd (b. 1866), the first Catholic graduate of the Manchester (New Hampshire) Training School in 1886, found immediate employment in the local high school. So too did Martha C. Doyle (b. 1869) who joined the faculty of Boston's Girls' High School upon her graduation from the Boston Normal School in 1890. But the woman born in the 1870s and 1880s envisioning a career as a secondary school teacher or as a school administrator in major cities increasingly needed both a liberal arts degree and a normal school diploma.

Although Midwesterner Catherine McPartlin (b. 1878) was able to advance to a Minnesota high school principalship with a B.A. from the state university (1905), her contemporaries in more populated states needed additional academic credentials. For example, Mary A. Lawton (b. 1876) of New York had already earned a Ph.B. (Cornell, 1898) when she enrolled in the New York State Normal School for a degree in pedagogy, essential for teaching in a local high school. Similarly, Lillian C. Dunn (b. 1881), a 1903 Cornell graduate, proceeded to Plattsburg Normal School before undertaking her life's work as mathematics teacher in Trenton (New York) High School. The pattern was the same, but in reverse order, in the case of Marie A. Dunne (b. 1882), a distinguished Chicago teacher and administrator. After graduating in 1897 from the Chicago Normal School, she found it desirable for career mobility to earn a Ph.B. thirteen years later at the University of Chicago.

By the 1930s, women anticipating leadership positions in public education typically needed at least a master's degree. Elizabeth C. O'Daly (b. 1910) was one of these. Upon graduation from Hunter College in 1931, she proceeded immediately to acquire an M.A. at New York University (1933). Her extensive experience as teacher and principal qualified her in 1958 for an assistant superintendency in New York City junior high schools. Several years later she was supervisor of three Brooklyn school districts.

Catholic women were also taking faculty and administrative positions in the nation's normal schools. Ella R. Baird, an 1898 graduate of the Oswego (New York) Normal School, moved from a school principalship in Burlington, Vermont to serve successively as principal of normal schools in Poughkeepsie, New York and Toledo, Ohio. A generation later, a normal school diploma and on-the-job experience were insufficient preparation for such posts. Connecticut native Margaret Kiely held B.A. and M.A. degrees from Columbia (1916, 1924) and, while serving as director and principal of the Bridgeport Normal

School, continued her graduate study at Columbia where she received her Ph.D. in 1930. Thus qualified, she was offered a deanship at Queens College (New York) in 1937.

The doctorate was becoming a must for normal school faculties by the 1930s, and Catholic women in numbers responded to the challenge, often while teaching full time. Typical was Julia C. Harney, who earned three degrees from New York University between 1918 and 1931, advancing successively in her field, first, as principal and, in the 1940s, as faculty member at the New Jersey Training School for Teachers.

Another relatively accessible occupation for women with some education was library work, and Catholics were soon well represented in this field. Before the 1860s, training tended to be received on the job, and there was little upward mobility for women, especially in the large city libraries. For example, Caroline E. Poree (b. 1842), a convert at thirty-eight, had only a public school education before commencing her life's work. For nearly four decades she held the title of "assistant" in the periodical department of the Boston Public Library, presiding over the men's reading room. Yet Michigan-born Marie H. Harlan (b. 1859), with the same education as Poree, but employed in a rural location, advanced to head the Langdon, North Dakota, Public Library.

Opportunities expanded in large cities for those born about 1900. Mary L. McCabe of New York, an Elmira College graduate with library science certification from Syracuse University (1916) was librarian of the Corning, New York, Public Library by 1922. And Joyce E. Nienstedt of Wisconsin, with a B.A. and a library science diploma from Lawrence College and the University of Wisconsin respectively (1932, 1938), by 1946 headed the Iowa City Public Library. Sarah L. Wallace (b. 1914) of Missouri, a college and library science graduate of the College of St. Catherine (1935, 1936), enjoyed a career spanning nearly thirty years with the Minnesota Public Library. In 1963 she was appointed publications officer at the Library of Congress and editor of the *Quarterly Journal of the Library of Congress*.

By specializing within the field, others were able to find attractive positions. For example, Helen S. Moylan, a 1912 Radcliffe graduate, worked as assistant librarian at the Harvard Law School until 1916 when she moved to the University of Iowa Law School Library, heading it by 1922. While working as librarian in the law library at George Washington University, Helen Newman (b. 1904) of Washington, D.C., enrolled in the law school (Ll.B. and Ll.M., 1925, 1927). In 1942 she had become associate librarian and in 1947 librarian of the United States Supreme Court. Massachusetts native Katherine McNamara (b. 1898), a graduate of New Rochelle College (1917), joined the staff at the Harvard University School of Landscape Architecture Library after earning her library certification (Simmons College, 1918). She became its librarian in 1924. Similarly, Elizabeth E. Biggert (b. 1915) of Ohio, with a B.A. from St. Mary of the Springs College (1937) and a library science certificate from Western Reserve (1938), headed the Economics Library at the Battelle Memorial Institute in 1956.

Catholic women continue today to gain recognition in this field. Best known is China-born Yen Tsai Feng (b. 1923) who emigrated to the United States in 1946, a year after graduating from Shanghai University. In addition to a Ph.D. (University of Denver, 1953), she earned an M.S. in library science at Columbia University (1955). After advancing to increasingly responsible positions in the Harvard College Library and the Boston Public Library, Feng in 1977 was named librarian at Wellesley College and, in 1980, librarian of Harvard College.

Some librarians have also held positions on university faculties. Marie G. Blanchard (b. 1874) of Pittsburgh earned a library school certificate from Carnegie Institute of Technology (1913) and taught there and at Pennsylvania State University until 1928 when she assumed the posts of librarian and dean of women at Duquesne University. Anna C. Kennedy (A.B., Vassar, 1915), with a journalism degree from Columbia (1916) and certification from the New York State Library School (1924), was well qualified to become in 1929 supervisor of school libraries for the New York State Department of Education. Like those aiming to teach in normal schools, women born after 1900 needed advanced degrees for faculty appointments in schools of library science. Librarian Genevieve M. Casey (b. 1916), for example, prepared to teach in her field by earning a master's degree at the University of Michigan at the age of forty. By 1968 she was associate professor of library science at Wayne State University.

Despite remarkably rapid advances made by Catholic women in public school teaching and librarianship, the fact remains that by the time they were entering these professions in large numbers, both had been clearly labelled as "women's fields." Late nineteenth century Catholic women who wished to enter male-dominated professions found opposition still severe and they were restive under narrow social and church definitions of appropriate work choices for females. Once again Mary A. Dowd voiced their dilemma:

> There is a large class between the home-makers and religious who can be neither the one nor the other. The church, in its infinite wisdom, has never said that a woman must marry or enter the convent. . . . This class, including all others obliged to support themselves, have the moral right, and should have the social and legal right, to enter whatever professions or fields of labor they choose and are capable of filling. . . . If the superior wisdom of the church had set the seal of disapproval on this movement,

we would have known it long ere this; but, as it is, we are free to advocate, as Catholics, what we believe to be one of the greatest reform movements of the age.[40]

Although Catholic women had made major contributions to the field of education at its lower levels, they were far less successful in breaching the male preserve of higher education. Those aspiring to a teaching career at the college or university level needed Ph.D. degrees and these were relatively inaccessible to most laywomen until the twentieth century. Their heavy concentration in "female specialties" was the result not only of discrimination in access to graduate programs, but also of efforts by academic women themselves to professionalize various aspects of traditionally domestic responsibilities. Such focus on academically marginal fields indicates lingering uncertainty about the legitimacy of pursuing a scholarly career. Most of the early Catholic laywomen in higher education were found in these traditionally female fields. The career of Mary D. Chambers (b. 1865) demonstrates that at the turn of the century few qualifications were demanded by universities of those teaching female subjects like home economics. Although she had not yet earned a college degree she was in 1903 a professor and department head at Milliken University in Illinois.

Other pioneers in higher education came to it after significant careers elsewhere. Eleanor Kelly (b. 1879), a 1902 graduate of the Thomas School of Music and Art, had been a music superintendent in Iowa and Michigan public schools before taking a graduate degree at Cornell University in 1913 and joining the faculty of Hillsdale (Michigan) College. By 1920 she had left college teaching to become director of a conservatory of music. Similarly, after many years as an Ohio teacher, Mary G. Waite (b. 1877) earned a Ph.D. in childhood education at Yale and, at age fifty, commenced her career at the University of Cincinnati. Eugenie Andruss Leonard (b. 1888) also was past fifty when she earned a Ph.D. in education at Columbia and became dean of women at Catholic University.

Since language teachers were less likely to be required to hold the Ph.D., Catholic women made significant strides in these fields. Frances Arnold (b. 1888), for example, earned a B.A. and an M.A. in Spanish (1910, 1923) at the University of Maine, and at age thirty was a professor there. Paris-born Helen Fouré (b. 1889), educated at the Institut de Phonétique, taught French at Ohio State University, and Louise Delpit, also born and educated in France, moved to Smith College as associate professor of French in 1908 after several years in high school teaching.

Women fully realized that by choosing male-dominated fields of study they would probably be unable to advance in regular faculty ranks except at women's colleges. In conventional fields like education, nursing, and social work they had at least some prospect of achieving professorial rank. Thus social work, sociology, education, and psychology were especially popular fields of study among women aiming for careers in higher education. Butler University graduate Dorothy L. Bork (b. 1903) undertook graduate study at Fordham's school of social work before her appointment as dean of the Boston College School of Social Work in 1944. And 1927 graduate of the College of Notre Dame (Maryland), Mary E. Walsh (b. 1905), joined the Catholic University sociology department at the age of twenty-eight after earning her graduate degrees there. Dorothy Abts of Nebraska (b. 1908) and Dorothea McCarthy (b. 1906) of Minnesota were also on the faculties of Catholic University and Fordham in the 1940s in the fields of social work and psychology. Although restricted by field, these Catholic women, and many like them, made significant contributions to the development of Catholic lay and religious professionals and, more broadly, to the progress of Catholic higher education.

The situation was not very different in secular universities. Traditional female fields of specialization opened doors for many laywomen. A typical example is Magdalene Kramer, a 1920 graduate of Trinity College, who earned her doctorate in speech at Columbia Teachers' College and then joined its faculty. The same specialty was chosen by Charlotte G. Wells of Nebraska (b. 1912), who, with a Ph.D. from the University of Wisconsin (1941), was by 1946 an associate professor at the University of Missouri.

Nursing, too, promised teaching opportunities for ambitious Catholic women. An especially popular institution among nurses seeking academic degrees to supplement their R.N.'s was Columbia Teachers' College. Eugenia F. Spalding (b. 1896) of Indiana earned both B.A. and M.A. degrees at that institution (1932–34), returning there, after a period in teaching and public health, as professor of nursing education. A contemporary, Agnes Gelinas, also earned degrees at Columbia (1928, 1933) before moving to head the department of nursing at Skidmore College. Mary K. Mullane (b. 1909) followed them at Columbia and, after long experience as administrator and teacher of nursing, assumed the deanship of the University of Illinois College of Nursing. Ethel M. Tschida (b. 1914) earned a B.S. at St. Mary's College in Indiana (1924) as well as an M.A. at Columbia before her 1954 appointment to the Cornell University Hospital School of Nursing faculty.

Faculties of teachers' colleges also provided positions for women completing graduate work in education. Inez Specking (b. 1895) of

Missouri, a graduate of Harris Teachers' College, returned to teach at her alma mater after earning a Ph.D. at Stanford University (1931), and Lulu M. Spilde (b. 1894), a graduate of South Dakota Teachers' College also returned to her college in 1925 as dean of women. Fourteen years later, with an Ed.D. from New York University, she left to become professor of education at St. John's University. Convert Annabelle M. Melville (b. 1910), a graduate of Albany State College for Teachers (1931), studied history at Catholic University (Ph.D., 1949). By 1953 she was a professor of history at Bridgewater (Massachusetts) State College and has since gained recognition for her exceptional studies of leading figures in the American church.

After 1900 the emerging Catholic women's colleges provided faculty openings for women in traditionally male fields of specialization. These institutions had been founded by religious communities of women and from their inception laywomen faculty proved critical for their success. Many held advanced degrees from excellent universities and did much to set standards for the fledgling colleges. Rose Smith, for example, held B.A. and M.A. degrees from the University of Illinois (1911, 1916) and a Ph.D. from the University of Wisconsin (1926). She began her long teaching career at the College of St. Teresa in Minnesota in 1915. Twenty-five years later, Trinity College students were benefiting from the lectures of another typical laywoman, economics and sociology professor Eva J. Ross. A native of Ireland, Ross held a B.Comm. from London University (1930) and a Ph.D. from Yale University (1937).

Barnard College graduate Helene Magaret (b. 1906) earned her Ph.D. at the University of Iowa in 1940 and taught at the College of St. Teresa and later at Marymount College in New York. This pattern of movement among the Catholic women's colleges was not uncommon. However, since most administrative posts were filled by nuns, laywomen aspiring to them usually had to apply elsewhere. One such was Mary P. Holleran (b. 1905) of Connecticut, a 1929 graduate of the College of Mt. St. Vincent in New York and of Columbia University (Ph.D., 1948). After teaching for fifteen years at St. Joseph College in Connecticut, she departed in 1953 to become dean at Hampton Institute in Virginia.

Although their contributions to the education of women are frequently overlooked in discussions of the Catholic women's colleges, it is indisputable that faculty laywomen, accepting low salaries and carrying heavy teaching loads, have had an enormous impact on the progress of the Catholic women's colleges. While early hostility to hiring Catholics has disappeared in most American colleges, discriminatory treatment in hiring and promotion of women, especially in male-dominated fields, still pervades American higher education.

Thus Catholic women's colleges continue to benefit from the presence of exceptionally talented laywomen on their faculties.

Catholic women made more progress in entering the many state teachers' colleges and Catholic colleges than in finding acceptance in elite coeducational and women's colleges. Nonetheless, by the 1920s their representation was growing in these quarters as well. One of the first and still the best known is Helen C. White, the only Catholic laywoman listed among leading teacher-scholars in *Notable American Women*. A Connecticut native, White (b. 1896) earned B.A. and M.A. degrees at Radcliffe College (1917) and a Ph.D. in English at the University of Wisconsin (1924). She joined the university faculty upon completing her graduate work, and her appointment in 1936 as full professor made her the only woman at that rank in the college. A respected scholar and novelist, White served as president of the American Association of University Women in the 1940s and of the American Association of University Professors in the 1950s and remained for decades an influential figure in American higher education.

White's younger sibling Olive also had a distinguished career in higher education, specializing like her sister in English. After earning three degrees at Radcliffe she moved to Bradley Polytechnic Institute in Illinois where she commenced a long career as faculty member and later dean of women. Another humanities scholar was Mary L. Shay (b. 1894), a B.A. and Ph.D. graduate of the University of Illinois (1917, 1930) who was professor of history at her alma mater from 1930 until her retirement in 1963. While few laywomen in the early decades of the twentieth century taught science in coeducational universities, an exception was Elizabeth C. Crosby (b. 1888) of Michigan. A convert at the age of forty-nine, she taught anatomy for many years at the University of Michigan after completing her Ph.D. at the University of Chicago in 1915.

Laywomen were taking more faculty positions in secular women's colleges by the 1920s. Hunter College in New York City stands out among these institutions for its relatively high Catholic representation. For example, Elizabeth M. Lynskey, a B.A. and M.A. graduate of the University of Minnesota (1919, 1920), who held a Ph.D. (1929) from the Brookings Graduate School of Economics and Political Science, joined the Hunter political science department in 1927. In the same year, the history department hired Georgiana P. McEntee, a 1918 graduate of the College of Mt. St. Vincent with an M.A. and a Ph.D. from Columbia (1919, 1927). Eleanor G. Clark (b. 1895) graduated from Oberlin College (1918) and from Bryn Mawr College (M.A., 1919, Ph.D., 1928), where she taught from 1923 until 1930. In that year she became a Catholic and also moved to the Hunter faculty. A Hunter alumna of 1934, Margaret R. Grennan (b. 1912), returned a year later with an M.A. from Columbia to begin her career in the English Department, earning the Ph.D. in 1943. Another 1943 Columbia Ph.D., Madeleine H. Rice, accepted a faculty appointment at Hunter the same year.

Teaching positions opened up in other women's colleges as well. Helen S. Corsa (b. 1915) graduated from Mt. Holyoke College (1938) and earned a Ph.D. at Bryn Mawr (1940), moving to the Wellesley faculty in 1948 after several years at Russell Sage College. And Mary C. Rose (b. 1916), who earned her Ph.D. at Johns Hopkins in 1949, was professor of philosophy at Goucher College by 1953. Phyllis J. Fleming (b. 1924) of Indiana, after graduating from Hanover College, earned her Ph.D. at the University of Wisconsin in 1954. A member of the Wellesley faculty after 1953, she became professor of physics in 1967 and was appointed dean the following year. Her career differed in several critical respects from that of her counterparts of earlier generations. Her field of specialization was not traditionally female, she progressed quickly toward the Ph.D., and she held a faculty appointment at a secular liberal arts college. By the 1960s, as more Catholic women attended the best graduate schools and became less concentrated in "women's fields," their representation grew on faculties of major colleges and universities across the country.

By the end of the nineteenth century, prestigious male-dominated professions like medicine and law were requiring formal academic credentials for entrance, and women's still-limited access to graduate and professional schools became a major barrier to their progress in these fields. In general, Catholic women were not well represented among early physicians. The economic status of the average Catholic family in the mid-nineteenth century was not conducive to the fulfillment of unusual professional career aspirations of daughters. Ironically, by the 1920s, when greater numbers of Catholic women were acquiring means as well as motivation to pursue medical careers, the American Medical Association and the medical schools had imposed rigid and highly restrictive quotas on the admission of women. At Boston University, for example, while the 1898–1918 graduating medical classes were 30 percent female, not a single woman was listed among the graduates in 1939.[41]

One of the earliest Catholic women physicians was Jane Wall Carroll (b. 1848) of New Jersey. Despite family obligations entailed in raising ten children, she earned her M.D. at the University of Buffalo Medical School in 1891 at the age of forty-three. We know that she practiced in Buffalo and that she went on to take two degrees in law. However, few young women from ordinary Catholic families of this period could emulate her, and it is not surprising that converts figured prominently among Catholic health professionals of the nineteenth century.

Mary Gove Nichols (b. 1810), who became a Catholic at forty-seven, was an early and influential figure in the medical field, although she was not a physician. An advocate of health reform for women, she preached widely on preventive medicine and hygiene.[42] Another early physician-convert, Sarah Hackett Stevenson, was the first woman member of the American Medical Association. She arrived in Philadelphia in 1876 as a representative to the American Medical Association meeting. "Only her initials had been sent in with her name so her arrival was a shock. A motion to refer names of women delegates to the Judicial Council was tabled and she became the first woman accepted by that body."[43] A pioneer in many ways, Stevenson, who died in 1909, was the first of her sex to be appointed to the Cook County (Illinois) Hospital staff and to the Illinois State Board of Health and was a motivating force behind the establishment in 1880 of the very popular and successful Illinois Training School for Nurses.

The labor shortage faced by midwestern and western states in the late nineteenth century contributed to greater tolerance of women in traditionally male roles there than in the East. For example, Hannah M. Graham (b. 1874) earned her M.D. in 1900 at Northwestern Medical College, becoming the first woman surgeon appointed to the staff of the Indianapolis City Hospital. Kentucky native Florence Meder (b. 1877) was a high honors graduate of Louisville Medical School in 1898. Although her original specialty was in diseases of women, she soon became interested in the medical treatment provided in public institutions for the insane. Her appointment in 1909 as assistant physician at one of these hospitals was hailed as "the first promotion a woman physician has received in Asylum service in the state of Kentucky."[44]

Seventeen medical schools exclusively for women opened between 1848 and 1895, providing an increasingly important route to the M.D. degree. Before 1900 only a few Catholic women were found in these institutions. Perhaps the best known was Lillie R. Minoka-Hill, born in New York of Indian-white parentage in 1876. A convert at age twenty, she graduated from the Woman's Medical College in Philadelphia in 1899. Upon her marriage in 1905 she moved to Oneida, Wisconsin, to begin a long medical career among Indians and whites. Her deep concern for her poorer patients brought her considerable attention. It was demonstrated creatively in such innovations as her "kitchen-clinic" where patients who could not meet the standard fee were able to pay in kind.

A strong social service orientation marked the careers of many early Catholic women physicians, in part because opportunities for independent practice were limited. New York-born Teresa Bannan (b. 1868) undertook medical training at the New York Woman's Medical College after graduating from Syracuse University. During her long career she worked as a Red Cross physician during World War I and served as physician for the Syracuse Department of Health. Public health captured the interest also of Boston native Helen I. Doherty, who received her M.D. in 1895 from the Woman's Medical College in Philadelphia. She taught at the Harvard School of Public Health, served as director of the New Hampshire State Board of Health and also as field agent for the Social Hygiene Board of the U.S. Department of the Interior. A few women, like Elizabeth A. Riley, a Tufts graduate (M.D., 1897), turned to proprietary medicine. After teaching gynecology and surgery at her alma mater for eight years and gaining managerial experience as superintendent of the Women's Charity Club Hospital in Boston, Riley purchased and managed the Bay State Hospital.

An exceptional Baltimore family produced two physicians, Jennie Nicholson Browne (b. 1876) and Mary Nicholson Browne (b. 1879), and a scientist, Ethel Nicholson Browne (b. 1885). Graduates of Bryn Mawr College, Jennie and Mary followed their father's profession, both earning M.D.s in 1902 at the Woman's Medical College in Baltimore. They practiced medicine in Baltimore and were acknowledged for their socially progressive ideas in health service. Jennie served as physician for city charities and as city health officer, while Mary was clinician in gynecology at the Johns Hopkins Hospital and obstetrician in an evening clinic. Ethel graduated in 1906 from the Women's College of Baltimore (later Goucher College) and, after receiving her Ph.D. in biology at Columbia (1913), found employment as a research biologist.

For women born after 1890, the route to a career in medicine became more structured, with college more often preceding medical training. Although Bertha K. Hobart (b. 1889) of Ohio had already graduated from the Tennessee Medical College at the young age of twenty-two, Isolde T. Zeckwer's longer educational path was to become the accepted one. Born in 1892, she was a 1915 Bryn Mawr graduate who earned her M.D. from the Woman's Medical College in Philadelphia in 1918, specializing in pathology. Research appointments at the Mayo Clinic and Harvard University continued until 1927, after which she moved to the University of Pennsylvania, where by 1936 she held the rank of assistant professor.

Some pioneer women physicians had first embarked upon a traditionally female profession before finding their way to a medical career. For example, Adelaide D. Hoeffel of Wisconsin (b. 1867) graduated from Wisconsin State Normal School before enrolling in Hahnemann Medical College where she earned her M.D. at the age of thirty-six. Interested in children, she pursued a career as a pediatrician at Children's Memorial Hospital in Chicago. Mary O'Malley (b. 1867) also studied medicine after completing the Brockport (New York) Normal School program, becoming in the mid-1930s clinical director of St. Elizabeth's Hospital in Washington, D.C. Iowa native Mary A. Kileen (b. 1872) followed a similar path: After graduating from Iowa State Teachers' College, she took her M.D. at the University of Michigan in 1904. Her original interest in teaching remained, reflected during her busy medical career in Dubuque in her willingness to offer courses at two local Catholic women's colleges.

Pediatrics and psychiatry attracted many young women, since these specialties were considered more appropriate for their sex and hence promised relatively better prospects for rewarding practices. For example, Margaret M. Nicholson (b. 1899) of Virginia received B.A. and M.D. degrees (1922, 1925) from George Washington University. She practiced pediatric medicine in Washington, D.C., taught at Georgetown University Hospital, and served as chief of the cardiology department at Children's Hospital. New York native Edith A. Mittell (b. 1899), an M.D. graduate of the Long Island College Hospital (1922), gained an excellent reputation in treating children and, in time, was named a fellow of the American Academy of Pediatrics.

One of the earliest Catholic psychiatrists was Anita M. Muhl (b. 1886) a graduate of Indiana University (M.D., 1920) and of George Washington University (Ph.D., 1923). A strong supporter of women's higher education, she served on the auxiliary board of regents of Trinity College. Another was Annette Clark Washburne (b. 1898) who, after graduating from the University of Illinois College of Medicine in 1929, joined the faculty of the University of Wisconsin, becoming professor, director of neuropsychiatry, and director of student health. Dorothy D. Dowd (b. 1904) of Ohio, a graduate of Trinity College (1926) and Vanderbilt University (M.D., 1930), worked as senior physician at the Boston State Hospital before opening a private practice in psychiatry in the 1940s. In 1950 she became an associate professor at Georgetown University.

Catholic women physicians found increasing opportunities in municipal hospitals, state health agencies, and charitable institutions. An early example is gynecologist Millicent M. Cosgrave, New Zealand native, 1902 graduate of the University of Cooper Medical School, and faculty member at Stanford University after 1918. For decades after 1910 she served as physician for various homes, clinics, and missions in the San Francisco area. A much more formal pattern marked appointments of city physicians of the next generation. Frances C. Rothert (b. 1897), for example, earned her medical degree at Columbia (1922). After seventeen years as medical director of the Southwest Region, United States Children's Bureau, she was named director of maternal and child health, Arkansas State Board of Health in 1944.

Black women always faced far greater obstacles than their white counterparts in their efforts to enter the medical profession. But these did not deter such remarkable Catholics as Lena Frances Edwards (b. 1900) of Washington, D.C. After graduating from Howard University Medical School in 1924, she married a classmate and together they opened a joint practice and raised six children. After working at the Margaret Hague Hospital in Jersey City for six months in 1931, Edwards was informed by the chief of staff that some of the other physicians objected to her presence there. According to Edwards:

> He said to me, "We're having a little difficulty because you're on the staff of the hospital. You must remember that you have two handicaps: first, you're a woman, and secondly you're a Negro." And I said, "Well, God gave me both of those things, and I don't think there's a human being who has the right to judge me for what He did. You'll find I do my work properly, so you're going to have to find a better excuse for not wanting me."[45]

Edwards became a member of the International College of Surgeons and of the American Board of Obstetrics and Gynecology and in 1954 joined the Howard University faculty. Six years later she moved to St. Joseph's Mission in Hereford, Texas, where with her own resources, she opened a maternity hospital for migrant workers and became one of the medical profession's strongest champions of high quality care for the poor. Edwards' unselfish sharing of her resources, time, and skill in the service of migrant workers was honored in 1964 when she received the Presidential Medal of Freedom, the nation's highest civilian award.

Wider opportunities for movement to male-dominated medical specialties emerged for women born after 1900. Caroline A. Chandler (b. 1906) of Pennsylvania became a Catholic in 1929, the year she graduated from Barnard College. After earning her M.D. at Yale (1933), she taught pediatrics at Johns Hopkins University. After 1949, however, she was senior surgeon with the U.S. Public Health Service. The medical themes of her popular juvenile novels encouraged many girls to aspire to professional careers. German native Ruth H. Wichelhausen (b. 1908), became a Catholic in 1934, the year she earned her M.D. at Göttingen. She left a research position at Johns Hopkins Medical School to become in 1946 chief of arthritis research at the Veterans Administration Hospital in Washington, D.C.

Nursing had long attracted large numbers of working-class Catholic women, some of whom advanced professionally by entering military and government service. A typical early example was Julia M. Leary of Rhode Island (b. 1869), who saw active duty in 1898 and during World War I. She later served on the Board of Managers of the New York State Reformatory. By the 1930s, educational requirements for leadership positions in nursing had already moved beyond the R.N., and Catholic women were among those meeting them. For example, nurse Mary W. Sweres (b. 1890) of Wisconsin earned a B.S. at the University of Chicago (1923) in order to further her career as senior bacteriologist for the U.S. Government. And nurse Ruth A. Houghton (b. 1909) was already in her forties when she took up the challenge of earning B.S. and M.S. degrees at Catholic University and Boston College (1951, 1958). In 1957 she was the first nurse to achieve the rank of captain in the Navy, and a year later she became the director of the Navy Nurse Corps.

Serious careers in law were rare among American woman as late as 1880, since few law schools admitted female students. And while medical schools opened by and for women were tolerated because women had traditionally cared for the sick, no such history of female involvement existed in the male preserves of law and business. Thus few law schools for women emerged to compensate for discrimination in established institutions. Before 1900, Catholics were not numerous among women entering the field. An exception was Ellen Hardin Walworth (b. 1832) of Illinois, who became a Catholic at her marriage in 1852. After her divorce in 1871, she began to study law while supporting herself and six children. A graduate of the Women's Law Class at New York University and an authority on parliamentary law, she lobbied creatively for a national archives. She is remembered today as one of the first three women elected to a New York school board in 1880 and as a founder of the Daughters of the American Revolution in 1890.

Married women who attempted to pursue a serious career in law in these years were not usually successful. The experience of Texas-born Hortense Ward (b. 1872) reveals the critical importance of a supportive husband for a career-minded wife. Married at the age of nineteen, Ward was soon dissatisfied with domesticity. She left home to work as a stenographer, a step that contributed to her divorce in 1906. Her interest in law developed after her marriage to a lawyer in 1909. Enrolling in correspondence classes, she went on to become the first woman to pass the Texas bar examination. In 1915 she again made history as the first woman in the state to appear before the U.S. Supreme Court, and was long remembered for her vigorous lobbying for legal reform in the area of married women's rights. A 1913 Texas bill passed to protect married women's property was dubbed the "Hortense Ward Act."

By 1900 women were making more progress in entering the legal profession and Catholic women were well represented among these pioneers. New Orleans native Ophilia G. Beals, an LL.B. graduate of Washington State University (1901), was the first woman to practice law in Seattle. She also worked tirelessly to improve the lives of Seattle's citizens by founding the famous Fruit and Flower Mission, a charity serving the urban needy. On the east coast, Susan C. O'Neill graduated from the New York University Law School (1897) and became in 1901 the first woman to practice before the Connecticut Supreme Court. Another young Catholic, A. Winifred McLaughlin (b. 1882), who studied law at Fordham and New York University, was the first woman to pass the bar examination in New Hampshire. And Gertrude F. Handrick (b. 1871), a 1911 law graduate of Baldwin University in Cleveland, earned distinction as the first female member of the Cleveland Bar Association.

Like early Catholic physicians, women lawyers did not always set out to have law careers. Many had enrolled in normal schools or "business colleges" in anticipation of traditional careers as teachers or office workers. New Yorker Helen T. Hooley, after graduating in 1893 from Eastman Business College, worked as a secretary in a law firm where she developed an interest in the law. After studying independently in her spare time, she was admitted to the Herkimer County (New York) bar in 1902 and became in 1906 the first woman named clerk of the county surrogate court. Irish-born Mary O'Toole (b. 1874), after completing courses at a New York business school had the distinction of becoming the first female court stenographer in Steuben County. But this work did not satisfy the ambitious young woman for long, and she proceeded to earn LL.B. and LL.M. degrees (1908, 1914) at the Washington (D.C.) College of Law. After practicing in Washington for seven years, she was named in 1921 the first woman judge in the Municipal Court of the District of Columbia by President Harding, an office to which she was reappointed in 1925 and 1929. Born in the 1870s, Katherine R. Williams taught school for eighteen years after attending the Wisconsin State Normal School. She was able to move out of teaching by studying law independently and passed the bar examination in 1912. Many women born after 1900 followed similar two-stage career paths. Mary M. Wilkinson (b. 1911) of Missouri worked as a legal secretary after graduating at nineteen from Wylie Business School. Soon eager for more challenging and remunerative work, she enrolled at Memphis University, earning her law degree in 1937.

Catholic women lawyers were also counted among women holding judiciary appointments. The first female judge in New York state was Jean H. Norris, an LL.B. and LL.M. graduate of New York University Law School. After practicing in New York City until 1919, she was appointed judge successively in the Woman's Day Court, the Family Court, and finally the District Magistrates Court. Noted for a keen social consciousness, she was particularly active on behalf of delinquent girls and female ex-prisoners. After nearly two decades in private practice, Anna J. Levy, a graduate of Loyola University Law School in Los Angeles, was appointed in 1940 judge in the Juvenile Court of New Orleans and, nine years later, judge in the First City Court. During her long career she served also as director of the Department of Public Welfare.

Public service was an integral part of the career of Mary H. Donlon, a 1921 graduate of Cornell University Law School. Although she worked as partner in a law firm, she was convinced that women should take a direct role in politics, since it was "really only the housekeeping processes of government."[46] In 1945 she headed the New York State Workmen's Compensation Board and, at her appointment in 1955 as judge in the U.S. customs court, she became the first New York woman to receive a lifetime appointment in a federal court. A long-term member of the Cornell University Board of Trustees, Donlon promoted women's professional advancement at her alma mater by endowing a chair for a female faculty member.

Another pathbreaking Catholic woman lawyer was Helen P. McCormick (b. 1889), a 1913 graduate of Brooklyn Law School, who was, at her appointment as assistant district attorney in New York State in 1917, the first woman in the country to hold such a position. Other Catholic women soon followed in her footsteps. Sophia O'Hare, admitted to the bar in 1913 after studying law through University of Pennsylvania extension courses, became deputy attorney general of Pennsylvania in 1927 and secretary of the commonwealth in 1939. Mildred Lillie (b. 1915) of Iowa, a graduate of the University of California Law School (1938), was twenty-seven when she assumed the post of assistant attorney general for Los Angeles. In 1958, the same year that she became a Catholic, she was named judge of the California District Court of Appeals and shortly thereafter a member of the Judicial Council of California.

In contrast to their growing representation in judicial and state offices, fewer Catholic women chose to specialize in criminal law. One of those who did was Emelia Schaub (b. 1891), a graduate of the Detroit College of Law (1924), who had the distinction of being the first woman in Michigan to defend a client successfully against a murder charge. Their slow acceptance in legal specialties like criminal law propelled significant numbers of women into government work.

A good example is Louise F. McCarthy (b. 1902), who graduated from Trinity College in 1923 and earned both LL.B. and LL.M. degrees at the University of Pennsylvania (1926, 1929). After a few years with a law firm and with the Federal Emergency Administration of Public Works, she became in 1935 Chief Counsel for Pennsylvania for the Works Progress Administration. Similarly, Eleanor McDowell (b. 1913), a graduate of the College of New Rochelle (1934) and of George Washington University Law School (1944), worked as an attorney and treaty adviser for the State Department. Genevieve Blatt of Pennsylvania earned three degrees at the University of Pittsburgh, the last a J.D. in 1937. Before her appointment as judge of the Commonwealth Court of Pennsylvania, she served as chief examiner for the Civil Service Commission in Pittsburgh and as state secretary of internal affairs.

By the 1930s, women lawyers were more likely to join their male colleagues in stepping from private law practice into politics. Although public activity by women was still frowned upon in the early decades of the twentieth century, universal suffrage made it increasingly difficult to argue that highly educated women had no place in politics. Given the historic propensity of Catholic women lawyers for government employment, some wanted political involvement. Geraldine F. Macelwane (b. 1909) of Michigan, a Toledo University Law School graduate, began her law career in 1937 as assistant prosecuting attorney in Lucas County, Ohio. She was first elected judge in 1951 in the Toledo Municipal Court and subsequently in the Court of Common Pleas. After graduating from St. Mary-of-the-Woods College and earning a master's degree at Butler University, Marie T. Lauck (b. 1912) commenced the study of law only after years of work as a probation officer. At the age of forty-three she was admitted to the bar, and four years later she won election to the Indiana House of Representatives and in 1965 to the state senate. Florence K. Murray (b. 1916), a Boston University Law School graduate, served two terms in the Rhode Island Senate before her appointment as associate justice of the Rhode Island Superior Court in 1956. Catholic women born in the 1920s enjoyed greater acceptance as candidates for public office and more ambitious young lawyers found short-term political service attractive. Texas-born Frances T. Farenthold (b. 1926), for example, a graduate of Vassar (1946) and of the University of Texas Law School (1949), left her law practice for the Texas House of Representatives (1968–1972) and served as president of Wells College in New York from 1976 until 1980.

Women lawyers were less welcome on law school faculties. One early law professor was Elizabeth B. Lane (b. 1876) of Kansas, who earned an 1899 LL.M. from the Illinois College of Law (later the law department of DePaul University) and was listed on its faculty in 1910. Miriam T. Rooney, a 1920 graduate of Portia Law School in Massachusetts also held a Ph.D. (1937) from Catholic University and a second law degree from George Washington University (1942). With these formidable credentials, she secured an appointment as a lecturer at the Columbus School of Law at Catholic University.

Economic constraints and racial discrimination made it extremely difficult for black women to advance in this field. The varied career of Florence M. Hornback (b. 1892) of Ohio hints at the limited nature of opportunities for the ambitious black woman lawyer. After working until 1918 as a social worker in the Cincinnati Department of Public Welfare she enrolled in law school, graduating in 1921 from McDonald School of Law. Until 1927 she worked as supervisor and attorney for the Bureau of Catholic Charities, at which point she decided to abandon the law in favor of a teaching career in social work. At thirty-five, she commenced a long struggle to acquire the necessary credentials, earning a B.S. in 1930 at Xavier University in Los Angeles, an M.A. at Columbia University, and a Ph.D. at New York University (1941). Finally, Xavier, the nation's only black Catholic university, offered Hornback a regular teaching appointment in its school of social service.

Entry of Catholic women in significant numbers into the relatively new field of social work began in the first decades of the twentieth century. Before 1900, Catholic social workers might more appropriately be characterized as philanthropists than as participants in the labor force, since most were wealthy volunteers. A good example is Emma Forbes Cary (b. 1833), member of a prominent Boston family and convert to Catholicism at the age of twenty-two. Her extensive volunteer work in Massachusetts penal institutions led to her appointment in 1882 as commissioner of prisons in Boston, a post she filled for twenty-five years.

Twentieth-century Catholic women made significant advances as social work professionals, mainly by finding work in governmental agencies. Irish-born Ellen C. O'Grady followed a familiar female path by marrying shortly after her graduation from a New York high school in 1885. After her husband's death in 1899, however, she entered the labor force as a probation officer and welfare worker in New York City courts, working especially with women and girls. The experience deepened her awareness of the plight of poor women and she established the "Friend in Need Day Nursery" where working mothers could leave their children. By 1918 O'Grady was deputy police commissioner, the first woman to hold such a post in the United States. Courtroom experiences also affected Anna L. Smith (b. 1878) who worked with women offenders in a Chicago morals court from 1914 until 1923. After spending the next four years as clerk of Cook County, she was appointed Chicago's commissioner of public welfare in 1927.

Some ambitious women, born before 1880, were able to enter the field and advance to positions of influence without much formal training. This was particularly the case in western states and territories where the professionalizing trends increasingly evident in the major cities of the East had not yet taken hold. Kate Barnard (b. 1875) was raised in the Oklahoma Territory, and like many of her contemporaries wanted to undertake a "useful" career after convent school. Her parish priest's admonition that as a daughter and an only child her responsibility was to remain at home and keep house for her widowed father, while typical, did not sit well with Kate. Instead, the young woman proceeded to develop for herself a remarkable career. Enlisting the aid of female friends and sympathetic male organizations, she founded the United Provident Association for the support of Oklahoma's homeless. As its director, she was soon giving public speeches, writing newspaper articles, and organizing unskilled, unemployed men into a Federal Union, which was later affiliated with the American Federation of Labor. At the age of thirty-two, she won election by a large majority as the first commissioner of charities and corrections in the new state of Oklahoma. Although reelected in 1910, she did not seek a third term in 1914. In the face of fierce opposition, Barnard remained throughout her career an adamant and eloquent champion of compulsory education, the legal rights of orphans, and the abolition of child labor.[47]

The official church message on women's proper forum, as reflected in Catholic newspapers and journals, did not change between 1865 and 1914. It was simple and direct: "All arguments to the contrary notwithstanding, the proper sphere for woman is still universally held to be the domestic one, and she will always be regarded as sadly out of her place in politics."[48] But such pronouncements were increasingly viewed by thoughtful women as unreasonable and anachronistic. Such women set out to fill political posts, either by election or appointment. Mary T. Norton (b. 1875) of New Jersey, daughter of Irish immigrants, began her adult life in a conventional way, working as a secretary in New York City until her marriage. The death of her child precipitated her involvement in public service and political office. A strong advocate of the rights of working women and of child labor legislation, she was in 1924 the first female Democrat elected to the House of Representatives in her own right and the first of her sex to represent an eastern state (New Jersey) in Congress. Her political career continued until 1951.

For several years between her high school graduation and her marriage in 1900, Milwaukee native Mary O. Kryszak (b. 1875) taught school. Thereafter she worked as assistant manager of *Polish News* (1908–1922) and editor of *Polish Women's Voice* (1921–1939). From this base, Kryszak moved swiftly to a leadership role within the Wisconsin Polish-American community as a champion of the interests of working citizens. Her election to the state legislature in 1928 made her the first woman Democrat to hold state office.[49]

Political careers became increasingly accessible and popular choices among Italian and Irish women, and by the 1940s Catholics were well represented among female office holders, some as members of the United States Congress, others as mayors of large cities. Mary C. Dondero (b. 1894) served as New Hampshire state senator for ten years before her election in 1945 as mayor of Portsmouth, and another Catholic, Eileen Foley (b. 1918), followed her in these posts, first as mayor and then as state senator. Ella Grasso (b. 1919), daughter of Italian immigrants, and a Mt. Holyoke College graduate (1940), worked briefly for the War Manpower Commission before beginning a long political career. After winning elections to the Connecticut legislature and serving as secretary of state and in the U.S. House of Representatives, Grasso made history in 1975 in her election as governor of Connecticut, the first of her sex elected governor of a state in her own right.

The long career of Agnes G. Regan demonstrates a developing awareness within the church of the need to train Catholic women formally for the field of social work. Born in California in 1869, Regan was educated in Catholic schools and was an 1887 graduate of San Francisco Normal School. After thirty years as teacher, administrator, and board of education member in her home state, where her efforts on behalf of teachers' rights bore fruit in the passage of the first teachers' pension law in the state, Regan moved in 1920 to Washington, D.C., to commence a twenty-year tenure as executive secretary of the National Council of Catholic Women. In 1921 she helped to found the National Catholic School of Social Service for Women, a two-year master's degree program, which in the 1940s was incorporated into the curriculum of Catholic University. Drawing on her professional experience in education and her keen awareness of the nation's social problems, Regan became a major figure in mobilizing Catholic women on behalf of progressive social legislation and causes.

The significance of educational preparation for success in the field of social work became more evident among Catholic women born after 1880. One leading social worker was Nebraska native Jane M. Hoey (b. 1892), a Trinity College graduate (1914), who by 1916 had also earned an M.A. from Columbia and a diploma from the New York School of Social Work. Her professional competence earned her such respect that in 1936 she was appointed the first director of the Bureau of Public Assistance of the Social Security Board, a position she held for seventeen years. As a national leader in the field of social welfare, Hoey worked indefatigably for the rights of minorities and women and supported a guaranteed annual income. In 1953 she was dismayed when her position was redesignated as an elected rather than an appointed one, believing as she did that administrators of government social agencies should be appointed solely on the basis of professional qualifications. Since she refused to retire or resign, she was fired.[50]

A contemporary of Hoey's and probably the best known Catholic woman to enter the field of social service was Massachusetts native Mary E. Switzer (b. 1900). Raised in a poor Irish-American family, she attended Radcliffe College (B.A., 1921) as a day scholarship student. Her long career in government social service commenced in 1923 and by 1950 she was director of the Office of Vocational Rehabilitation. Passage of the 1946 National Mental Health Act has been attributed to Switzer's influence and persistence. The citation of the Albert Lasker Award in Medicine (1960) aptly described her as "the prime architect of workable rehabilitation services for the nation's physically handicapped."[51] Switzer's position as administrator of social and rehabilitation services in the Department of Health, Education, and Welfare, which she assumed in 1967, represented the highest ranking government post filled by a woman who had earned it by making progressive advances in the federal civil service.[52] HEW Secretary Elliott Richardson called Switzer "an unforgettable spirit," and historian Jonathan Hughes partially captures that spirit in his simple description:

> The young woman from Newton and Radcliffe College achieved a career in the ordinary civil service that is astounding to recall. But, really, it is easy to remember her: Whenever you see a ramp by a stairway in a public building or a parking space reserved for the disabled, think of Mary Switzer.[53]

There were other Catholic social workers in responsible federal positions in Switzer's era, among them Louise McGuire. Well prepared for her career with both a master's degree and a law degree from Catholic University (1933, 1940), she began as director of social work for the juvenile court in Washington, D.C. and in time became chief of the handicapped worker section, Wage and Hour Division of the Labor Department.

More often, Catholic women were found in leadership positions in state social agencies. Mary A. Cotter (b. 1882) of Massachusetts, with a B.A. and M.A. from Radcliffe College, began her career in various social agencies in her home state. By 1926 she was named deputy commissioner of institutions in the department of child welfare in

Boston and in 1934 director of social service in the city's public welfare department. A generation later, the career of California native Marion A. Joyce (b. 1902) paralleled Cotter's. She also graduated from Radcliffe (1922), later earning an M.A. from Columbia (1928). After distinguished service as a Massachusetts social worker in the 1930s, she was appointed director of the Massachusetts Division of Child Guardianship in 1939. Her expertise as well as her longstanding interest in the professional training of social workers was recognized in her appointment as associate in public welfare at the Simmons College School of Social Work. Massachusetts also benefited from the career of Mary E. Spencer of Boston, a Barnard College graduate who earned a Ph.D. at Columbia (1934) and then an Ed.D. at Harvard. By 1947 she was chief of the Bureau of Health Education, Massachusetts Department of Public Health and in 1953 also a lecturer at the Harvard School of Public Health. Mary L. Gibbons (b. 1896) of New York was another typical professional in this field. After completing her professional training at Fordham University School of Social Service in 1921, Gibbons acquired experience as a worker and supervisor in a number of New York social agencies for sixteen years before her appointment as first deputy commissioner of the New York State Department of Social Welfare.

Without question, the most difficult field for women to enter, except at its very lowest levels, has always been business. Here the record of Catholic women was similar to that of the majority of American women, although as a group Catholics entered the field somewhat later. An exception was Margaret Brent (b. 1601), one of the first businesswomen in colonial America. This single woman arrived in Maryland in 1638 and soon made her mark as a landowner and astute business agent. An outspoken and active participant in public life, she was the first woman to request publicly that she be given the vote. One of her late-nineteenth-century successors was New Yorker Elizabeth Marbury (b. 1856), a convert to Catholicism in middle age. By 1888 Marbury had become a successful international business agent for writers and actors, dealing with such essential matters as copyrights and royalties. She represented members of the French "Societé des Gens de Lettres" in both the American and British markets and served as president of the American Play Company. Chicago native Minnie S. Randall (b. 1867), founder of the Vacuum Can Company, also gained prominence in the late nineteenth century as a business and charity figure. So, too, did public school educator B. Ellen Burke, who in 1889 edited a youth newspaper, the *Sunday Companion*, published by the Catholic firm, D. H. McBride and Co. In time, she purchased the paper, thereafter successfully publishing and marketing it herself.

Despite a relatively slow start, by the early twentieth century Catholic women were making their mark as business leaders in a variety of industries. In the publishing industry, for example, we find Helen G. Bonfils, born nearly four decades after publisher B. Ellen Burke, holding the position of chairman of the board of the *Denver Post*. Many women had begun with career ambitions in such "female" fields as teaching and nursing, recognizing better prospects in the business field only later. A good example of such a woman is Alice D. Walsh (b. 1880) of New York, who attended the New York City Normal School to prepare for a conventional teaching career. Instead she moved to a career in the male-monopolized construction industry. Described by her admirers as the "only woman builder in the world," she indeed oversaw construction of numerous public and private edifices, including "some of the most important buildings in New York, fifteen public schools, libraries, public baths, fire houses, loft and office buildings."[54]

Atypical in several ways was her contemporary, Eleanor Manning (b. 1884) of Massachusetts, who earned her B.S. in architecture at Massachusetts Institute of Technology in 1906. After working as a draftsman until 1913, she established a partnership with Lois L. Howe. Their Boston firm, Howe and Manning (later Howe, Manning, and Almy) proved successful and Manning became a popular lecturer on architecture for the women enrolled at Simmons College and Pine Manor School. By going into business for themselves, these women were able to avoid discrimination in pay and position that plagued most females who worked for established firms, and self-made successes were not uncommon. Female entrepreneurs frequently produced goods and services aimed at women or children. Pennsylvania-born Anne Fogarty (b. 1919), for example, studied briefly at Allegheny College and the E. Hartmann School of Design before commencing her career in fashion design. She established Anne Fogarty, Inc. in 1960, winning numerous awards for her work. Mundelein College graduate (1943) and Chicago native Jane Trahey, left the advertising department of the *Chicago Tribune* in 1958 to found her own advertising agency, Trahey Advertising, Inc., of New York and Chicago. And Joan G. Cooney (b. 1929), a 1951 graduate of the University of Arizona, became founder, executive director, president, and trustee of Children's Television Workshop in 1968. Her work as a writer for NBC and a documentary producer for educational television prepared her to establish her own business.

Others advanced to management positions within established companies. For example, Geraldine V. Stutz (b. 1924) of Illinois, another Mundelein College graduate (1945), worked as fashion editor for *Glamour* before becoming general manager and vice president of

I. Miller, Inc. By the age of thirty-three she was president of Henri Bendel, Inc. and in 1980 was managing partner and 30 percent owner of the company.

A smaller group of women worked their way up in family-owned enterprises. Many were relatively well educated. For example, California native Ramona Hayes Healy (b. 1900) held both B.A. and M.A. degrees from the University of Chicago (1921, 1932) and a J.D. degree from DePaul University (1945). With her husband, she operated two travel agencies in Chicago after 1923. Similarly, after graduating from Barnard in 1925, Mary A. Benjamin (b. 1905) joined her father in his business in autographs, letters, and historical documents, becoming in 1937 manager of the firm and editor of its trade paper.

Catholic women born in the twentieth century have entered a broader range of industries at a rapid rate and have enjoyed far more social approbation in the process than their predecessors. A widely hailed example from the banking industry is Wisconsin native Catherine Cleary (b. 1916), a graduate of the University of Chicago (1937) and of the University of Wisconsin Law School (1943). She joined the First Wisconsin Trust Co. in 1947, and in time became its president. In the course of her career, Cleary has served as assistant treasurer of the United States and assistant to the secretary of the treasury. Jessamine M. Durante (b. 1911) also found success in the same industry, joining Harris Trust Co. after graduating from the University of Chicago in 1922. She was by 1963 manager of women's banking and by 1971, a vice president of the bank.

Chicago native Julia Montgomery Walsh (b. 1923), a 1945 graduate of Kent State University, joined the Washington, D.C., brokerage firm, Ferris and Co. in 1955, to become senior vice-president in 1970 and vice-chairman of the board in 1974. With that background, she proceeded in 1977 to found her own investment company, Julia M. Walsh and Sons, with seats on the New York and American Stock Exchanges. Walsh holds the distinction of being the first woman to complete the Advanced Management Program at the Harvard University School of Business in 1962, and in the following decade became the first of her sex to sit on the Board of Governors of the American Stock Exchange.

Laywomen in the labor force have played a critical role in the development of the American church. Catholics, like other citizens, were certainly affected by American values of independence, self-reliance, and individualism as well as by the rising freedom of action that accompanied westward expansion and the growth of modern business. Catholic women were particularly influenced by the feminist and suffrage movements to question traditional values confining their legitimate ambitions to the home. The women discussed in this chapter, professional leaders and typical workers alike, all went outside the home to undertake gainful work. In so doing, they collectively changed the thinking of both men and women about women's place in society and in the church. In the interest of objectivity and truth, and to avoid an incomplete church history, scholars must consider the impact of working women on the membership and institutional progress of the church. Laymen prominent in secular pursuits have always been identified as "leading Catholics" and their experiences carefully assessed. Professional women must be accorded similar recognition. Thanks to thousands of laywomen over the period 1850 to 1950, the church today no longer limits appropriate life choices of its female membership to home or convent.

Catholic laywomen proceeded, often in the face of sex discrimination and ridicule, to enter all of the professions, progressing in each to positions of authority and influence, bringing the Catholic presence to every sector of American life and thereby enhancing the visibility and dignity of their church in periods when it was viewed with hostility in a wider society. Committed to improving the conditions of working women, to furthering educational opportunities for their sex, and to entering upon long-term professional careers, they played a critical role in forming the consciousness of later generations of Catholic women and in paving the way for their progress into every arena of American life.

While upward mobility for Catholic women in most occupations and professions was slow in coming, they continued to struggle for positions of influence. Their entrance into the traditionally male-dominated professions, accomplished with considerable difficulty in most cases, served to expand the vision of bishops, clergy, and laity, encouraging new perspectives on women's situation in church and society. Society and church traditionally pressured women into female-oriented fields, low in social prestige and in remuneration. Yet many women freely chose fields that provided direct opportunity to affect the welfare of society, thereby reflecting the Christian message of preferring those needing help the most. Of particular consequence for the welfare of the church was their unremitting labor for the progress of women and girls.

CHAPTER
5
A Question of Equality

James J. Kenneally

"After the slave—then the woman," promised the noted abolitionist Wendell Phillips. Fearful that a Republican congress, indebted to suffragists for their Civil War support, might do just that—enfranchise women after awarding the ballot to blacks—a national women's antisuffrage society was founded in 1870.[1] The organization's leaders, on behalf of "the majority of the women of the country," presented a petition to the Senate. Signed by one thousand women, this political document proclaimed their political unfitness, "because Holy Scripture inculcates a different, and for us, higher sphere apart from public life." Furthermore, claimed the signatories, the imposition of suffrage would undermine marriage, lead to the "infinite detriment of children," increase divorce, and harm working women.[2]

This protest reflected the perceptions of much of the nation, especially adherents of organized religion. To vast numbers of Americans the ideal woman was pure, pious, submissive, and domestic and should be confined to her own sphere of activity, a standard quite in keeping with the church. As early as the eighteenth century, Catholic girls were taught that ladies should possess those virtues and were warned that public affairs and public persons were not fit subjects for conversation. These precepts were repeatedly reconfirmed during the nineteenth and early twentieth centuries. Christian tradition held that such qualities were ordained by God, exemplified by the Virgin Mary, revealed by scripture and the natural law, and reinforced by biological differences. There evolved, then, distinct spheres of activity

125

for each sex. Man's was the world at large; woman's was as perpe-
tuator of the race and nucleus of the family, a role superior to that
of man, for her nobility could uplift that sinful creature.[3] As the Reverend Bernard O'Reilly, one of the nineteenth century's popular writers, pronounced, "The head of the house is man; the head of society
is man; the destroyer of the moral world is man; its restoration and
salvation must be through a woman."[4]

Many Christians strove to keep these spheres apart, for usurpation
by either sex of activities belonging to the other was unnatural. One
of the most serious threats to this established order was woman suffrage, an innovation that would wrest females from their place on
the pedestal and thrust them into the sordid and debased world of
politics. (Despite opposition from some ministers, Protestant clerics
supported woman suffrage in far greater proportion than people of
other professions.) Catholic journals, newspapers, and spokesmen, lay
as well as clerical, assailed this alleged reform for endangering social
stability and, more important, woman's redemptive mission. The
Chicago New World, reflecting the upper-class nature of the proponents, observed that, "Irish Marys, Italian Marias, and Polish Hildas"
may have been sent by God for saving the country from women graduates of our great universities.[5]

Many of the hierarchy were outspoken in their hostility toward
the ballot. Bishop Joseph Macheboeuf (Denver, 1869–1889) led the
fight against it in Colorado. In a series of lectures and sermons, some
of which were distributed throughout the state, he contemptuously
and inconsistently dismissed its advocates as "Spiritualists, divorced
women, and free lovers, . . . old maids disappointed in love," and
"short-haired women and long-haired men."[6] In an official letter read
in all churches, Archbishop Henry Moeller (Cincinnati, 1904–1925)
urged women to protect their dignity, refinement, and modesty by
rallying against the intrusion of suffrage into their domain.[7] The nation's most prominent Catholic, Cardinal James Gibbons (Baltimore,
1878–1921), frequently railed against suffrage, warning as early as
1886 that it would result in a loss of reverence for women. In a sermon
eight years later he declared, "Woman does not to-day exercise the
right of suffrage. She can not vote, and I am heartily glad of it. I hope
the day will never come when she can vote, and if the right is granted
her I hope she will regret it." The Baltimore prelate even had William
T. Russell, the bishop designate of Charleston, South Carolina (1917–
1921), greet the first national antisuffrage convention on his behalf
in 1916. In his message, later distributed as a pamphlet, Gibbons
maintained that he spoke for the dignity of women and asserted that
feminists would rob women of character and substitute masculine
boldness for feminine honor and character.[8]

Catholic opposition became even more strident when many suffragists directly contravened church teachings by endorsing birth control, challenged its view of property rights by espousing socialism, and denigrated its members by nativist rantings. The National American Woman Suffrage Association (NAWSA) in 1900 was able to list only six Catholic clergymen in the nation who supported the ballot, while as late as 1915 that organization's church-work committee singled out as one of the suffragists' most important tasks "the organization of Catholic women, that they will make their demands so emphatic the church will see the wisdom of supporting the movement."[9]

It is little wonder, then, that the founders of that first antisuffrage organization and initiators of its petition were both Catholic: Ellen Ewing Sherman (1824–1888) and Madaline Vinton Dahlgren (1825–1898). Like antifeminist activists for the next century they became enmeshed in a mass of contradictions; using political methods to protect women from political burdens and assuming a public role to proclaim that their major responsibility lay in the privacy of the home.

Ellen Ewing, the more traditional of the two, came from a prominent Catholic family and married William Tecumseh Sherman, a West Point graduate. Adhering to conventional middle class norms, she followed her husband wherever his business or military career took him and concentrated on raising the children (one of whom became a Jesuit priest). A devout Catholic, she undertook a campaign against the evils of "round dancing" and raised money for charitable endeavors, making her Washington home a mecca for the poor. On the surface she possessed all of the virtues of the nineteenth-century lady, however, Sherman found neither domesticity nor submissiveness entirely satisfying. She had no qualms about expressing political views or urging her husband to rebuff efforts to nominate him for the presidency. Furthermore, she intervened with Lincoln on his behalf and publicly defended his military record from "slanderous" attacks by a southern newspaper. On the other hand, she rejected her husband's advice in 1860 to invest in slaves; ignored his disapproval of "ladies selling things over a table" to manage a Catholic booth in one of the nation's largest Civil War Fairs; undermined his Indian policy by helping establish the Ladies Catholic Indian Mission Association; and embarrassed him when he was commander in chief of the armies by flying a papal flag with black crepe from their Washington home when Rome was seized by the Italian state in 1870. To the complaints of the Italian ambassador, the general replied that he only lived in that house.[10]

Like most antisuffragists, Sherman was able to reconcile ladylike values, religion, and self-worth. She therefore acted to preserve traditional values from the changes suffrage would bring.

Her Visitandine-educated partner, Dahlgren, was even more outspoken in contesting the evils of suffrage, for she was completely at ease in the city of Washington, having functioned as hostess for her father in congress. Furthermore, her first husband had served as assistant secretary of the interior and her second, Admiral John Dahlgren, also made his home in the nation's capital.

Widowed in 1851, she began writing to support herself and her two children. In 1870, left with three additional children on the death of Dahlgren, she resumed her writing career while pressing congress for a pension based on his ordnance inventions. Her early works consisted primarily of translations and essays, many of which were antisuffrage. Traditional views on women were revealed in her *Etiquette of Social Life in Washington* and in her novels, which assailed divorce, miscegenation, liberalism, public schools, coeducation, and of course women's rights.

Dahlgren turned her home into a salon for literary figures and intelligentsia. Young scholars, politicians including James A. Garfield, members of the diplomatic corps, clergy, and established authors gathered at her dinner parties for lively conversation, often political.

Most of her boundless energy, however, was devoted to protecting family life from the inroads of feminists. By 1871 she had been identified by the suffragists as their leading opponent. The ballot, an "outcropping" of socialistic and communistic schemes, she claimed, would undermine Christian civilization by luring women from the home. Furthermore, possession of this right would logically demand that females bear arms. Women really did not need the vote, she asserted, for as mothers they formed male voters and as wives they influenced their husbands.

In refuting those who urged suffrage as a remedy for the exploitation of working women, Dahlgren contended that the vote would do more harm than good by ending chivalry and courtesy. Working conditions should be improved by excluding men from pursuits more proper for women, paying equal wages, transporting women from crowded cities to labor-short areas, and most importantly encouraging marriage by establishing endowments for the young and by taxing bachelors. She felt that to be a breadwinner was permissible for women, but also that females must be taught from infancy that their mission was to fulfill men and that equality was unnatural, otherwise they would be as unhappy and bitter as the suffragist leader Elizabeth Cady Stanton.[11]

Because of her deep-seated convictions, Dahlgren was reluctant to defend her views in public. Neither she nor Sherman appeared before the 1871 congress to protest a proposed suffrage amendment. The following year, she claimed that to participate in a debate at the national woman suffrage convention would violate "female modesty."

Essays, however, were a use of God-given talents consistent with "home life and its duties." In time she became less reticent. In 1878 she was the only remonstrant before the senate elections committee, and when her friend Garfield was elected president she audaciously suggested a cabinet appointee. "Perhaps, as a woman, I have no right to speak, but I feel that I may write as a friend."[12]

Many suffragists accepted the basic assumptions of critics like Sherman and Dahlgren and, as a result, argued that precisely because woman was unique she should have the ballot. It was relatively easy to advance this proposition because the antisuffrage ideology contained the seeds of its own destruction: if females were so pure, so pious, so superior, it was only logical to uplift society by extending their influence to the world about them. Motherly qualities could reform government and spawn interest in education, playgrounds, and public health. (To some extent, Catholics had operated on these assumptions for centuries. Nuns had been perceived as ideal for teaching children, blacks, and Indians, for administering orphanages, and for nursing the infirm and aged.) Furthermore, some contended that the home could be protected from the evils assailing it—drunkenness, inadequate wages, and a decline of public morality, for example— only through extending the ballot to women. Many women then, labeled "social feminists" by the historian William L. O'Neill, agitated for the ballot, not because they were proponents of women's rights, but because they were advocates of reform.[13]

Catholic suffragists, too, followed this line of reasoning. In newspapers and magazines, from pulpits and lecture platforms, the vote was hailed as a means of purifying government, guarding the family, and bettering the community. Woman, one supporter proclaimed, should imitate the virtue of the Virgin Mary, not her habits of life, and Mrs. Leonora S. Meder, president of the Catholic Women's Protectorate of Chicago, predicted that "woman will do for politics what St. Patrick did for Ireland when he drove out the snakes. Women will drive out the grafters."[14] A lawyer and chair of a Brooklyn woman suffrage society, Helen P. McCormick, related Catholicism to suffrage by contending that society was an extension of the female sphere and that woman's natural interest in "social and democratic movements is a response to the urge of mother love that is experienced by every normal woman, whether married or unmarried."[15] The Reverend Edward McSweeney of Mount Saint Mary's College touched all such reasoning in a letter to the New York *Sun*, asserting that suffrage was in woman's sphere as the home had become coextensive with the city, country, and world. Her participation would purify politics and soften the rough ways of society, influencing men of intelligence and refinement to return to the polls.[16]

Even some members of the hierarchy favored furthering the influence of women by awarding the ballot. Bishop John Lancaster Spalding (Peoria, 1877–1908) declared as early as 1884 that he saw no harm in experimental suffrage because these "natural educators of the race" were the most religious, most moral, most sober portion of the populace and might succeed, where men had failed, in elevating American life.[17] Surprisingly, the conservative bishop of Rochester Bernard J. McQuaid (1868–1909), endorsed this view. At a celebration paying tribute to Catholic women engaged in educational work he proclaimed, "It fills me with joy when I think of the many changes that will be brought about when women have the right of suffrage. They will defy the politicians, and vote as any Christian man should and would vote if he had the moral courage."[18] When suffrage appeared on the ballot as an amendment to the state constitution, Bishop Austin Dowling (Des Moines, 1912–1919) urged its support, not only because working women needed the vote to protect themselves, but because government needed the motherly qualities of women as much as it needed the deliberative powers of men.[19] Bishop John S. Foley (Detroit, 1888–1918), in order to take the schools out of politics, signed a petition to enable women to vote for school inspectors, although he opposed complete suffrage.[20]

Many Catholics believed that temperance was one of the most important reforms that could be achieved with the help of suffrage extension. This position was championed by the *Brooklyn Examiner* in 1885, in San Francisco by Father George Montgomery in 1891, and by the president of the Catholic Total Abstinence Society of Boston, Father Thomas Scully. Repeatedly linking suffrage with the end of saloons, Scully cooperated with the Massachusetts Woman Suffrage Association, had Alice Stone Blackwell, editor of the *Woman's Journal*, lecture in his church, and testified for a constitutional amendment before the Massachusetts legislature.[21]

Although the Catholic Total Abstinence Society was slow to accept women members and reluctant to use political methods, its long-time third vice president was a woman (usually officers were priests) and a dedicated proponent of the female vote as a means of reform. This was Leonora Barry Lake (1849–1930), a former organizer for the Knights of Labor, (K of L), and one of the most effective women in the temperance movement. A tireless worker and compelling orator, in 1898 alone she gave 160 lectures, traveling 20,215 miles by rail and 180 by team, frequently relating suffrage and temperance. Ironically, however, Lake's bishop, John J. Glennon (St. Louis, 1903–1946), was opposed to women reformers and disapproved of females in the temperance movement.

Despite the reform orientation of the suffrage movement, some prominent Catholic women never ceased their opposition to it. Among the most outspoken were Martha Moore Avery (1851–1924) and Katherine E. Conway (1853–1927). A well-known convert from socialism, a zealous advocate of the rights of labor, and a founder of the Catholic Truth Guild of street corner preachers, Avery assailed suffrage "as an up-to-date temptation suggested by the prince of devils" and urged Boston's Cardinal William O'Connell to establish a Catholic anti-suffrage society.[22] Conway, an essayist, author of twenty books, and editor of the *Boston Pilot* and *The Republic*, was an officer in the New England Women's Press Association and a member of the Board of Massachusetts Prison Commissioners. Yet she believed women could have no vocation to public life and as a result was an active member of the Massachusetts Anti-Suffrage Society.[23]

Many of the suffragists shared the values of their opponents and often their family, class, and educational background as well. Among these Catholic suffragists were Mary McGrath Blake (1840–1907), Jane Campbell (1845–1928), Mary E. Smith (1849–1918), Sarah Irwin Mattingly (1852–1934), Mary C. Crowley (1857–1921), Eleanor O'Donnell McCormick (1867–1931), and Janet E. Richards (?–1948).

The Irish-born Blake, mother of eleven and wife of a Harvard-trained physician, stressed the gentleness and domesticity of women in essays and poems. However, she not only supported suffrage but ran for public office in 1900.

Philadelphia's Jane Campbell, poet, club woman, and historian, although believing that females instinctively preferred home life, was convinced the ballot was necessary for justice. Founder (1882) and long-time president of Pennsylvania's largest and most influential suffrage society, she began every meeting with a prayer. She edited a journal, best described as "consciousness raising," in order "to keep women informed of the various opportunities that are open to them; of the political status in different parts of the world, and of their work in Literature, Art, Science, and Education." Campbell testified before the legislature, spoke before national and state conventions, in her late sixties participated in open-air meetings with the "radical" Lucy Burns, and at age seventy-two joined a delegation attempting to persuade Cardinal Gibbons to change his mind on the issue.[24]

Under the pen name Christine Faber, Mary E. Smith, a southern-born New York school teacher, wrote many articles and twelve novels featuring strong women characters. Her *Original Girl*, most unusual for nineteenth-century Catholic fiction, defended woman suffrage as a means of improving politics. She personally aided Henry George, a reform candidate, in his bid to become mayor of New York in 1886. In a more traditional mode, she became guardian of the orphaned children of her friend, the sister of the controversial priest Edward McGlynn.

Sarah Mattingly, a North Carolinian and graduate of Nazareth Academy in Bardstown, Kentucky, was a prominent educator in Washington, D.C. Mother of two children and a pioneer suffragist, she frequently contributed to one of the early feminist publications, *Kate Field's Washington*.

Mary Crowley graduated from Sacred Heart College, Manhattanville, in New York. She edited the *Catholic Mission Magazine* and *Annals of the Propagation of the Faith*, wrote novels, collaborated on the *Memorial History of Detroit*, where she lived for many years, and was a strong advocate of woman suffrage.

Eleanor McCormick was so successful in her teaching that she was elected county superintendent of education. With the leisure resulting from her marriage she organized the Memphis Symphony, served as president of the Tennessee Federation of Women's Clubs, and became a suffrage worker.

A member of the Daughters of the American Revolution, Janet Richards was a lecturer and a contributor to the *Washington Post*. She devoted much energy to woman suffrage, addressing national suffrage conventions, toiling for the reform in Maryland, Delaware, New York, New Jersey, and the state of Washington and as a delegate to the International Woman Suffrage Alliance at Amsterdam in 1908, Stockholm 1911, and Rome 1923. In 1917 she was the official spokesperson for the group of women who met with Cardinal Gibbons on the question.

One of the weaknesses of the early suffrage movement was that its most ardent supporters, drawn from the middle class, were unable to interest wage-earning females. The latter, if not opposed, were at best apathetic to the proposal, being concerned primarily with the immediate problems of pay and working conditions. Failure to reach this group became all the more significant when from 1900 to 1910 the number of employed women soared from less than five million to nearly eight million—21 percent of the work force. The leading unions, such as the K of L, the American Federation of Labor (AFL), and several of its affiliates, advocated suffrage as but *one* way to improve the lot of female employees. However, as unions were reluctant to commit scarce resources to organizing women whom they believed to be in the work force only temporarily, the ballot became the primary means of ameliorating oppressive conditions for many females. Some Catholic reformers, too, although still believing woman's normal role was as wife and mother, started to justify suffrage as a means of protecting working women—"potential" mothers.[25] More important, leaders from several unions and the Women's Trade Union

League (WTUL, a cross-class alliance of feminists and wage earners), many of whom were Catholic women, began to agitate zealously for the ballot. Obliteration of class divisions on women's issues had begun.

The first Catholic woman to argue along these lines was Leonora Barry, also the first full-time female labor organizer in the United States. A thirty-seven-year-old widowed mill worker, she traveled throughout the country promoting the K of L, pressuring for protective legislation, and pushing for the ballot. Barry represented the Knights before the Women's Suffrage Association of Detroit and at the International Conference of Women in 1888. Despite her advocacy of justice for women, Barry was not a feminist; she claimed that understanding political, economic, and social conditions made for better mothers and wiser wives. When she married Obadiah Lake in 1890 she resigned her union position to pursue more "ladylike" activities, lecturing on suffrage and temperance, canvassing Colorado for the vote in 1890 and 1893, and becoming a mainstay of the Catholic Total Abstinence Society.[26]

One of the founders of the WTUL and the first woman organizer for the AFL, Mary Kenney O'Sullivan (1864–1943), was a devout Catholic. A Hull House resident and president of a bookbinders' union, she organized shirtwaist workers and cab drivers in Chicago, lobbied for labor legislation in Illinois, and unionized garment and bindery workers in Massachusetts and New York. After her marriage to O'Sullivan, a labor reporter and AFL representative, she continued her efforts for suffrage and unions and increasingly linked the ballot with work reform. She testified for the vote before a congressional committee, campaigned for it in Illinois, and before a Massachusetts legislative committee in 1908, as a trade union representative, accused female antisuffragists of insensitivity toward wage earners and their working conditions. Moreover, she castigated opponents of suffrage as enemies of the people, comparing them with scabs and strikebreakers. At a WTUL convention she described suffrage opponents as "women of leisure who by accident of birth have led sheltered and protected lives," and then censured them for "selfishly obstructing the efforts of organized working women to obtain full citizenship."[27]

Another booster of suffrage and labor was Elizabeth Maloney (fl. 1903–1913), who in 1903 founded a waitress's union, which she headed for many years. She also organized waitresses nationally for a year and served on the executive board of the WTUL. A member of the Illinois Industrial Survey Commission, she lobbied for eight-hour and minimum wage legislation as well as for the ballot, one of her major concerns. Maloney, who negotiated contracts barring employers from using offensive language, kept a print of the Sistine Madonna in union headquarters so that waitresses "can see what woman can be and learn to respect yourselves accordingly." If "picturesque" language were used by a worker she was not allowed to wear the union button where it could be seen.[28]

As a young woman in Minnesota, Eva MacDonald Valesh (1874–1952) was influenced by nearby Dominican nuns and was likely inspired in her pursuit for justice by her Catholic faith.[29] Valesh, who lectured throughout the Midwest for the K of L, the Farmers' Alliance, and the People's party, was also a newspaper reporter specializing in exposing abusive working conditions. Early in life she became convinced that the ballot and justice were inseparable. In 1900 she was hired by the AFL, organized women, including those in the Federal Bureau of Engraving and Printing, addressed labor meetings and conventions, often as a surrogate for AFL president, Samuel Gompers, and edited the AFL journal, *The Federationist*. When Gompers refused to put her name on its masthead, she resigned, and somewhat disillusioned with unions, she increasingly concentrated her energies on suffrage.[30]

After being blacklisted for her role in the New York laundry workers strike of 1912 and after serving thirty days in the Tombs (the city prison of New York) for picketing with striking Panama hat workers, Margaret Hinchey (fl. 1913–1926), the "Irish vote-getter," became a suffrage organizer for the National American Woman Suffrage Association (NAWSA). She spoke in factories, at subway excavations, on docks; she toured the Bowery and upstate New York, always preaching the same message: the need for suffrage to protect women wage earners, especially the unskilled and helpless. Dubbed the "Billy Sunday of the suffragists" by the *New York Times*, she was particularly effective at winning over unskilled workers and frequently addressed her coreligionists in union halls, churches, and church clubs and carnivals. In 1914 she led a delegation to Washington in a fruitless effort to persuade President Woodrow Wilson to support a national suffrage amendment.[31]

Many second generation Catholic women were able to climb from the ranks of the unskilled into middle-class occupations. Particularly attractive to these ambitious women was teaching. From New York to California they flooded that profession. Bright, articulate, and self-supporting, these women refused to tolerate pay discrimination and turned to unions and the ballot as a means of correcting that injustice. In Chicago, Margaret Haley (1861–1939) and Catherine Goggin (1855–1916), both Catholic (Goggin was high trustee of the Women's Catholic Order of Foresters), founded the Chicago Teachers' Federation in 1897. (Haley had entered the profession as a result of promising to dedicate her life to all children when praying for the survival of her sister's only child.) Together, Haley and Goggin demanded equal pay for women and tax reform as a means of meeting the additional expenses this would entail. The federation, under their direction, endorsed school board candidates and forced the National Educational Association to select a woman presiding officer and to become more responsive to the needs of female members. Above all, it enthusiastically embraced suffrage. Haley used the issue of the injustice of pay differentials to recruit colleagues to that cause and even converted the mayor of Chicago (and future Illinois governor) Edward F. Dunne, to the suffragist cause. Furthermore, she campaigned for the vote in California in 1911 and Ohio in 1912.[32]

For fifteen years the president of the Interborough Association of Teachers (with over 15,000 members) and sometime assistant superintendent of schools in New York, Grace Strachan Forsythe (1863–1922) also pushed for equal pay and for the right of married women to teach. She led campaigns against politicians who failed to support such measures and, to increase her political influence, worked for the ballot. She founded and chaired the teacher's branch of the Empire State Suffrage Campaign Committee, urged teachers to defy convention and march in suffrage parades, implored clergymen to support the reform, and addressed NAWSA conventions. Forsythe also did philanthropic work with the Young Women's Catholic Association of Brooklyn.[33]

As unionists, social feminists, and upper-class reformers joined the suffrage ranks, women increasingly challenged their clerical opponents—the majority of churchmen. Mrs. Frank J. Mott, a prominent charity worker in Denver, told an interviewer, "But it makes no difference who says these things that are ascribed to Cardinal Gibbons. . . . We know that families are not broken up, nor is divorce sought on account of equal suffrage. In fact I believe it is exactly the reverse."[34] In Chicago, Haley defied the church lobbyist who opposed her efforts to obtain the initiative and referendum. In response to clerical opposition to the suffrage amendment in Ohio she averred, "The Church doesn't oppose progress. . . . If I believed it did, I would not belong to it."[35] Mrs. Margaret H. Rorke of New York compiled a brief book designed to correct any impression that the church was officially opposed to the vote and to encourage Catholic support for suffrage. One of the first documents in it was a letter from Gibbons's secretary stating that the question was open and left by the church "to her children as they think best."[36]

Thus by the second decade of the twentieth century it was impossible to assert that there was a "church position" on the issue. Despite the continued protests of critics, many priests supported prosuffrage amendments to state constitutions, and churchmen found no deleterious effects on family life or on society in suffrage states.

Bishop James J. Keane (Cheyenne, 1902–1911, Dubuque, 1911–1929) visited Los Angeles when a state amendment was before the voters and asserted that forty-three years of female suffrage in Wyoming had convinced him that women voted as intelligently and conscientiously as men. Furthermore, based on his experience, Californians should have no fear that enfranchisement would lure women away from the home or church.[37] During that campaign, the Reverend Joseph M. Gleason, pastor of a parish in Palo Alto, addressed a huge rally in San Francisco where box seats were reserved for notable Catholics. Gleason, a constitutional scholar and member of the advisory board of the American Historical Association, contended that suffrage was no threat to the dignity of woman. Instead he argued that the ballot should be extended to give decency a chance and to strengthen the fight against corruption. But more important, he felt it was a matter of justice that woman be man's equal in politics.[38]

Bishop Thomas J. Conaty (Los Angeles, 1903–1915) gave the opening address at a Catholic fair in Santa Monica where suffragists had erected a booth for each woman suffrage state in the union. His diocesan paper, *The Tidings*, edited by Alice J. Stevens, even approved of "The New Woman" and her right to vote.[39] The California suffrage amendment carried with considerable Catholic support and, although the paper of the San Francisco diocese had opposed it, Archbishop Patrick W. Riordan urged pastors "to take a seasonable opportunity to advising our new electors to register that they may be at all times prepared to give their service in making California a model state, and of handing down to the children that come after a tradition of righteousness and unselfish patriotism."[40] Needless to say, Riordan's counsel was frequently cited by Catholic supporters in nonsuffrage states.

In the East, a Catholic society for woman suffrage was established in Buffalo in 1915, and in the same year, in New York City, Father Thomas Murphy, formerly of St. Patrick's Cathedral, endorsed the ballot. Among that city's most outspoken suffrage advocates was the Reverend Joseph H. McMahon, who supported suffrage extension in his sermons and who publicly described the purpose of the feminist movement as the betterment of women, a danger to neither morality or religion. In 1912, two of McMahon's parishioners, Sara M. McPike, an executive secretary in an advertising firm, and Winifred Sullivan, a lawyer, established the St. Catherine Welfare Association at the local convent. Through a vigorous educational program the association fostered suffrage as well as other reforms for the social and economic betterment of women and children. In 1915, to demonstrate that the church was not opposed to enfranchisement, McPike's organization sponsored a Catholic day where Carrie Chapman Catt, president of

NAWSA, was the featured speaker. McPike, who led five hundred Catholic women in a 1917 suffrage parade, also was one of the delegates that met with Cardinal Gibbons hoping to persuade him to cease his opposition to suffrage because of the protection needed by working women. (After the amendment was ratified, McPike continued her efforts on behalf of women, undertaking a campaign against the *Catholic Encyclopedia* for its demeaning approach to females, urging women to join the Democratic party, and serving as secretary to the state labor commission, the first woman in such a position.)[41]

Preaching on behalf of the reform in Bayonne and New Brunswick, New Jersey, were three pastors, one of whom was rector of an Italian parish whose congregation was traditionally antifeminist. The Reverend James J. McKeever of Newark, who believed in suffrage because it would better the condition of women, was an advisor to the Women's Political Union. In 1915 the Catholic Women's Suffrage Committee was established as part of the union under the leadership of Mrs. Howard Garis, a writer of children's stories. The committee's objective was to convince Catholics that suffrage would cure the ills of political and social life.[42]

In 1893 the Catholic Woman's League was established in Chicago for "the advancement and promotion of the general good of humanity in accordance with the principles of the Catholic Church." The league, whose members were required to be single, staffed settlements and day nurseries, provided jobs for immigrants and shelters for homeless girls. It also "militantly" promoted the ballot to achieve its reforming goals, despite the antisuffrage stance of the diocesan newspaper.[43]

In Pennsylvania, too, prominent Catholics rallied to the reform. Scranton's bishop, Michael J. Hoban (1899–1926), announced that for forty years he had favored allowing at least women of property to vote on tax and bonding issues. Adelaide Delany, a University of Pennsylvania graduate and editor of the woman's department of the *Philadelphia Record*, was an articulate public exponent of the ballot. Under the presidency of Dr. Eveleen Douredowic, the Catholic Woman Suffrage League was established in Philadelphia to obtain for women the same right as men to govern themselves.[44]

In 1918, when the question appeared on the ballot in Michigan, Detroit's bishop, Michael Gallagher (1918–1937), reminded the men of that state that if German women had been enfranchised there probably would have been no war. Moreover, he urged Catholics to vote for the amendment and thereby remove the "blot from our constitution, that insult to the position, intelligence, and dignity of woman—the denial of the ballot—and write instead equal suffrage to man and woman alike."[45] That same year in Massachusetts, home of the oldest continuous antisuffrage organization in the nation, a Catholic woman's suffrage society was established with branches throughout the commonwealth. Quite appropriately it was named the Margaret Brent Guild after the first suffragist in the New World. Brent, a Catholic, demanded two votes in the seventeenth-century Maryland assembly: one for herself as a freeholder and one as the proprietor's attorney.

In order to harmonize suffrage even further with Catholicism in nonsuffrage states, these organizations frequently cited clerical appeals to residents of suffrage states to vote. These entreaties, often made by churchmen who had opposed the reform previous to the enabling legislation, emphasized the moral obligation of good women to vote and were repeated everytime a new state extended suffrage. Typical was an editorial in the *Catholic World* exhorting Catholic women "for God and country" to outvote "the Socialist, the feminist, the pacifist and the radical."[46]

To some, the ladylike approach of petitions, lobbies, speeches, and conventions had proven ineffective; demonstrations were needed to move the public. Teresa O'Leary Crowley (1874–1930), lawyer, mother of three, and suffragist from age sixteen, was one of the first women to conduct outdoor meetings (1908) and to lead a suffrage march through the streets of a major city. Furthermore, she addressed conventions, testified before legislative committees, and demanded fairer treatment from newspaper editors. More significantly, she chaired the legislative committee of the state suffrage association, directing a campaign that ousted six antisuffrage legislators including the president of the Massachusetts senate who ascribed his defeat to her activities. A few years later, Crowley and a special nonpartisan committee established by her were instrumental in the defeat of one of Massachusetts's antisuffrage senators and in the election of the first Catholic to represent the state in that chamber: the suffragist enthusiast, David I. Walsh. Two years later, after the ratification of the Nineteenth Amendment, Crowley retired from public life devoting her talents to her law practice and her family.[47]

Another attorney, Mary O'Toole, president of the District of Columbia Equal Suffrage Association from 1915 to 1920, also organized street meetings and protest parades promoting equal pay as well as the ballot. Furthermore, she canvassed Maryland for the amendment, crisscrossing the state and conducting rallies from her automobile. O'Toole was later appointed a municipal court judge by President Warren Harding.[48]

To some suffragists, even public demonstrations seemed inadequate. Inspired by the sensational exploits of English militants and the American tour of one of their leaders, Emmeline Pankhurst, they began to turn to confrontation and a form of militancy. Margaret Foley, a former trade union officer, was hired by the Massachusetts Woman Suffrage Association. She conducted many street-corner rallies and even ascended in a balloon to shower the crowd below with prosuffrage literature. In 1911 she was sent abroad to study with the radicals. After her return she tailed antisuffrage politicians across the state, haranguing their crowds, disrupting their rallies, and contributing substantially to the defeat of some of the best known office holders in the commonwealth. Her tactics were so successful in Massachusetts that she later crisscrossed the nation for suffrage as a representative of the NAWSA, staying overnight in unheated shacks of midwestern mining camps. On her return, Foley chaired the Organizing and Industrial Committee of the Margaret Brent Suffrage Guild, conducting rallies in church halls and meeting with priests and nuns on behalf of the ballot.[49]

The most radical of all suffragists, if radicalism is measured by the number of days one has been jailed for a cause, was Lucy Burns, a Catholic, later described by her confessor as "as gentle a woman [as] I have ever met."[50] In 1909 Burns abandoned her studies for a doctorate at Oxford to join the militant wing of the English suffrage movement, which later awarded her a medal for valor as a result of several arrests and prison hunger strikes. Back in the United States together with Alice Paul, an American student with whom she had been jailed in England, she established the Congressional Committee of the NAWSA to concentrate on a national constitutional amendment rather than state-by-state campaigns. In time the committee split from the national and was reorganized as the National Woman's party (NWP) to make militancy a relevant part of the struggle. Burns was the first of a long line of suffragists arrested for picketing the White House. When her demand to be treated as a political prisoner was refused, she engaged in a hunger strike and was subjected to the pain and indignity of force-feeding. Convinced that it was necessary to "devote all our efforts toward freeing the women of the United States," Burns refused to substitute war work for suffrage and continued her assaults on "Kaiser-Wilson." Many believe the massive publicity engendered by the Woman's party, speech burning, demonstrations, picketing, and arrests, was a major factor in passing the amendment. After its ratification, an exhausted Burns retired from public life. "I don't want to do anything more. I think we have done all this for women, and we have sacrificed everything we possessed for them, and now let them . . . fight for it now. I am not going to fight anymore."[51]

The constant pressure of the NAWSA, the dramatic activities of the radicals, the spirit generated by the progressive movement, and most important, the participation of women in wartime activities resulted in passage and ratification of the suffrage amendment. Churchmen now made national appeals exhorting women to vote and thereby to offset radical voting. Even Cardinal Gibbons urged them to exercise the franchise "as a strict social duty," and in the pastoral letter of 1919 the American bishops averred that the vote of woman, if cast with care, could purify and elevate our political life. At its first meeting, members of the National Conference of Catholic Women (NCCW) were warned to register and save the country, while a year later, in 1922, the convention resolved to use the ballot to defend the "principles sacred to Christian Civilization."[52]

Yet little had really changed. Suffrage had been bestowed as a reward for contributions to the war effort, or because women's perspective was needed in government, or to purify politics, or for purposes of reform. Since Americans seldom had perceived suffrage extension as a right, the reform was consequently deceptive; perceptions of the role of women were basically unchanged.

As a result, the NWP, the "radical" wing of the suffrage movement, saw approval of the Nineteenth Amendment, not as the century-long culmination of a struggle for political rights, but only as a step toward equality. Shortly after ratification, its executive committee resolved to continue to struggle for women, concentrating on the removal of legal disabilities. To achieve this end the party sponsored equal rights legislation in several states and promulgated a manifesto for a federal equal rights amendment (ERA) which read: "Men and women shall have equal rights throughout the United States and every place subject to its jurisdiction. Congress shall have the power to enforce this article by appropriate legislation."

The objectives of the NWP and the institutional church conflicted, for churchmen remained traditionalists. The bishops' pastoral letter of 1919, acknowledging that woman's sphere was no longer confined to the family and urging her to vote, nevertheless reaffirmed conventional roles. Woman was to rule the home and through gentleness and dignity, qualities in which she excels, "reach the hearts of men and take away their bitterness, that they may live henceforth in fellowship one with another—this is woman's vocation in respect of public affairs, and the service which she by nature is best fitted to render."[53] The clergy persisted in their reluctance to recognize women's right to employment. The Bishops' Program of Social Reconstruction of 1919 insisted that the numbers of women in industry be kept as small as possible and, to encourage employers to hire males rather than females, demanded that women be paid equally with men.[54]

To advance Catholic social goals while preserving established values, the National Council of Catholic Women (NCCW) was formed under the direction of the National Catholic Welfare Conference (NCWC). It was hoped that by centralizing and unifying a campaign for morality, marriage, motherhood, and home, "the foundation stones of the national structure," the NCCW would offset the aggressiveness of feminists, which, since enfranchisement, threatened Catholic norms.[55]

As early as 1922 the NCCW denounced the ERA. During the nineteen-twenties, thirties, and forties, the conference lobbied against it. Members of the organization, most frequently its executive secretary, Agnes G. Regan (1869–1943), testified before congressional committees alleging that it removed protection from working women and endangered the family.

Regan had served as a teacher, principal, and member of the board of education in her native San Francisco. In 1920 she was appointed representative of that diocese to the organizational meeting of the NCCW. Shortly thereafter she was elected vice president and appointed executive secretary (a position she held for twenty years) and assistant director of the National Catholic School of Social Service. Deeply committed to social reform, she worked to interest Catholic women in social legislation and supported vacation schools, aid to immigrants, the child labor amendment, and the liberalizing of immigration laws. She cooperated with Mary Anderson of the Women's Bureau in obtaining protective legislation for working women and as a result was opposed to an ERA. She believed that such legislation violated "history, science, and philosophy" in attempting to change the "fundamental differences" between men and women.[56]

Representatives of the conference's parent organization, the NCWC, and of other Catholic groups also claimed the amendment would endanger the role of mother, wife, and even husband. Leading Catholic journals joined in this attack. Furthermore, many Catholics, both lay and clergy, defamed the amendment by indirection. Repeatedly they assaulted the immorality and "unnatural" goals of feminists and berated working women for ignoring their main duty, the home, and denying the values of marriage and motherhood.

The NWP was, initially, not very concerned with its Catholic opponents. During its first decade-and-a-half the party was more patronizing than harsh toward them. It sorrowed for those "subjected people [i.e., Catholic women] who acquire the psychology of subjection" and contrasted the subservience of American women with those in St. Joan's Alliance, an English Catholic feminist organization.

The two Catholics whose NWP activities were most publicized were Mary A. Murray (1868–1952), a founder of the party and chair of its industrial council, and Maggie Hinchey, the former suffragist enthusiast. Murray who had reconciled her obligations as mother of five children with her need for employment by working evenings, became infuriated when New York's protective legislation outlawed night work for women. President of the Women's League of the Brooklyn Manhattan Transit Company, she was a valuable spokesperson for the party in challenging union and social feminist objections to the ERA. Murray contended the amendment would eliminate the discriminatory protective laws supported by the AFL as a means of reducing the number of females in industry and thereby cut competition with men. Charging that such legislation was really "poor working-girl stuff from sympathetic men" she rejected it as a "substitute for social justice."[57]

Murray lambasted regulatory measures before legislators at Albany. She also toured the west on behalf of the ERA, and testified for it at congressional hearings over a period of twenty years and before the Resolutions Committee of the Democratic National Convention in 1936. She also led a demonstration of three hundred NWP women to the White House in 1926 where she presented President Calvin Coolidge with an ERA petition. When Father John A. Ryan of the NCWC addressed the NCCW contending that the majority of women workers received "a special benefit" from regulatory laws and that the ERA represented a "doctrinaire habit of thinking," Murray immediately replied that "*Dr.* Ryan [italics mine] does not speak for the masses of Catholic women."[58]

Hinchey, who had supported the NAWSA and WTUL, broke with the latter in 1918 for embracing regulatory legislation for transit workers, legislation that resulted in the dismissal of 1,500 female employees. Returning to laundry work, she searched for an organization "that will stand by working women, that we can trust and won't sell us out," a group that will support the right of females to choose for "themselves when and where they want [to] work eight or nine hours day or night just the same as men."[59] Hinchey discovered such an organization in the Woman's party with its espousal of the ERA. She became an officer in the party's Industrial Council and a lobbyist for the amendment during the 1920s. She also met with Coolidge, beseeching him to support the measure that would "prevent the adoption of protective laws which cost us our good jobs to give us others more poorly paid."[60] In those early years of the NWP, Murray and Hinchey were the only members whose Catholicism was conspicuous. But their religion was incidental; their importance to the party was as wage earners challenging criticism of the ERA by organized labor and women reformers.

The coming of World War II, like World War I, liberalized many attitudes on women. The first favorable subcommittee report on the ERA, that of the house in 1939, was repeated in the house and senate in 1941, and a favorable plank was included in the Republican platform of 1940. Winifred C. Stanley, one of the few Catholic congresswomen, endorsed it shortly after her election in 1942 as New York State's representative at large. Nevertheless, this former assistant district attorney joined her fellow Republican congresswoman, Connecticut's Clare Booth Luce (soon to become a Catholic), at a Women's National Press Club dinner in proclaiming that homemaking was woman's greatest career.[61]

As a result of growing support for the ERA Catholic opposition became more strident. The NCCW and diocesan, archdiocesan, and state councils of women mounted campaigns against it and Catholic lobbyists threatened retaliation at the polls. At least three Catholic congressmen abandoned the measure in the face of this onslaught. The views of Catholic advocates such as the novelists Margaret Culkin Banning and Kathleen Norris, who did publicity work for the ERA, and May Merrick, the president of the Christ Child Society, were lost in the tumult. Emma Guffey Miller of the Democratic National Committee attributed the House Judiciary Committee's negative report of 1943 to NCCW pressure and urged the Woman's party to challenge directly the stand of the church.[62]

Catholic ERA supporters had been encouraged by Bishop Edmund J. Fitzmaurice (Wilmington, Del., 1925–1960) chancellor of the Philadelphia diocese (1914–1920) before his consecration as bishop (1925) by Philadelphia's Cardinal Dennis Dougherty. A close friend of Florence Bayard Hilles, a civic and social leader in Washington and later chair of the NWP, and of Marie Lockwood, Delaware WP chair, Fitzmaurice delivered the invocation at the 1941 Eastern Regional Conference. After describing party members as having been called "to high and holy living—to consecrated service," he besought all "noble souls" to join in the war against discrimination and injustice and concluded by begging God to hasten the day when women would enjoy equality with men.[63] Fitzmaurice never again publicly upheld the amendment, probably because he had become "a source of dissatisfaction among leading Catholic groups." Nevertheless, he sustained Catholic women in their quest. He suggested that they attempt to get support from Cardinal Dougherty and encouraged them to organize on behalf of the proposition.[64]

Although Dougherty was approached within a week of Fitzmaurice's suggestion, it was three and a half years before he publicly backed the amendment. The suggested organization was established only with slightly less difficulty. By the spring of 1943 Dorothy Shipley Granger (b. 1899), ignoring her husband's injunction for "caution" lest she become "vulnerable" because of her efforts, had tried on at least two occasions to form Catholic women into a vehicle for advocating the

ERA. Her lack of success may have been because she attempted to recruit Catholic women of prominence rather than feminists who happened to be Catholic.

A direct descendent of Adam Shipley who came to Maryland in 1668, Granger, whose mother died when she was four, was always close to her father. He encouraged her voracious reading habits and fostered an abiding sense of responsibility to state and church by teaching her "if a person has anything to give at all it belongs to the community." At the time of these efforts Granger was one of Baltimore's leading insurance agents, having previously led a successful career as a department store buyer. (From 1950 to her retirement in 1969 she was public relations director for the city's Bureau of Sanitation, was active in civic and cultural groups, including the International Federation of Catholic Alumna (IFCA), and three times was named woman of the year by various Maryland organizations.)[65]

In August 1943, at NWP headquarters, Granger succeeded in forming an association by drawing upon lists of Catholic WP members provided by state chairpersons. Named for St. Joan of Arc, who was hailed as the patron saint of feminism, the Saint Joan's Society was designed to coordinate efforts of Catholic women in their struggle to realize the ideals of Joan and to emulate her example by securing equality before the law. Dues were one dollar a year, annual meetings were held in Washington, a board of directors was chosen from five different states, and Bishop Fitzmaurice's invocation was used on the society's letterhead.

Saint Joan's publicly endorsed the ERA straight away, and as early as September the organization was included in a list of proponents submitted to Congress. Members lobbied, petitioned, and were quick to object publicly when Catholic adversaries gave the impression they represented a monolithic church. The society also played a significant role in the Democratic party's adoption of an ERA plank in 1944.

Although contesting the positions of many leaders of the institutional church, Saint Joan's tried to avoid needless antagonism of the hierarchy. When the pastor of Saint Dominic's, Baltimore, suggested that members of the altar and sanctuary society join the organization, Granger immediately reproved him for fear that the resulting publicity would alienate the bishop.[66] But circumspection was not enough. The column "Father Quiz in Matters Catholic" in the nationally circulated *Our Sunday Visitor* not only contended that good Catholics should oppose the ERA but charged the NWP with deception for creating the Saint Joan Society, "allegedly composed of Catholic feminists."[67] Furthermore, the IFCA and the NCCW warned their members that the society did not have episcopal approval; before joining, women should consult their bishop. Emotions ran so high that when it was revealed that Mrs. Vina M. Betterley, newly elected state officer in the Catholic Daughters, was state chair of the Florida Women's party, her life was made "a hell" by those Catholics who equated birth control with equality for women. Betterley resigned her WP office but continued her membership.[68]

Even Granger became discouraged, describing a session before the NCCW as "beautifully refined torture" during which the "boys who made the Inquisition, rolled in their graves in envy."[69] She concluded that a favorable committee report from Congress was impossible unless Catholic opposition could be stopped and enough courageous Catholic women who were not afraid of the church could be rallied to the cause. In order to ease the fears of such women, individual Catholics and Saint Joan's members attempted for two years to persuade the papal delegate to proclaim that the ERA was not a matter of faith, that Catholics were free to support it. But the archbishop refused to become involved in what he described as a political issue—legislation of a controversial nature. Futile attempts were also made to obtain the same commitment from Archbishop Michael Curley (Baltimore, 1921–1947) who also headed the archdiocese of Washington.

Meanwhile, representatives of Saint Joan's and the Woman's party, acting on Bishop Fitzmaurice's suggestion, began writing and visiting Cardinal Dougherty in 1942. They were pleasantly received but obtained little satisfaction. However, about a year later, nuns of the Assumption Convent in Miami succeeded in arousing his support for the proposal. Ethel E. Murrell, lawyer and Florida NWP chair, and her attorney husband helped the religious community establish an academy and interested the nuns in the ERA. They in turn discussed the issue with a receptive Dougherty while he vacationed at their convent. Continued correspondence and meetings with Murrell and Saint Joan's members eventually resulted in his telling the women he was "in full accord with the ERA." However, Dougherty refused permission to publicize his views, for "it might seem to the public that I was rebuking certain of my co-religionists, some perhaps, of high ecclesiastical rank."[70] Not until 1945 did the cardinal make his views public when he gave NWP officers a letter of unqualified support praising President Harry S. Truman and the House Judiciary Committee for approving the ERA. This missive proved to be the highlight of the senate hearings and its release before the committee "caused a minor sensation" according to the *New York Times.*[71]

Dougherty's approbation made it easier for women to reconcile faith and feminism: NCWC meetings avoided the ERA, and it was not until the 1980s that the Catholicism of the amendment's proponents was seriously questioned. The letter also apparently influenced

Catholic members of the House Judiciary Committee, but neither it
nor the endeavors of Saint Joan's seemed to have much effect on
Catholic pressure groups. For the rest of the 1940s the NCCW, the
Catholic press, and organizations such as the Catholic Daughters,
Daughters of Isabella, and archdiocesan councils of women, repeated
charges that the ERA would create a "spurious equality," weaken, if
not destroy, the family, and invalidate protective legislation, thereby
endangering potential mothers.

The conservativism of the 1950s, with an emphasis on home, children, and the suburbs, reinforced these judgments and overwhelmed
ERA supporters. Although an amendment passed the senate in 1950
and again in 1953, it included a rider preserving protective legislation,
a provision unacceptable to feminists, and from 1949 through 1970
the house did not even hold hearings on the measure. Church opposition continued but it was no longer as significant as during the wartime years because now it was but one voice among many. Consequently less and less was heard from specifically Catholic proponents,
including Saint Joan's, which gradually faded away.

The historian Arthur Schlesinger, Sr., has described American political history as following a conservative-liberal cyclical pattern. So,
too, it seems with the quest for equality by women. The rigidity of
the Federal period was succeeded by the mid-nineteenth-century
awareness of women's issues and an improvement in female property
rights; the restrictions of the Gilded Age paved the way for the Progressive era and suffrage; the doldrums of the Great Depression were
offset by wartime opportunities; and the baby-boom of the fifties was
the precursor of the feminism of the sixties and seventies. Some manifestations of these changing attitudes were the Equal Pay Act of 1963,
the Civil Rights Act of 1964 (whose employment provisions were originally extended to women—in an effort to defeat the measure), the
establishment of new societies, such as NOW (the National Organization for Women, 1966), and a whole spate of consciousness raising
books, chief among which was Betty Friedan's *The Feminine Mystique*
(1963). Encouraged by the empathy of John XXIII and Vatican II on
the status of women, Catholic feminists applied new perspectives even
to the church. The changing climate was reflected in works such as
Sidney Callahan's, *The Illusion of Eve* (1965), Sally Cunnean's, *Sex:
Female; Religion: Catholic* (1968), and Mary Daly's, *The Church and
the Second Sex* (1968), and in the establishment of the United States
Section of Saint Joan's Alliance (1965, see below).

In 1923 when the Vatican ruled that any organization calling itself
Catholic needed the consent of the ordinary to be represented at
"neutral" meetings, the Catholic Woman Suffrage Society of England,
to preserve its independence, changed its name to Saint Joan's Alli-

ance. Its stated purpose, however—"to establish political, social, and economic equality between women and men"—remained the same as it had been since its founding in 1911. During its struggle for social justice, the alliance spread into Latin America and Europe as well. In 1959 it began a campaign to promote increased opportunity for women to participate in the church, requesting the deaconate in 1961 and in 1963 welcoming ordination. The same year a *Commonweal* article on the alliance aroused the interest of many Americans. As a result, at the initiative of two longtime members, Georgiana McEntee, a professor at Hunter College, and Frances McGillicuddy, Saint Joan's consultant to the Economic and Social Council of the United Nations, a United States section was established. The organization, which soon became national in scope, pressed for equality for women in church and state and ardently supported the Equal Rights Amendment.[72]

The ERA, seemingly laid to rest by the negative report of President John F. Kennedy's Commission on the Status of Women (1963), was resurrected in 1967 at the insistence of NOW. Passed and sent to the states for ratification in 1972 it provided that: "Equality of rights under the Law shall not be denied or abridged by the United States or any State on the basis of sex. Congress and the several States shall have power, within their respective jurisdictions, to enforce this article by appropriate legislation." This proposal was warmly greeted by Catholics. According to Gallup polls during the 1970s and 1980s, the Catholic majority supporting it exceeded that of Protestants favoring it.

Representatives of Catholic organizations such as Saint Joan's, the National Coalition of Nuns (with over 1,300 members), and Women Theologians United testified for the measure at congressional hearings and accused the opposing NCCW of representing neither an authentic Catholic position nor Catholic women. These groups, along with the Canon Law Society of America and the National Conference of Catholic Charities, continued their support by pushing for ratification. One individual instrumental in the amendment's passage was Congresswoman Margaret O'Shaughnessy Heckler (b. 1931). The child of Irish immigrants and graduate of a Catholic college and law school, this mother of three was the first woman elected in her own right to the House from Massachusetts. Active in veterans' measures and child welfare concerns, Heckler was also cofounder of the bipartisan Congressional Caucus for Women's Issues. She championed the passage of the ERA as a means of correcting injustices to working women.

Some Catholics rallied behind ratification in a dramatic fashion. The outspoken McGillicuddy, president of Saint Joan's, initiated a "Bundles [of feminist literature] for Bishops" campaign, and was as a result likened to a "buzz saw" by Archbishop Leo Byrne of Saint

Paul (1967–1974). Members of this organization picketed Saint Patrick's Cathedral, New York, protesting the lectionary readings from Saint Paul on a wife being subject to her husband. The following year, representatives of Catholic Women for the ERA, dressed as female saints, posted a "woman's proclamation" on the doors of both Saint Patrick's and Saint Peter's, Cincinatti, calling on the Catholic community to conform to Christian principles by supporting the ERA.[73]

Unlike a generation before, nuns in the 1960s actively joined with their lay sisters. In Florida a pro-ERA nun publicly prayed with two Catholic senators who had begun to waiver in their support. In North Dakota, Sister Glenna Raybell headed the ratification campaign. The National Assembly of Women Religious and the Leadership Conference of Women Religious (representing about 90 percent of religious communities) commended it. Sister Maureen Fiedler of the liberal Quixote Center wrote and lobbied for it. Network, the Washington-based group of sisters drawn together by social justice and feminist concerns, was one of the most active ERA supporters, producing brochures, providing testimony before state legislatures, and frequently coordinating religious efforts.[74]

As most of working women's "protective legislation" had been invalidated by the 1964 civil rights act, opponents no longer were able to argue that the amendment would be detrimental to female wage earners. Instead they assailed it as an unnatural threat to the family and society. In 1970, when urging Congress to reject it, the NCCW, as it had done for a decade, described the proposal as "a threat to the nature of woman which individuates her from man in God's plan . . . an idea of woman foreign to the Christian concept."[75] Following its passage, Archbishop Byrne, chair of the Bishops' Ad Hoc Committee on Women and Society in the Church, expressed fear that ratification would destroy the unity essential to stable families. An extensive effort to prevent ratification was undertaken by those sharing these views. The NCCW organized massive letter-writing campaigns to state legislators, distributed anti-ERA literature in schools, and bussed children to state capitals to demonstrate. The Knights of Columbus, Holy Name Societies, and Catholic Daughters, who passed resolutions against it, actively publicized their apprehensions.

These fears were exacerbated by American bishops. In 1972 and again in 1975 they declared that the amendment should be "closely scrutinized" because of its "doctrinaire character and broad sweep," which may destroy family relationships. A clerical columnist in a national Catholic newspaper under the caption "Equal Rights Amendment: A Catholic View" even interpreted this warning to mean that support of the ERA was "an untenable position for any Catholic who is responsive in a loving and reasonable way to the genuine teaching of the Church."[76]

Traditionalists also found their position strengthened by the tumult ensuing from the Supreme Court decision legalizing abortion (*Roe* v. *Wade*, 1973). Those who advocated a "right-to-life" amendment to the constitution were assailed by NOW and other feminist organizations identified with the ERA. Scholarly presentations asserting that abortion and equal rights were two separate issues were ignored by both camps. In the town of Kankakee, Illinois, priests warned parishioners that the church opposed the ERA because of its connection with abortion; in Chicago, feminists now found it difficult to rent space in Catholic buildings; some congregations in the Joliet, Illinois, diocese filled out anti-ERA postcards during mass, which were gathered in collection baskets and mailed from the rectory to the legislature. The Florida Catholic Conference collaborated with the organization Stop ERA. The bishops of New Orleans, Tallahassee, and Saint Louis also made their opposition public.

Emotions were so heated during this period that the hierarchy became more cautious than ever. In 1978, a member of the Bishops Committee on Women in Society and the Church disclosed that his group was going to seek authorization to issue a pro-ERA statement. This news resulted in an outpouring of protest mail to the bishops, much of which had been encouraged by the NCCW. As a result the forty-eight member administrative committee of the National Conference of Catholic Bishops unanimously refused permission for the pronouncement because of "uncertainties as to its [ERA's] legal and constitutional consequences for family life, the abortion issues, and other matters." It then reaffirmed its policy statement of 1972 and 1975. The committee was even denied permission to state its position that abortions and the amendment were two separate issues.[77]

However, the spirit of Cardinal Dougherty was not entirely dead. During the last month available for ratification, June 1982 (Congress had extended the original approval period from seven to ten years), with the support of only three more states needed to make the ERA part of the Constitution, twenty-three bishops in an unprecedented action issued a joint statement: "Each of us speaking in his own name, calls upon legislators . . . to approve the Equal Rights Amendment."[78]

The bishops' announcement, however, was far too late. Phyllis Stewart Schlafly (b. 1924), who personified the resurgent conservatism of the late seventies and early eighties, led a crusade against the ERA. Credited by many as the individual most responsible for the amendment's defeat, Schlafly dismissed endorsement by nuns with the observation they would not suffer from its most harmful effects: the draft and the abolition of laws requiring husbands to support wives. A conservative activist and "right-to-life" exponent, Schlafly claimed that the feminist goal was really independence from men and therefore concluded that "lesbianism is logically the highest form of the ritual of women's liberation."[79]

Schlafly, the daughter of a Saint Louis engineer, attended Catholic schools until her sophomore year in college when she transferred to Washington University and worked nights at an arms factory to earn tuition. After receiving an M.A. from Radcliffe (1948), she was employed first by the American Enterprise Institute in Washington and later by a bank in Saint Louis until her marriage to John Schlafly, a wealthy lawyer. Ms. Schlafly then abandoned the work force and became a homemaker, but remained active in community causes and Republican politics, running for the United States Senate on three occasions. Her six children were no impediment to these pursuits; each of them, while still nursing, was brought by her to political conventions.

In the 1960s, Schlafly obtained a national reputation, broadcasting, lecturing, and writing books and articles for conservative causes. Not until her husband "nudged" her did she perceive the ERA threat to women and initiate her Stop ERA crusade. By 1978 she had established branches in forty-five states and had begun to master the media and excel at public relations. Repeatedly she denounced the amendment as a "tremendous ripoff of the legal rights of homemakers" that would weaken the family, lead to abortion and lesbianism, and subject girls to the draft and combat duty. Furthermore, according to Schlafly, the ERA would probably force the church to abandon single-sex schools and to ordain women (a step that would have delighted many Catholic proponents). She also established the Eagle Forum to lobby against women's liberation and developed a subscription list of 35,000 for the *Phyllis Schlafly Report*, an antifeminist publication. In time she claimed 50,000 committed anti-ERA followers, who could call upon thousands of others for concerted action. Leaving no stone unturned, Schlafly asked those attending her Eagle Forum leadership to pray for the defeat of the ERA; she herself recited a daily rosary for this purpose. While leading this struggle she returned to school to obtain a law degree. Her amazing career has been summed up by one of her critics as follows: "Ideologically she is an inherent contradiction; a paradigm of feminism she rails against it; a superbly accomplished career woman who recommends staying home and baking cookies; a wide-ranging intelligence committed down the line, to the entire panoply of political reaction."

When the deadline passed, still three states short (thirty-five of the necessary thirty-eight states ratified), the amendment was immediately reintroduced into Congress and was quickly and soundly defeated. Partisans on both sides attributed the drubbing to the National Right to Life Committee, which opposed passage unless an anti-abortion proviso were incorporated, a position supported by the U.S. Catholic Conference and reaffirmed by them in 1984.[80]

The defeat of the ERA did not, of course, end the struggle of women for equality; if anything it intensified it. The conflict honed political skills and organizational talents, drew many into the governmental process for the first time, and raised the consciousness of millions. For some Catholic women it overlapped with the quest for equality in the church, as inequality in state and religion were regarded as manifestations of the unjust male power structure.

CHAPTER
6
Reformers and Activists

Debra Campbell

*I*n the popular American Catholic imagination in which women have traditionally fallen into two categories, nuns and mothers of large families, female Catholic reformers and activists appear to be anomalies of recent vintage, symptoms of the "protestantization" of the Church in North America or outgrowths of Vatican II. Recent American history textbooks have begun to include the stories of a whole network of nineteenth-century Protestant women, including the Grimké sisters, Elizabeth Cady Stanton, and Frances Willard, whose activities in the abolitionist, temperance, and woman suffrage movements cause them to be considered the first generation of American feminists. The standard texts contain no references to individual Catholic women of the same period, except perhaps for intimations that they were the poor immigrants whose families the temperance reformers sought to salvage. Protestant women were drawn to abolition and temperance reform for a variety of reasons—religious, social, and political—and participation in these movements awakened them to the limitations being placed upon women's efforts by male reformers, fostered a sense of solidarity among women, and led to the fight for suffrage and equal rights. While Catholic women (and men) generally remained aloof from abolitionism, both because of the anti-Catholic undercurrents in the movement itself and because of the hierarchy's ambivalence regarding the morality of slavery, the temperance movement attracted growing numbers of Catholics during the heyday of temperance organizations, from the 1870s through the

152

ratification of the Eighteenth Amendment in 1919. Many Catholic women joined the nondenominational Women's Christian Temperance Union, as well as a multiplicity of Catholic reform organizations to combat drunkenness, poverty, and economic injustice and ease the plight of the ever-growing urban immigrant population. These experiences taught them a great deal about what they had in common with their non-Catholic sisters and raised new questions concerning the role women should play in church and society.

Catholic women's involvement in turn-of-the-century progressive reform paved the way for the emergence of a spectrum of new, distinctively Catholic forms of social activism between the 1930s and the 1950s, fostered by the small, communal social justice movements established by Dorothy Day and Catherine de Hueck Doherty, by imported and indigenous Catholic Action movements like the Grail and the Christian Family movement, and by an expanding network of freelance women activists whose leaders included the publisher Maisie Ward and Dorothy Dohen, editor of *Integrity* magazine. Since the late 1960s, this evolving tradition of Catholic women's activism, in combination with the new inclusive ecclesiology that surfaced at Vatican II, and with an emphasis upon theology as a means of liberation, informed by the Third World experience and recent American feminism, has given a whole new meaning to the term Catholic activism.[1]

During the period between the establishment of the American Catholic hierarchy in 1789 and the present day, the involvement of Catholic women in organized social reform movements in the United States has been affected by three factors: the changing needs of the church, Catholic attitudes toward reform movements not sponsored by the church, and Catholic perspectives on women's proper role in the home, the church, and the nation, propagated in sermons, popular literature, and the Catholic press. While the first factor, the changing needs of the ever-expanding immigrant church, represented a mandate for Catholic involvement in social reform, especially from the 1820s to 1920s, the other two factors—Catholic attitudes toward non-Catholic reform efforts and women's role in home and society—served to inhibit Catholic women's reform activities. Many Catholics questioned the motives of non-Catholic reformers and social critics whose work they considered excessively secular and materialistic, lacking the necessary spiritual component, and occasionally, merely a smoke screen for Protestant proselytizing among the Catholic immigrant poor. Meanwhile, Catholic attitudes toward women, like those of middle-class, nineteenth-century Americans in general, reflected a basic ambivalence toward women's right (or duty) to reform society.

In *The Mirror of True Womanhood* (1878), by Father Bernard O'Reilly, a popular handbook written expressly for Catholic laywomen, this ambivalence is apparent. O'Reilly states unequivocally that the home is "the sacred sphere within which God has appointed that true women should exercise their sway." He places the home at the very foundation of society, and warns that if the home is not safe and holy, the social order is endangered. In fact, O'Reilly maintains, a wife is, in a very real sense, the "savior" of her husband and sons, the one who keeps them on the straight and narrow path, and reminds them of what God and the church demand. In O'Reilly's words:

> No man ever lived a right life who had not been chastened by a woman's love, strengthened by her courage, and guided by her discretion.

Although O'Reilly denies that any Catholic woman "animated by the Spirit of her Baptism" would claim to need "any other sphere of activity than that home which is her domain, her garden, her paradise, her world," he also affirms that every Catholic housewife has the responsibility to care for any needy person who comes to her door, reserving for the poor the same "reverence" with which she would treat Christ. (Mere "kindness" is insufficient.) Reflecting upon the growing ranks of the poor in the nation's industrial areas, O'Reilly urges Catholic women to *organize* into parish associations that could work in collaboration with the women religious already engaged in caring for the needy.[2] For O'Reilly, and the clerical constituency he represents, woman's role as servant of the poor in her neighborhood was merely an aspect of her housework; it did not enlarge her sphere of activities. For Catholic laywomen, however, this first sanctioned step into the neighborhood around the parish could lead in a variety of directions and far from the hearthstone.

Catholic laywomen did not join organized social reform movements in large numbers until the final quarter of the nineteenth century, a period historians have called a watershed in the history of the American Catholic community, the dawn of "Catholic social liberalism," and the birth of a "Catholic social gospel."[3] Until this period, women religious, rather than laywomen, were the primary caretakers of the poor and the needy. Although many congregations confined their efforts to the field of education, often at the urging of bishops and priests, others established a whole spectrum of programs and institutions to meet the needs of the poor, the sick, and the aged. For example, the Holy Family Sisters, established in 1842 in New Orleans by Henrietta Delille (1813–1862), a free woman of color who had already tried twice (unsuccessfully) to form an interracial community of sisters, cared for the material and religious needs of slaves and poor blacks, ran an orphanage and a hospice, nursed the sick in their homes, and eventually established a school for black girls. As their names might imply, the Sisters of Mercy and the Sisters of Charity paid special attention to the needs of the poor in the growing cities and towns. Mother Mary Baptist Russell (1829–1898), an Irish immigrant who became the superior of the San Francisco Sisters of Mercy in 1854, creatively met each new challenge posed by the urban frontier. She established Saint Mary's, the first West Coast Catholic hospital, along with a night school, a shelter for unemployed, homeless women, the Magdalen Asylum for prostitutes, free primary and secondary schools for students of both genders, and a home for the aged. The legendary Ohio Sister of Charity, Sister Blandina Segale, faced a different set of challenges on the receding western frontier as she opposed lynching and the "might makes right" mentality prevalent in new settlements in Colorado and New Mexico in the 1870s.

The efforts of women religious could be rendered even more difficult by powerful ecclesiastics who prejudged the sisters' activities and failed to lend their support. John Hughes, Archbishop of New York in the mid-nineteenth century, "only tolerated" the work that the local Sisters of the Good Shepherd were doing with delinquent girls because he was skeptical about the possibility of ever reforming a young woman after she had "lost 'the glory of her womanhood.' "[4] From the 1840s onward, the Sisters of Mercy ran "houses of protection" and provided vocational training for the growing numbers of single women flocking to the cities and larger towns in search of work, despite local pressures placed upon them to devote more energy to parochial education. These "houses of protection" anticipated the "preventive charity" fostered by Catholics (and others) at the end of the nineteenth century, efforts to change the social environment and expand the options of women and the immigrant poor rather than simply caring for the casualties of the current social system.

During epidemics, and especially during the Civil War, the void in health care that was filled by nursing sisters became especially apparent. Over six hundred sisters served as nurses during the Civil War. Some like Mother Angela Gillespie (1824–1887), who built and administered her own military hospital at Mound City, Illinois, as skillfully as she had administered Saint Mary's College in Illinois prior to the war, showed that women's talents in health care extended beyond nursing the sick and into the executive realm. The nursing sisters of the early nineteenth century foreshadowed and actually helped to bring about the professionalization of nursing in the second half of the century, which, like a parallel development, the professionalization of social work, opened up whole new arenas of women's activity in social reform. Both developments presented problems, however, to some Catholics, clerical and lay, who objected to paying individuals to do the corporal works of mercy. The need for professionally trained nurses was especially apparent in places where sisters were unavailable. Convicted prostitutes in New York City in the nineteenth century were given two alternatives: a prison term or a stint of nursing at Bellevue.[5] Unfortunately, choice of the latter alternative did not bring with it the promise of adequate training for a nursing career.

Sisters were especially active in one cause dear to the hearts of the first generation of (Protestant) American feminists: the education of women. By the time educational reformers like Catherine Beecher, Emma Willard, and Mary Lyon had established their pioneering seminaries for women in the 1820s and 1830s, Catholic sisters had been educating young American women in female academies for a century. The first Catholic female academy in what is now the United States was run by the Ursulines in New Orleans starting in 1727. Despite the suspicions of outsiders concerning the motives and activities of sisters running schools for girls—which could flare up into local violence as they did in 1834 when an Ursuline convent in Charlestown, Massachusetts was burned by an angry mob—Catholic female academies proliferated. By 1852 there were one hundred Catholic female academies across the nation run by numerous religious orders and congregations, many with European roots. These academies were by no means concerned exclusively with the academic training of young women, but neither were the female seminaries run by Lyon and Beecher during the second Great Awakening. Nevertheless, Catholic female academies provided a precedent to be used by later advocates of Catholic higher education for women. The College of Notre Dame in Maryland, which became the first Catholic women's college in the United States in 1896, had its roots in an academy established in 1863. In one important instance, the needs of local children and the apparent absence of sisters who could care for them gave rise to a new congregation of women religious; the Oblate Sisters of Providence, the first American black congregation of sisters, was established in 1831 by Elizabeth Lange (c. 1800–1889) and three other black women to provide an education for the children of the black community in Baltimore.

The history of laywomen's involvement in social reform during the first century after the establishment of the hierarchy remains virtually undocumented. Certainly, the role played by laywomen in social causes was far more limited during the period prior to the final quarter of the nineteenth century than that of women religious. Nevertheless, some laywomen, generally women of means, made important contributions as journalists, philanthropists, and educators. Their work, like that of women religious, was important not only in itself, but also because it expanded the horizons of the Catholic community and suggested new arenas in church and society in which laywomen and women religious might fruitfully and appropriately serve. Joanna

England (d. 1827), who worked with her brother, Bishop John England of Charleston, on the *U.S. Catholic Miscellany*, published from 1822 until 1861, was the first woman in a long line of rarely acknowledged female American Catholic journalists of the nineteenth and early twentieth centuries. Georgia Hamlin (1845–1917) of Boston wrote for the *Herald* and the *Tribune* and replaced Mrs. John Boyle O'Reilly (pen name Agnes Smiley) as editor of the Children's Department of the Boston *Pilot*. By the turn of the century, women were on the editorial staff of three Catholic publications in Boston. Katherine Conway wrote for the *Pilot* from 1883 to 1908, assuming the job of editor for the final three years. Susan L. Emery served as editor of the *Sacred Heart Review* in Cambridge, and Mary Josephine Rogers (1882–1955) was coeditor of the Maryknoll magazine *Field Afar* with James Anthony Walsh in Boston from 1909 until 1912 when she moved to New York state to establish the Maryknoll Sisters of Saint Dominic.

Most female Catholic philanthropists were wealthy women who fulfilled their obligation to show reverence for the poor by diverting some of their money (or that of their husbands and sons) to the needy or to worthy Catholic causes: convents, schools, or other institutions. Sometimes charity could become a family tradition, as it was in the case of three generations of Catholic women of Belgian lineage, Sylvia Parmentier (1793–1882), Adele Parmentier Bayer (1814–1892), and Rosine Parmentier (1829–1908) of Brooklyn who cared for the needy, visited the sick, including sick sailors at the City Hospital, and acted as patronesses for orphanages, Indian missions, schools for blacks, missionary priests, and the local Sisters of Saint Joseph. Ellen Boyle Ewing Sherman (1824–1888), wife of General William T. Sherman, established a dispensary of food and clothing for the poor in the nation's capital, which she ran with the help of Sister Paula, a Holy Cross Sister. Ewing encouraged the poor to "pay" by saying the rosary together on the premises. Mrs. Sarah Peter (1800–1877) of Cincinnati, who was received into the church in 1864, helped to establish the local Convent of the Good Shepherd even before her conversion, and went on to support the work of several other groups of women religious in Cincinnati. She traveled to the Franciscan motherhouse in Aachen in 1857 to find sisters to work in Cincinnati hospitals and to care for indigent poor in the open air.

Not all female Catholic philanthropists of the nineteenth century came from wealthy homes. Margaret Gaffney Haughery (1813–1882), "the Bread Woman of New Orleans," was a self-made woman who ran her own dairy and bakery. Born into a poor immigrant Irish family, Haughery, who had lost her husband and only child in an epidemic in the 1830s, became a familiar figure among the poor of New Orleans, as she both sold and dispensed free bread from her company wagon (which she drove herself). Besides contributing to homes for the poor, the aged, and the sick supported by Protestant and Jewish as well as Catholic organizations, Haughery gave generously to families and individuals of all creeds and races stricken by epidemics, injured in the Civil War, or rendered homeless by floodwaters. As a single woman with her own business, Haughery could approach the freedom of movement and freedom from conventional domestic confines enjoyed by women religious, a freedom that married women, even wealthy ones, often could not exercise.

Finally, nineteenth-century Catholic laywomen made important contributions in the field of education. Although Catholic female academies were generally staffed by sisters, laywomen became public school teachers in large numbers, a development that would further complicate the hierarchy's efforts to promote parochial education in the wake of the Third Plenary Council held in Baltimore in 1884. Teaching was especially popular among unmarried Irish women from the second generation onward. By 1870 20 percent of all New York City public school teachers were Irish women, most of them Catholic. This pattern would prove increasingly true by the turn of the century, not only in New York, but in Chicago and San Francisco as well. Bernard O'Reilly acknowledges this in *The Mirror of True Womanhood*, when he laments the plight of the overworked and underpaid public school teachers whom he calls the "daughters of the people." These Catholic laywomen, who played such a visible role in their communities, could become scapegoats for anti-Catholic nativism, even late in the nineteenth century. In *The Mauve Decade*, Thomas Beer recounts the story of an Irish Catholic woman in Massachusetts who had to swear that she was Unitarian in order to obtain a position in a local school. She returned home from the ordeal only to find "a gang of Christian women rifling her trunk in search of a nun's veil or penitential emblems."[6]

For many nineteenth-century laywomen, the experience of teaching school opened their eyes to their own potential and the injustices in their local communities, as well as in society at large. For some of these women, teaching led to other commitments and other careers. The labor activist "Mother" Mary Harris Jones (1830–1930) started out as a teacher, as did the journalist Eleanor Donnelly. Some teachers, like Kate Kennedy (1827–1890), Margaret Haley (1861–1939), and Catherine Goggins, moved from teaching itself to organizing schoolteachers. Kate Barnard (1875–1930), who worked as a teacher in rural schools in Oklahoma in the 1890s, went on to become that state's elected commissioner of charities and corrections early in the twentieth century. Some of these teachers-turned-reformers, like Kate Kennedy, moved out of the church as they became more involved in social reform. Others, like Mother Jones, moved out, and then, dramatically, back into the church later in life. From the mid-nineteenth century until well into the twentieth century, Catholic laywomen educated themselves to serve as teachers in the public school system, an acceptable profession for an unmarried Catholic laywoman. Like the volunteer efforts of married laywomen who cared for the neighborhood poor, it could lead to organized reform endeavors that were considerably less acceptable to some members of the Catholic community. Teaching, while considered appropriate for single women, was not considered nearly as appropriate for married women, especially mothers, who were expected to quit their jobs, if at all feasible financially, and devote all their time to domestic duties.

During most of the nineteenth century, women religious had far greater opportunities to actively promote social change than laywomen, but this situation changed rather abruptly in the final quarter of the nineteenth century. The reasons for this shift in laywomen's options are complex and numerous; they include the growth of labor unions, the arrival of the new immigrants from southern and eastern Europe, the achievement of middle-class status for increasing numbers of Catholics from Irish and western European backgrounds, and escalating efforts to organize the Catholic laity to meet new challenges to the sanctity of the family, the stability of the community, and the future of a Christian America. In their confrontations with the problems posed by an increasingly industrialized society and a growing population of immigrant poor, Catholics had two alternatives: cooperation with non-Catholic reformers and the launching of new exclusively Catholic movements and institutions that would, in some sense, compete with their Protestant, Jewish, or nondenominational counterparts. Some chose one or the other option; many chose both. By the turn of the century, however, the hierarchy focussed its attention upon promoting Catholic organizations for social service and reform; local clergy and even lay leaders followed suit.

An important factor in the Catholic church's response to the demands of an immigrant church in a rapidly industrializing American society was the increasing polarization of the Catholic community into two factions: liberals (also called Americanizers) who sought the rapid assimilation of the Catholic church and its immigrant constituency into the American mainstream and the conservatives whose closer ties to the immigrant community caused them to have a greater appreciation of the benefits of ethnic solidarity and the dangers to the faith posed by assimilation. Liberals tended to have more contact with non-Catholic reformers and more inclination to become actively involved in struggles to end urban poverty and economic injustice. Conservatives, while not denying the needs of the poor immigrants,

tended to encourage the traditional Catholic approach to the problems
of the poor: the voluntary practice of the corporal works of mercy by
sisters and laypeople who had attained at least middle-class status.
Liberals became part of the broad reform coalition taking shape in
the 1880s that found room for Catholics and Protestants, Social Gos-
pellers and members of labor unions, temperance advocates and pop-
ulists. Led by Archbishop John Ireland of Saint Paul, Minnesota,
Bishop John Lancaster Spalding of Peoria, Illinois, John Keane, rector
of the Catholic University of America, the Paulists, and others, the
liberals urged cooperation and dialogue with non-Catholics and an
activist posture in social reform. They popularized and worked to
implement Spalding's conviction that the major importance of Leo
XIII's pioneering social encyclical *Rerum Novarum* published in 1891
was its affirmation "that the mission of the church is not only to save
souls but to save society."[7] The conservatives, led by Archbishop Michael Corrigan of New York and Bishop Bernard McQuaid of Rochester, New York, with the strong support of the midwestern German
bishops, urged caution. Their main concern was that the Catholic faith
not be compromised or watered down by contact with non-Catholics.
They took seriously the lament of the Reverend Anton Walburg of
Saint Augustine's parish in Cincinnati, a self-proclaimed representative of the Catholic immigrants, who insisted in 1890 that two-thirds
of all Catholic immigrants left the church after arriving in the United
States, and that more could be expected to do so in the future. Although the German Central Verein had a strong social reform agenda,
women did not play significant roles in the movement.

In fact, both liberals and conservatives realized that contact between Catholics and non-Catholics was inevitable. It is not surprising
that the age of accelerating immigration which brought over one million newcomers to the United States each decade from 1880 to 1900,
and over two million during the years between 1901 and 1910, also
witnessed great strides in the growth of labor unions. Terrence Pow-
derly, a Roman Catholic who served as grand master of the Knights
of Labor during its boom years during the 1870s and 1880s, sought
the cooperation of workers of all religious faiths in their common
struggle against economic injustice, and worked to eliminate the
Knights' oath of secrecy in order to remove a major stumbling block
to Catholic membership. When Leo XIII sided with Cardinal Gibbons against the opponents of organized labor, he paved the way for
the strong support for labor unions that would characterize American Catholicism at least through the 1930s. He also opened up a new
arena in which laywomen of the working classes might struggle for
social justice.

By 1890 four million women in the United States had joined the work force; over half were employed in factories or domestic service. During the late nineteenth century, these female factory workers were disproportionately young, married and either immigrants themselves or of immigrant parentage, and for the most part they were Catholic or Jewish. As early as the 1830s, the plight of women workers was obvious to Harriet Martineau, a British author touring the United States, who commented upon the ill effects of American chivalry upon women who were forced to earn their daily bread. Martineau noted that "where it is a boast that women do not labour, the encouragement and rewards of labour are not provided."[8] Women in the work force, aware of the same problem, had already begun to band together to demand equal treatment and improved working conditions. During the Civil War, a labor shortage and a sudden need for expanded production encouraged further organization into local societies such as the New York Working Women's Protective Union. Nevertheless, half a century later, the vast majority of women laborers remained underpaid, in the least skilled jobs, and, for the most part, unorganized. Both church and society encouraged women to think of their work outside the home as a temporary solution to especially serious financial problems, a lifestyle to be abandoned for domestic life as soon as possible. Because they viewed themselves as temporary workers, most women did not see the need to organize. Moreover, some women were offended by the manner and rhetoric of the left wing of American labor. During the famous "bread and roses" strike in the Massachusetts mill town of Lawrence in 1912, "Wobblies" (members of the International Workers of the World) wielding placards reading "No God, No Master" alienated a sizable constituency from their cause.

Although the church has consistently supported the right of workers to organize in social encyclicals from *Rerum Novarum* (1891) to *Laborem Exercens* (1981), these documents also betray a basic opposition to women's involvement in occupations "less fitted for women." The following remarks written by William Stang, bishop of Fall River (Massachusetts), in 1905 describe the position the papacy has consistently taken and help to explain female Catholic laborers' ambivalence toward their work:

> Married women should not be permitted—a case of extreme necessity excepted—to work in factories. . . . The law of nature requires that a mother give her whole care and time to her children and her home. To violate this law would mean to ruin home life and thus sap the foundation of society.[9]

The extent to which turn-of-the-century American Catholic women heeded the hierarchy on this point varied from one ethnic group to the next. Irish, German, and Polish women generally followed this advice and stayed home after marriage, often supplementing the family income by taking in boarders or doing piecework. Italian women, who rarely worked outside the home after marriage, sometimes did so in garment or textile factories in the company of female relatives. Whole French Canadian families worked together in textile factories, an experience that appears to have unified the families rather than fragmenting them. Women of the laboring classes were sensitive to the implications of industrial and economic injustices for their families. Mother Jones was successful not only in organizing the workers but also in organizing their wives into "armies" who opposed scabs with their broomsticks, dishpans, and mops. In 1910 Italian builders' wives in Buffalo, New York marched two hundred strong, with babies in arms, to ask the mayor's intervention in a strike in which Polish scabs and police violence were being used. These women, who generally preferred to confine their activities to their homes, braved arrest for disorderly conduct, and took to the streets in order to save their husbands' jobs and ensure the safety of their children.[10]

Given the high concentration of Catholic women in the laboring classes, it is not surprising to find them among the ranks of the union leaders and organizers, nor to learn that some were treated less than cordially by the more conservative priests and bishops. Leonora Barry (1849–1930), appointed general investigator for the Knights of Labor's Committee on Women's Work in 1886, was a tireless organizer between her first and second marriages. While she could withstand opposition from her own bishop, who disapproved of women reformers, and persevered even after a priest called her a "lady tramp," she suspended her organizing activities immediately upon marrying her second husband Obadiah Lake in 1890, chiefly because she sincerely believed that women should not work outside the home except in cases of dire necessity. Some women showed that they could combine motherhood and a career in the labor movement despite hierarchical skepticism. Elizabeth Flynn Rodgers (1847–1939), a Catholic woman who led the first local Chicago women's assembly of the Knights of Labor, starting in 1881, helped to promote the idea of women's membership in the Knights and to cultivate the relationship between the Knights and the Women's Christian Temperance Union. A mother of twelve who brought her two-week-old baby to the national convention of the Knights of Labor in 1886, Rodgers worked hard to counteract women's reluctance to unionize.

Mary Kenney O'Sullivan (1864–1943), who began organizing shirtwaist makers and cabbies in Chicago in the 1880s, served as an organizer for the American Federation of Labor, starting in 1891. Cofounder of the National Women's Trade Union League (1903) and an active suffragist, prohibitionist, and member of the Women's International League for Peace, formed in the aftermath of the First World War, O'Sullivan proudly combined motherhood and activism. She picketed for the garment workers and shoe workers while pregnant. She remained a faithful Catholic and a sodality member.

O'Sullivan has been contrasted to Mother Jones, the legendary United Mine Workers organizer, a "fallen away" Catholic who embraced socialism and then, much later, returned to the fold. In May 1930, she celebrated her hundredth birthday by delivering a radio speech in which she warned would-be women reformers not to allow the capitalists to manipulate them by turning them into "ladies," a term she equated with useless "parlor parasites."[11] Although for much of her life Jones was not a *Catholic* organizer, her belated return to the church is worthy of consideration for those who wish to understand the compatibility of the Catholic ideal of womanhood with the life-style of the labor activist as well as the compatibility of socialism with the Catholic faith in the early decades of the twentieth century.

At least in the mind of Leonora Barry Lake, volunteer work in the temperance movement was closer to the church's ideal of womanhood than the life of a professional union organizer. Ironically, however, Catholic laywomen's involvement in the Catholic Total Abstinence Union (CTAU) and the Saint Vincent de Paul Society taught them lessons at least analogous to those learned by their Protestant counterparts in the abolitionist movement. When they attempted to combat drunkenness and poverty within these two Catholic organizations at the turn of the century, Catholic laywomen experienced the drawbacks of dual membership in the laity and in the "second sex." Temperance was not a movement that Protestant (or Catholic) Americans generally associated with the Catholic church. The CTAU, a federation of local Catholic temperance societies, some of which had been in existence since the 1840s, only slowly won sufficient clerical support to launch a national movement; its first meeting took place in Baltimore on February 22, 1872. It was an organization dedicated to reform by moral suasion, not legislation. In 1878, six years after its first meeting, the members of the CTAU decided to admit ladies' auxiliary societies as "honorary members," but it was nine more years before the female representatives of these societies were allowed to appear at annual conventions in lieu of their spiritual advisers or male surrogates. The proceedings of the annual meeting in 1889 note that male delegates were "intrigued" by their female colleagues' request to be known as "women's, not ladies' societies."[12]

This small hint and certain of the speeches delivered at the annual conventions during the 1890s and early 1900s point to the women's consistent and sometimes painfully courteous struggle to persuade the clergy and laymen that temperance was a cause in which all Catholic women might fruitfully and fittingly be engaged. At the 1890 convention, Sallie A. Moore of the Philadelphia Union lamented that even a superficial comparison between the female membership of the CTAU and the Women's Christian Temperance Union (WCTU), with which she herself was "proud to claim affiliation," showed that something was amiss in the CTAU. Moore accused the CTAU's members, and especially an unnamed "famous missionary priest," of propagating the popular illusion that "total abstinence is ... very good for a certain class; ... but ... it is an insult to the intelligence of a body of Catholic women to ask them publicly to take the pledge of total abstinence." Moore insisted that this kind of approach contradicted Catholic teachings on self-denial, encouraged talented Catholic women of the upper classes to remain within "the bonds of conservatism," and allowed the potential of many Catholic women to go unrealized.[13]

Eleven years later, in 1901, Leonora Barry Lake issued a plea for clergy and laymen to start encouraging—or perhaps, stop discouraging—Catholic women's organized temperance activities. "If a woman is allowed to charm us with her singing, why should she not be permitted to move us with her eloquence?" Lake began. She then proceeded to ask forthrightly whether women were the guardians of religion or not:

> Who have built the churches? If you answer truly you must say "the women." Who makes the man go to Mass of a Sunday morning? Who sends the children to Sunday School? The woman. . . . Good priests and laymen—bring the woman into our movement.

Lake goes on to say that although there were "splendid women waiting for a word of encouragement," they were instead receiving "a little cold water [that] ... takes the life out of them." She reminds the clergy that "One 'God bless' from a priest goes further with women than if a dozen other people applauded their efforts,"[14] and leaves her listeners with the distinct impression that those "God blesses" were infrequent invocations.

In an article that appeared in the *Catholic World* in 1893, Alice Timmons Toomy likewise suggested that Catholic women's temperance work was being undermined by institutional resistance and attitudes within the church. Toomy affirmed that: "Tens of thousands of our ablest Catholic women are working with the WCTU and other non-Catholic philanthropies, because they find no organization in their own church as a field for their activities."[15] As Leonora Lake later implied, Catholic women's aloofness from the CTAU indicated that however open to women the organization professed to be—and even Frances Willard of the WCTU remarked upon the apparent equal status of women in the CTAU[16]—the CTAU did not attract nearly as many Catholic women as the semi-Protestant WCTU. While one reason for the relative appeal of the WCTU among middle- and upper-middle-class Catholic women might well have been its (more socially acceptable) Protestant constituency, another aspect of the WCTU's atmosphere that appealed to reform-oriented Catholic women might have been the warm welcome they received and the freedom from worry about what the priests and bishops were thinking.

It was one thing for the clergy and bishops to promote temperance in an immigrant church whose economic and social problems were clearly linked to alcohol abuse. It was another to encourage Catholic laywomen to organize on an equal basis in reform societies with men. Bishop Stang, who readily admitted in 1905 that alcoholism might be "the social question of the hour," insisted nonetheless that women's proper role in temperance reform was far different than the one played by women in organizations like the WCTU or the CTAU. Stang maintained that the proper site of women's temperance activities was "the kitchen and the table." According to Stang, "the most valiant temperance reformers" were "not those . . . women who agitate on the public platform," but rather those "who stay at home and know how to cook dinners and feed men well and make homes bright and restful."[17]

From Stang's perspective, the women who devoted long hours to organized temperance activities were part of the problem rather than part of the solution. Cardinal Gibbons expressed the same sentiments in an article entitled "The Restless Woman," which appeared in *The Ladies' Home Journal* in January 1902. Gibbons, appalled by the degenerating situation in American family life, which he perceived to be following in the wake of the rising divorce rate and the emergence of "the new woman," placed the major portion of the blame squarely upon "the restless woman" who "chafes and frets under the restraint and responsibility of domestic life." Even the woman who joins a club "or perhaps two or three clubs" endangers the future of the American family, according to Gibbons, when she disappoints her husband who "after the labors of the day . . . rightly expects to find a comfortable home, where peace, good order and tranquility reign," and is instead "filled with sadness and despair."[18] Of course, Gibbons's contention that women were joining clubs and societies wholly out of selfishness and restlessness, and to the clear detriment of home life was strongly opposed by women reformers who reiterated that the safety of the home was their major concern. Rallying to the cry of "home protection," the many followers of WCTU leader Frances Willard adopted the slogan "Do everything" to signify that all of their efforts in the political arena, in the temperance and suffrage movements, the peace movement, women's education, and the fight against prostitution were on behalf of the home. Women reformers agreed with Bernard O'Reilly that woman's efforts to help the unfortunate in their neighborhood were merely an extension of her domestic duties; they merely expanded their concept of what constitutes their neighborhood.

By the turn of the century the question of Catholic women's duties in the home and society had blossomed into a debate over the compatibility of feminism and suffragism with Catholicism, a debate with far-reaching ramifications. The position taken by Cardinal Gibbons was unequivocal: he declared women's rights advocates "the worst enemies of the female sex," who valued "masculinity" over motherhood. He inveighed against woman suffrage (except in municipal elections on issues related to the home), and predicted that if woman "thrusts herself into politics and mingles with the crowd, she must . . . surrender perhaps wholly, at least in part, that reverence now paid her."[19] Gibbons saw all of women's potential gains in the political arena as severe threats to her domestic, moral, and spiritual influence, with tragic implications for the future of the family and society at large. Moreover, if Catholic women were to emulate the "restless woman," the clubwoman, and the political reformer, rather than their true exemplar, the Blessed Mother, Gibbons understood that this would have massive implications for the future of the Catholic church.

When Cardinal Gibbons aired these opinions in the pages of the *Ladies' Home Journal* in 1902, the debate over Catholic women's proper sphere was well underway. In a special issue of the *Catholic World* published in 1893 in the wake of the Catholic Women's Congress, held in conjunction with the Columbian Exposition in Chicago, both sides of the question were addressed by outspoken Catholic laywomen. Journalist Eleanor Donnelly argued that "the average woman can have but one mission, one kingdom—that of the home," and but one model, the Virgin Mary, whose "life was a hidden one, altogether free from self-assertion." In the same issue, another female Catholic journalist and author, Katherine Conway, joined the chorus, rejoicing that Catholic women have exhibited "no consciousness of distinctly feminine—as apart from human—interests to be agitated for, . . . no morbid consciousness of womanhood." Catholic women, Conway maintained, have naturally and without coercion chosen to cooperate with men in charitable and reform activities under the church's guidance rather than embarking upon any unnatural "isolated and independent effort on the part of women."[20]

Needless to say, Donnelly and Conway lent their support to the antisuffrage movement, which was becoming increasingly organized by the 1890s, thanks to the groundwork laid decades earlier by two Catholic laywomen, Madeline V. Dahlgren and Ellen Ewing Sherman, whose antisuffrage petition presented to Congress in 1870 might be seen as the symbolic starting point of organized antisuffragism in America. As Sherman's involvement indicates, Catholic "antis" could also be very active in the traditional Catholic version of social reform, the performance of the corporal works of mercy in one's immediate neighborhood. Moreover, the support lent by Conway and Donnelly shows that laywomen with careers in the public sector could quite comfortably champion the cause of the antisuffragists. The case of Martha Moore Avery (1851–1929), a former socialist and convert to Catholicism whose public lectures opposing both socialism and woman suffrage were encouraged by her archbishop, William Henry O'Connell of Boston, illuminates the issues—and inconsistencies—involved in the Catholic female flank of the antisuffrage effort. Avery, a widow of moderate means and a powerful orator, spent much of her life on the public platform from 1890 until her death in 1929. From 1891 until 1902 she had served first as a promoter of the utopian ideals of Edward Bellamy and the Nationalist movement and then as an open-air propagandist for the Socialist Labor Party and Socialist Party of America. As Avery explained to Catholic audiences in the Boston area as well as to heterogeneous crowds gathered on Boston Common after her conversion to Catholicism in 1904, she transferred her loyalties from the socialist camp to the Catholic church when she became convinced that the church was the only institution that could save the endangered nuclear family, the bulwark of western civilization.

In essence, Avery took it upon herself to mount the public platform in order to affirm the need to defend the traditional family in which man was the natural head. Like many of her colleagues in the antisuffrage movement, Avery was convinced of both the necessity and the fragility of natural differences between the sexes ordained by God. Since she affirmed that God willed, and natural law required, that man and woman must be complementary, "the man to lead, the woman to help," Avery especially feared that woman suffrage would upset the delicate balance between the genders and cause unnatural role reversals. "If the natural law is violated," she warned, "we must suffer the consequences. . . . If men lose the heroic, we must expect women to be strident, thus maintaining a complementary, though very unlovely, difference between the sexes."[21]

The vocal majority of the American Catholic population followed the lead of Gibbons, Conway, Donnelly, and Avery and repudiated both "hard core feminism," which sought women's equality and the vote for their own sake, and "social feminism," which sought women's equal rights primarily as a means to a more just, humane, and religious society.[22] There were a few notable exceptions, however, including the liberal bishop John Lancaster Spalding and anomalous Catholic suffragists like Lucy Burns (1879–1966) and Margaret Foley (1875–1957) who could, with clear consciences, openly affirm both the truths of their Catholic faith and their conviction that women had the same political rights as male citizens. The views of the vast undocumented majority of American Catholic women are more difficult to discern. Given the large numbers of women religious and the increasing numbers of laywomen involved in social reform activities beyond the domestic realm during the latter part of the nineteenth century, as well as the attraction of a sizeable group of Catholic women to the WCTU, the epitome of social feminism, it is reasonable to assume that the antisuffragists did not speak for as many Catholic women as they claimed.

Even within the institutional church there were those who urged women to venture beyond the home and pool their efforts with other women for their own and the common good. The turn-of-the-century "brick and mortar" priests who facilitated the institutional expansion of the immigrant church encouraged the proliferation of parish societies. In *The People of Our Parish* (1900), Lelia Hardin Bugg quipped that American Catholics were "being 'clubbed' into model behavior if not into premature translation of glory" and recounted an impressive list of organizations found in a typical urban parish. She included a vast selection of groups primarily or exclusively for women: sodalities; devotional societies specializing in guardian angels, souls in purgatory, the rosary, and the Sacred Heart; service clubs like the Altar Society and the Queen's Daughters; auxiliaries to the Catholic Foresters and other men's groups; numerous reading circles; and a women's industrial club. "Father Ryan believes that in union there is strength," Bugg's protagonist affirms, "and he evidently wants all the . . . strength . . . he can get."[23] At least some of these organizations might be seen as attempts to provide Catholic equivalents of popular Protestant women's organizations. For example, the Queen's Daughters, established in Saint Louis in the late 1880s by a convert, Mary Hoxsey, represented the Catholic counterpart of a Protestant service club, the King's Daughters, which offered religious instruction and cooking and sewing classes and also ran a home for working women. This popular organization was endorsed by the hierarchy in 1896 and had sixty branches by the First World War.

The major challenge to the immigrant church was clearly the material and spiritual care of the growing population of urban poor, a challenge widely acknowledged by clergy, religious, and laypeople alike. The church was polarized, however, on the question of what

Catholics should do to help the poor. By 1910 the American Catholic church had almost 1,200 charitable institutions. The new age of the professional social worker was dawning, but the conservatives among the clergy and the Catholic press remained skeptical concerning the professionals whom they viewed as mercenaries who benefited from the poverty and ignorance of others. This skepticism waned a bit in the decades after the First World War when sisters experimented with the new techniques of the professional social workers, for sisters, by definition, were unselfish and respectable. Until 1910, the year the National Conference of Catholic Charities (NCCC) was established as an umbrella organization for the numerous local agencies working with the poor, the only broad-based Catholic organization seeking to combat the ill effects of urban poverty was the Saint Vincent de Paul Society, which had established its first United States branch in 1845.

The story of women's involvement in the Saint Vincent de Paul Society parallels that of women in the CTAU, and quite probably that of women's participation in many Catholic and non-Catholic voluntary organizations in which women were honorary or auxiliary members who had to struggle to become full-fledged partners with the men. Women in the Assumption Parish in Brooklyn were assisting the local (men's) Saint Vincent de Paul Society strictly on their own initiative as early as 1856, ten years before the Vincentians ever met as a nationwide movement. As late as 1911, however, women were barred from both "active" and "honorary" membership, although they could be "subscribers" or "benefactresses," sharing fully in the available indulgences and occasionally helping with the "friendly visiting." In a heated discussion of women's potential role in the Vincentians that took place at the national conference in Boston in July, 1911, Father William Kerby argued that women's auxiliaries should exist on an equal basis with men's societies whenever a male chapter could be found. He insisted that women were especially necessary in the field of "preventive charity" carried out through home visitations, because of women's expertise in domestic chores, nursing the sick, and child care, as well as women's natural tenacity, good humor, tact, and patience. This same position was argued strenuously by James Wise, a Boston Vincentian, at the society's international convention held in Saint Louis in September, 1904. While Wise understood why some viewed the admission of women into the society as a "radical innovation" and a departure from the founder's intentions, he believed that it would actually be a "progressive step" that would enhance both membership enrollments and efficiency. Kerby's and Wise's appeals went unheeded, however, and women failed to win equal status in the movement.[24]

Because the NCCC was a federation of existing member-societies that already included women, women fared better. Henry Somerville of the English Catholic Social Guild left the fourth annual meeting of the NCCC with a strong impression that the women were the progressives, much more familiar with the latest literature on social work than the men, who tended to be both conservatives and Vincentians.[25] The progressives Somerville heard at the conference had emphasized the preventability of poverty and the need to combat the social, economic, and political situations that created or exacerbated the plight of the immigrant poor. Quite possibly the visibility of single women among the progressive reformers advocating child labor laws and other legislative solutions to social problems heightened the anxiety of conservatives like Edward Maginnis who, in 1913, in the Philadelphia *Catholic Standard and Times*, bitterly condemned the intrusiveness of "freak, childless women shedding crocodile tears for the God-loving children of the poor."[26]

This suspicion of the new methods wielded by the "new woman" helps to explain the relative unpopularity of the settlement movement among American Catholics, despite the support of a number of liberal and conservative bishops and the good example set by the Cincinnati Sisters of Charity at Santa Maria Institute, established in 1897. The prototypical American social settlement, Hull House, established by Jane Addams and Ellen Gates Starr in Chicago in 1889, became associated with a wide variety of progressive reform movements sponsored by social feminists and perhaps discouraged many Catholics from considering settlement work an authentically Catholic solution to urban problems. Converts like Marion Gurney, the former Episcopalian who organized Saint Rose's settlement for Italian and Bohemian immigrants in New York City in 1898, and Grace O'Brien, who supervised half a dozen Brooklyn settlements for Italian immigrants during the first decade of the twentieth century, were especially prominent in Catholic settlement work. The programs offered at Saint Rose's were fairly typical. Gurney began by offering evening classes in sewing, child care, and religion for women and English classes, initially open only to men due to a staff shortage. Over the years, Saint Rose's expanded its facilities and its staff to include English classes for women and more diversified vocational training, athletics (in a new gymnasium), folk dancing, and daytime religion classes. During the early 1900s, Ann Leary, a laywoman who had inherited a fortune from her brother, purchased several houses in Lower Manhattan and opened a settlement called the Pius X Art Institute, which she hoped would be the foundation for an Italian-American University. Meanwhile, in Los Angeles, four Catholic settlements to care for Mexicans opened under lay leadership between 1901 and 1930.

In Chicago, the presence of Hull House and the need for a Catholic alternative provided the incentive for the establishment of Madonna House in 1898 by members of the alumnae sodality of the Chicago Academy of the Sacred Heart as well as another settlement run by Rebecca Gallery in the Casa Maria neighborhood. Although there is a sense in which Catholic settlements in Chicago were in competition with Hull House, this competition never overshadowed the cooperation and mutual respect that characterized relations between Hull House and its Chicago Catholic counterparts. Catholics like the labor organizer Mary Kenney O'Sullivan had strong ties to Hull House. In fact, Ellen Gates Starr, cofounder of Hull House, converted to Catholicism in 1920.

An important source of support for Catholic settlements was the large number of Catholic laywomen who were public school teachers. Maria Lopez relied upon the help of this constituency at Casa Maria, a settlement for Spanish-speaking immigrants in New York City, as did Josephine Brownson at Weinman Settlement for Syrian immigrants in Detroit. Generally speaking, however, Catholic settlement work attracted only a tiny minority among Catholic laypeople. Because of Catholic skepticism concerning professional social workers and a general lack of encouragement given to lay workers, especially women, the number of Catholic settlements remained very modest: about fifty Catholic settlements established prior to 1930, in comparison to five hundred non-Catholic ones.

Although many Catholics reacted unfavorably to the growing specialization and professionalization apparent in the field of social service, Catholic sisters were generally not among them. By the turn of the century, sisters were involved in the same kind of work being done by settlement and social workers, including counseling prisoners, providing alternatives to state care for the criminally insane, establishing day nurseries, and other social service agencies. In this age of specialization, sisters, too, sought to specialize. The turn of the century witnessed the successful attempts of many American congregations to achieve pontifical status and thereby circumvent episcopal attempts to employ them in areas not of their own choosing. Both for women religious and for laywomen, the end of the nineteenth century ushered in a time of experimentation and growth as they strove to serve the church, and especially the poor and needy, without hindrance from ecclesiastical structures.

By the dawn of the twentieth century Catholic women's involvement in social reform had yielded new visions of the religious life focussed upon specific forms of social service. Margaret Tucker, a lay Catholic settlement worker, proposed establishing a semicloistered order of deaconesses who would specialize in settlement work. She hoped that this new group might mitigate the suspicion many Catholics had harbored toward paid professionals in this field. Her plans were interrupted, however, by the First World War and never came to fruition. In 1908, Rose Gurney, the pioneer Catholic settlement worker, became Mother Marianne of Jesus, foundress of the Sisters of Our Lady of Christian Doctrine, a congregation of women religious engaged in settlement work on New York's Lower East Side.

Similar concerns prompted Katharine Drexel (1858–1955), the daughter of a prosperous Austrian-American banker from Philadelphia, to establish the Sisters of the Blessed Sacrament for Indians and Coloured People in 1891. As Mother Katharine, Drexel built and staffed schools and vocational training centers for blacks and Native Americans across the nation, caring for a constituency whose needs had been overlooked by the immigrant church, overwhelmed as it was by the ever expanding population of urban immigrant poor. In 1925, Xavier University in New Orleans, a teachers' college launched by Drexel ten years before, was chartered as the first Catholic College for blacks in the United States. Rose Lathrop (1851–1926), the widowed daughter of Nathaniel Hawthorne and a convert to Catholicism, likewise established a congregation of sisters, the Servants of Relief for Incurable Cancer in 1899, to do the work she saw being neglected by church and society. Lathrop (Sister Mary Alphonsa) and her first collaborator, Alice Huber (Sister Mary Rose), pioneered in hospice work, first in the homes of the terminally ill, and later in two hospitals, Saint Rose's Free Home in New York City and Rosary Hill in Hawthorne, New York.

One final example of a new specialized congregation of sisters emerging to meet new needs and reflect Catholic women's expanding horizons at the turn of the century is the Maryknoll Sisters, launched by Mary Josephine (later Mother Mary Joseph) Rogers. Rogers had already taught at Smith College and in Boston schools and coedited a Catholic publication prior to her decision in 1912 to help establish a community of women religious to work with James Anthony Walsh's Maryknoll Fathers in the foreign missions. In keeping with her conviction that Maryknoll Sisters should be active contemplatives, Rogers went on to establish a second, purely contemplative community for Maryknoll Sisters in 1933. While the contemplatives prayed for their efforts, the active contemplatives taught, nursed, or engaged in social service work initially in the Orient, but later throughout the world and among cultural minorities in the United States. The Maryknolls and other congregations of nursing and missionary sisters had to work around Vatican regulations prohibiting sisters from providing maternity care, restrictions finally removed in 1936 thanks to the efforts of Dr. Anna Dengel.

The years between the 1880s and 1920s, which witnessed a new age of specialization and "preventive charity," also represent an era of organization-building in the Catholic church in the United States. The attempt to organize the laity bore fruit in two lay congresses held in Baltimore (1889) and Chicago (1893), as well as a parallel series of contemporaneous black Catholic congresses in which lay people played the dominant roles. Both the general lay congresses and the black congresses died out in the first half of the 1890s, essentially because they were not an episcopal priority and were, in fact, viewed as potentially dangerous by some clergy and bishops. Although women were not present at the first Catholic Lay Congress organized by the hierarchy to meet in Baltimore in 1889 in conjunction with the centenary of the American hierarchy, women were both visible and vocal at the second congress, planned by lay leaders to meet at the Columbian Exposition held in Chicago in 1893. The program of the second congress included several women speakers: Eliza Allen Starr on Christian art, Eleanor Donnelly on women in literature, Mary J. Onahan on "Isabella the Catholic," Katherine Conway on reading circles, Anna Sadlier on medieval women, and Elizabeth Cronin on convent school alumnae associations. Henry Spaunhorst's presentation on Catholic societies did not refer to activities of women, but ironically, another speech, "Young Men's Societies," by Warren Mosher, did. Mosher contrasted women's wholehearted support for societies promoting both piety and education to men's lukewarm interest. "There is a barrier growing up between Catholic men and women," Mosher affirmed, "the barrier of education and refinement."[27]

Perhaps the clearest signal of Catholic women's aspirations at the time of the congress was the establishment of the National League of Catholic Women by Alice Toomy, Eliza Allen Starr, and other participants. The League's stated goals were reminiscent of those of the WCTU and the settlement movement, the "do everything" approach to social reform. The league sought "to promote education by spreading Catholic doctrine; to promote philanthropy by encouraging temperance, and by forming day nurseries, kindergartens, protective and employment agencies, and clubs and homes for working girls." *The Pilot*, the Boston archdiocesan paper, noted with regret the league's resemblance to Protestant women's organizations and expressed a preference for a new specifically Catholic model.[28] There were some bright chapters in the history of the league, for example, the active Chicago and Pittsburgh Catholic women's leagues, both dedicated to cooperation rather than competition with non-Catholic social reform agencies, and the Portland (Oregon) league, established in 1908, which sponsored Caroline Gleason's successful fight in the state legislature for the first minimum wage law for women in the nation (1913). Generally speaking, however, the National League of Catholic Women failed to live up to the expectations of its founders and was over-shadowed by later organizations, especially the National Council of Catholic Women.

After the Catholic Lay Congress movement died in the 1890s, lay interest in a national organization focussed upon the short-lived American Federation of Catholic Societies (1901–1918). Although women had been charter members of some of the local societies, there was strong pressure exerted within the federation, expressed at the first national convention, to exclude women from membership. This effort was not successful, but it set the tone for the short future of the federation. Although one woman, Elizabeth Rodgers, served as treasurer of the federation for a brief period, she was the exception. Men dominated the federation so completely that concern was expressed in the official *Bulletin* in 1906 as to whether women were welcome at the annual conferences. As late as 1912 there was heated discussion on the floor at the conference concerning whether it would be advisable for women to withdraw and form a separate federation.[29] Ironically, it was during this same period that one of the member organizations, the Catholic Central Verein, established a National Catholic Women's Union (1916), which displayed remarkable vitality and growth into the 1930s. The Central Verein Women's Union launched a broad based reform program that included day care, assistance to working women, and health care, and not only eclipsed its male counterpart, the Gonzaga Union, but also served as a major catalyst in involving women of German-American extraction, who had previously been encouraged to confine their activities in social reform and "preventive charity" to *Kirchen, Küchen, und Kinder*.

The establishment of the National Catholic Welfare Council (NCWC) on the eve of the First World War, with its forward-looking social action department led by Father John A. Ryan from 1919 to 1945, ushered in a new era, a period of centralization and strong episcopal leadership that definitely closed the door on the age of localized, fragmented lay and clerical efforts. Historian Aaron Abell aptly characterizes the nature of this transition in a terse subtitle: "The Bishops Take Command."[30] The National Council of Catholic Women (NCCW), founded in 1920, incorporated existing Catholic women's organizations into this new centralized structure. Mrs. Michael Gavin, the first president of the NCCW, underscored the precedent set by her new organization: it was "not . . . a mere federation of women's clubs, but an organic part of . . . the National Catholic Welfare Council."[31] The structural link to the American hierarchy, which Gavin clearly perceived as a major breakthrough, turned out to be a two-edged sword. The NCCW, which has expended most of its energies in the area of education, promoting study clubs, and dialogue on social topics, as well as administering immigrant aid and the National Catholic Service School, has exhibited little inclination or ability to take a stand independent from the official position of the hierarchy on such pivotal issues as feminism, communism, abortion, women's ordination, and the ERA. Although the NCCW represents the church's official acknowledgement of women's ability to serve church and society in the public arena and even a hierarchical mandate for Catholic women's work as social reformers, activists, and occasionally lobbyists, its institutional ties appear to have inhibited its independent Christian witness.

The same process of official coordination and control of Catholic women's social reform efforts took place simultaneously on the diocesan level. When Cardinal William O'Connell of Boston wished to oppose child labor laws in a state referendum in 1924, he utilized specially trained pairs of laywomen chosen from each parish to help propagate his position. O'Connell, a strong proponent of diocesan organizations for laypeople of both genders, made very clear ground rules. As Martha Moore Avery noted in 1918, "the Cardinal laid down the *law* under which a Catholic club must operate. If . . . there are women who mean to work on their *own will, they are not wanted*. It was said as bluntly as that."[32]

By the 1920s the hierarchy had finally acknowledged women's desire to serve the church by reforming society, and had even established channels through which women's contributions could be organized and monitored. This was a major step away from the fragmentation (and relative freedom) that had previously characterized Catholic women's reform efforts. By the 1930s, however, it had become apparent that church organizations and agencies to train social workers or administer poor relief did not strike at the heart of America's social and economic ills, nor did they satisfy the growing need for a deeper sense of social solidarity and lay spirituality apparent within the increasingly educated, upwardly mobile Catholic population. Between the world wars, three grass-roots lay movements led by women, the Catholic Workers, Friendship House, and the Grail, transformed the social vision of the American Catholic community. Bolstered by a renewed emphasis upon the church as the Mystical Body of Christ and the nascent liturgical renewal led by Father Virgil Michel, O.S.B., of Saint John's Abbey in Minnesota, these three movements represent a clear departure from turn-of-the-century Catholic reform, and mark the emergence of a distinctive form of Catholic social activism. Without explicitly criticizing the spiritual and social limitations of the hierarchy's centralized efforts at social reform, all three movements pointed the way to an alternative vision based upon the conviction that the spiritual solidarity that bound together members of the Mystical Body of Christ had radical social implications that could only be realized in small communities.

The first of the three movements, the Catholic Workers, resulted from the collaboration of Dorothy Day (1897–1980), a former socialist and radical journalist, and Peter Maurin, a French peasant and itinerant prophet of personalism. Day, who had dutifully abandoned her former comrades after her conversion in 1927, felt deeply frustrated by the limits traditionally placed upon Catholic social activism. With Maurin she developed an alternative, a movement in which small groups of volunteers lived in urban "houses of hospitality," feeding the poor and supporting labor unions, striking workers, and the gradually emerging peace movement. Day was the central presence in the movement, and, throughout her lifetime, the most audible voice in the penny paper after which the movement was named. Like the Catholic settlement workers before them, members of Catholic Workers sought (and still seek) both to soothe the pain of the poor and to engage in "preventive charity" by providing a public forum for discussions on the roots of social injustice. They moved far beyond their progressive forbears, however, by their physical presence on the picket lines, their use of the techniques of passive resistance to protest the draft and the arms race, and their close connection to the drive for liturgical renewal.

Although Dorothy Day was by far the most visible woman in the movement, there were many others. "Houses of hospitality" attracted growing numbers of Catholic college graduates of both genders during the forties, fifties, and sixties. The vast majority of these volunteers were transient visitors, but they left the movement with a wider vision of their social and spiritual responsibilities, and firsthand experience of the church as the Mystical Body that would bear fruit in the renewal movements of the 1950s and 1960s. A few, like Michael Harrington, moved from the Catholic Workers out of the church and into the socialist camp. Despite her orthodox theology and patent piety, Day's pacifism, her socialist sympathies, and her occasional dissent from the position taken by her archbishop (e.g., during wars, as well as in the New York gravediggers' strike in 1949), made her a visible countervailing force within the church. Day represents an important precedent for the expression of conscientious lay dissent from the hierarchy on social questions, and paved the way for lay dissent on matters theological and ecclesiological.

A second movement, Friendship House, sought the transformation of American society by communal efforts to combat racism. Founded by the Russian émigré the Baroness Catherine de Hueck (Doherty) in Harlem in 1938, the movement spread to Chicago, Washington, D.C., Portland, Oregon, and Shreveport, Louisiana. Like the Catholic

Workers, de Hueck's movement provided an opportunity for middle-class, educated Catholic women to move beyond reading circles and discussion groups to implement change. Some, like Ann Harrigan (Makletzoff), a Brooklyn schoolteacher who quit her job to work full time in the Chicago Friendship House, and Monica Durkin, who sold her Cleveland insurance company to run a Friendship House farm intended to integrate blacks into rural Wisconsin, found in de Hueck's movement the possibility of a full-time career in the social apostolate. De Hueck played an important role in raising the Catholic community's consciousness of the racism in the church and in American society. Through its newspaper, *The Catholic Interracialist*, and the "outer circle," a group of laypeople on the periphery of the movement who shared its social concerns and its spirituality, the impact of Friendship House spread far beyond the core group and helped to stimulate Catholic women's involvement in the civil rights protests of the 1950s and 1960s.

The third movement, the Grail, had its origins in the Society of the Women of Nazareth, established by Jacques Van Ginneken, S.J., in the Netherlands in 1921, and was transported to the United States in 1940 by two Dutch laywomen, Lydwine van Kersbergen and Joan Overboss. Its goal was nothing less than to:

> . . . counteract in the world all masculine hardness, all the angles of the masculine character, all cruelty, all the results of alcoholism and prostitution and sin and capitalism, which are ultramasculine, and to Christianize that with a womanly charity.[33]

From its second headquarters, Grailville, a farm outside of Loveland, Ohio, the Grail, which earned the nickname "the Mystical Body in miniature," sponsored courses and retreats attended by Catholic women from across the nation that dramatized the vital link between involvement in the liturgy and the lay apostolate in the world. By the 1950s the Grail had achieved national stature in the United States: during that decade several thousand women participated in its programs, six hundred women (both married and single) were active members, and its core group of lifetime (celibate) members numbered close to one hundred. Grail centers opened in several U.S. cities, and its offshoots, the School of Missiology established in Grailville in 1950 and the Institute for Overseas Service founded in Brooklyn in 1956, began to train missionaries and social workers for active duty in the Third World. In the wake of its first national conference in 1962, the Grail reassessed its vision and entered a period of renewal. It welcomed the involvement of women from a multiplicity of religious backgrounds and focussed increasingly upon movements for social and economic justice. During the following decade, it became explicitly feminist, sponsoring conferences in feminist theology and related liturgical reforms.

It is significant that the Catholic Worker, Friendship House, and the Grail chose to operate outside of the network of Catholic Action movements promoted by the Vatican and the hierarchy, and without the "official status" enjoyed by the NCCW. All three movements burst the boundaries of Catholic Action as it was officially defined: "the participation of the laity in the apostolate of the hierarchy." In fact, most indigenous American Catholic movements described under the heading of Catholic Action functioned without the degree of clerical leadership envisioned in the Vatican's version of Catholic Action. This was certainly true of one of the most successful examples of American Catholic Action, the Christian Family Movement (CFM), established in Chicago in 1949 under the leadership of a married couple, Pat and Patty Crowley. Although it drew upon the traditional Catholic emphasis upon the need to reform society in order to preserve the family and gained some strength from the prior involvement of its founding members in the Young Catholic Students, an imported Belgian Catholic Action movement, the CFM was an important departure in several ways. It emphasized Catholic involvement with non-Catholics in wider movements for social justice in American society, all for the sake of the family. It self-consciously promoted lay leadership; the clergy played merely an advisory role. Finally, it provided the opportunity for married women to function as equal partners in a Catholic activist movement. CFM fell squarely in line with the priorities of Pius XII, who, three years before its founding, had reminded Italian women of their obligation to "[organize] the social structure" to enhance the quality of family life. However, it explicitly rejected the spirit of competition promoted by Pius XII and the need to reform society in an explicitly Catholic fashion to counteract the efforts of other men and women with other agendas.[34] In an age of escalating social activism, the CFM flourished, reaching a membership of 30,000 couples in the U.S. by 1958.

Although women served as leaders and enthusiastic participants in a wide variety of American movements referred to under the general rubric of Catholic Action or the lay apostolate, none of these allowed women or laypeople the same degree of initiative and autonomy as CFM, the Catholic Worker, Friendship House, and the Grail. Women played important roles in the social action groups organized by the NCWC to help victims of World War II, devoted their energies to the Cana Movement, which grew out of a retreat for married people held in 1943, were active in the Catholic Youth Organization and the Catholic Maternity Guild, both founded to meet the needs of the beleaguered

Catholic family during the Depression. All of these movements utilized laywomen's energies in programs led by male clergy.

During the 1940s and 1950s there also emerged, on the periphery of the Grail, the Catholic Worker, and Friendship House, a small cadre of "free-lance" female activists who lent their support to a number of Catholic causes and generated a new vision among Catholic laywomen through their writings and public appearances. Two important figures were Maisie Ward (1889–1975) and Dorothy Dohen (1923–1984). Ward, cofounder of the Catholic publishing firm Sheed and Ward with her husband Frank Sheed, spent much of the quarter-century after World War II addressing Catholic audiences in the United States on a wide variety of topics related to Catholic theology, history, and social thought. She became increasingly interested in social action during her final years, as she sought (at long distance) to provide better social services in India, to improve low cost housing in England, to help spread the Catholic Worker movement across the Atlantic and, in works like *Be Not Solicitous* (1953), to publicize the efforts of individual Catholic laypeople to be active in the social apostolate without jeopardizing the quality of their family life.

Dohen, a sociologist, did not shrink from criticizing the social and political implications of the inflated patriotism she perceived among the American hierarchy. As an author and editor of the magazine *Integrity*, she promoted a new ideal of lay social activism explicitly rooted in the theology of the Mystical Body. Moreover, she squarely faced and articulated the difficulties of being a single laywoman in the social apostolate, one who eschewed clerical movements in an effort to create her own niche in an increasingly organized American Catholic church. Like Protestant female abolitionists of the nineteenth century and women in the CTAU, Dohen quietly opposed sexism within the church as she struggled to function as a Catholic social activist. By her writings and personal example, she presented a new model of lay Catholic activism in the world, which viewed action as "preparation for contemplation" and judged personal sanctity by the degree to which individuals could establish a new harmonious social order better reflecting the reality of Christ's incarnation.[35]

Starting in the 1960s, the Catholic community in the United States witnessed a surge of social activism that has continued unabated into the present and in which men and women, clergy, lay, and religious are all involved. Certainly the Second Vatican Council, with its inclusive ecclesiology and the mandate for social change articulated in *Gaudium et Spes*, was an important factor in this development, but there were many others as well, including John XXIII's remarks on civil disobedience in *Pacem in Terris* (1963), the popular dissent that met the publication of *Humanae Vitae* (1968), and the Latin American bishops' acknowledgment of the church's duty to show a preferential option for the poor at Medellin, Colombia (1968). The 1960s witnessed the increasing visibility of women religious in social activism, prompted in part by reforms in sisters' education implemented by the Sister Formation Conference (1954), and in part by the increasing involvement of women religious from the United States in Latin America since the early 1960s in response to a request from the Vatican. The general direction of activism promoted by feminists, opponents of nuclear war, and civil rights advocates has had a tangible influence upon Catholic social activism, while the ecumenical movement, as well as precedents set by the CFM and others who encouraged Catholic cooperation with non-Catholic activists, has resulted in the corrosion of denominational boundaries separating activists. Catholic women, whose social agendas place them on the right as well as the left flank of the ideological spectrum, have come to appreciate the importance of broad-based coalitions for social change. Catholics are prominent on both sides of the prolife/prochoice conflict. Catholic women, slow to join the peace movement supported by social feminists at the turn of the century, have flocked to the cause since the 1960s. Building upon the witness of Dorothy Day and the Catholic Worker and that of Elizabeth Sweeney and Elizabeth Morrissey, among the women prominent in the Catholic Association of International Peace (1928) between the World Wars, Catholic women, lay and religious, have embraced the cause of peace as an essential component in a larger agenda of social reforms.

As the examples of Jean Donovan, Ita Ford, Maura Clarke, and Dorothy Kazel, killed in El Salvador in 1981, underscore, commitment to the poor and oppressed necessarily has political overtones. Catholic women, lay and religious, have been caught in the political and ecclesiastical crossfire during the past two decades as they have sought to act upon a radically updated version of Father O'Reilly's mandate to help the needy in an expanding global neighborhood. Mary Ann Sorrentino was excommunicated in 1986 for her work as executive director of Planned Parenthood in Rhode Island. Sisters who signed the 1984 *New York Times* advertisement affirming a plurality of Catholic positions on abortion have met with reprisals from the Vatican. Sister Margaret Traxler, who served as convener of the Justice Campaign, an interdenominational group that lobbies for federal funding for abortions for impoverished rape and incest victims, has had to resign under strong pressure from the Congregation for the Doctrine of the Faith. Sister Darlene Nicgorski, whose experiences in Guatemala in the early 1980s raised her consciousness about human rights violations in Latin America, was indicted early in 1985 by a federal grand jury for conspiracy and for transporting and harboring illegal aliens. Despite the sexism they found within the Catholic left, women accounted for at least 30 percent of its membership.[36]

American Catholic women have played an increasingly visible role in social reform and activism since the peak years of the immigrant church, beginning in the final quarter of the nineteenth century. They have had to struggle consistently to win the privilege of acting upon their Catholic faith in the social and political arena. The church's position on women reformers and activists can only be described as equivocal. Like Father O'Reilly's readers over a century ago, women of the 1980s are enjoined to show a reverence for the poor and oppressed without stepping out of their proper domain into the political arena. Even explicitly Catholic social reform movements have institutionalized Cardinal O'Connell's policy excluding "women who wish to act on their own will," while at the same time accepting contributions of time, money, and prayers from women who conform to the goals articulated by male leaders. Thus Catholic women's major contributions to Catholic social activism have been not in the institutional church but in smaller communal movements and informal expanding networks forged by communities of women religious, and by pioneers in Catholic social settlements, the Catholic Worker, the Grail, and Friendship House. The legacy of these movements can be tangibly felt in the prophetic positions taken by the American hierarchy in *The Challenge of Peace* and *Economic Justice for All;* however, only when the communal ecclesiology of these same groups finds its way into the leadership of the Catholic church can the aspirations of women activists and the cause of peace and justice be fully realized. As one sensitive observer of the workings of the American Catholic community, Lelia Hardin Bugg, wrote in 1900, "[History] is a magic mirror which shows two pictures and says, 'choose'."[37]

CHAPTER
7
Catholic Feminism: Its Impact on U.S. Catholic Women

Rosemary Rader, O.S.B.

*T*he previous chapters have dealt rather extensively with movements and trends within American culture which for Catholic women of the United States evoked some form of corporate or collective identity. There were two common threads interwoven throughout the historical narratives: the evidence that any movement develops within or is evoked by the historical conditioning of the times, and that during major period shifts or transition stages in American Catholicism many Catholic women, both lay and religious, were on the cutting edge, serving as agents of change when specific changes were deemed necessary. The historical data presented in the previous chapters demonstrates that women were often in the forefront when these changes were occurring. And although many women did play a role in maintaining the status quo (i.e., in resisting change), many others dared to be countercultural when it was a question of basic justice for individuals or groups.

The present chapter deals with Catholic feminism as a post–Vatican II phenomenon. Most of the previous chapters (particularly Chapters 5 and 6) posited proof that long before Vatican II there were outstanding individuals and groups who believed in a basic equality of races, sexes, and social classes. These leaders contributed significantly not only to the emerging sense of identity for Catholic women, but their strategies and processes became models for later implementation of ideals and practices related to issues of justice and peace. The focus of the present chapter deals more directly with events, groups, and individuals responsible for changes in attitudes and practices regarding the status and roles of women in U.S. Roman Catholicism after Vatican II. This necessarily demands a definition of Catholic feminism, a brief synopsis of the interrelatedness of the general feminist movement and religious feminism, and a broad (but by necessity, limited) survey of the chief U.S. Catholic exponents of feminist theory.

Catholic feminism must be set within the context of the general women's movement that has acquired international recognition. It is not a monolithic phenomenon in that it utilizes diverse theoretical frameworks and recognizes the legitimacy of various objectives, ideologies, and means of action. In its broadest definition Catholic feminism is that movement among U.S. Catholics which regards sexism (the exploitation and domination of one sex by the other) as an injustice to be eliminated if the "good news" of true equality in Christ is to become a reality. In its more positive connotations Catholic feminism can best be defined as the movement within the church that aims at the liberation of both women and men so as to allow their full and authentic response to the Spirit's call. It is an ongoing attempt to help bring about a radical renewal within the Catholic church, one that would celebrate the interdependence and collaborative efforts of men and women in building up the body of Christ, the church.

Catholic feminists, like the rest of society, are the products of their own historical conditioning. All are to a certain degree formed by the rapid changes that occurred in the post–World War II era when tradition and authority, already on shaky terrain since the seventeenth century, rapidly lost their preeminent positions as guardians of Western societies' morals and mores. Prior to the 1960s, in what some historians of U.S. Catholicism call the Institutional Period, U.S. Catholics, particularly women religious, identified rather closely with the Vatican. The focus was on strict adherence to traditional Catholic beliefs and practices. Loyalty to the pope and unquestioned obedience to Vatican commands and statements were considered by many to be direct obedience to Christ. But with the rapid changes in American society evoked by women's evolving roles in World War II, by the emergence of the feminist movement, and by greater emphasis on and greater accessibility of education for women, the older, more traditional concepts began to be questioned and loyalties began to shift.

There were varying attempts at adaptation, attempts to retain the basics but change ideals and patterns of socialization that no longer seemed relevant or compatible with a changing world. But when the energy demanded for either maintaining or changing ideals and structures proved disproportionate to results, many lost heart and began to search for other options.[1] Many women, encouraged by the openness of John XXIII and the changes made possible by the Second Vatican Council (opened in October, 1962), saw new hope for their own expanded ministries within the church.

Catholic women's alliance with the broader feminist movement and the call to church renewal through Vatican II resulted in a genuine revitalization process for many women. Although some resisted any changes, viewing them as a threat to the traditional beliefs and value system of their Catholic religion, others went through several stages of consciousness-raising, of reassessing old values in contrast to new needs and aspirations. There was a growing need for redefinition and restructuring of women's identity and positions within the church community. Many began to question the myths, symbols, and rituals of the Catholic institutional church that seemed to relegate women to a dehumanizing state of subordination.

With the increasing accessibility of historical-critical studies, and with the beginnings of critical feminist theories applied to the theological traditions of the Catholic church, women and men were nudged to envision new possibilities and new realities for women's roles and influence. The application of newly emerging critical feminist hermeneutical principles evoked the realization that theology, scripture, and tradition are expressed in human language, are derived from human experience, and emerge from culturally conditioned concepts and problems. Armed with the knowledge that "winners write the history," feminist historians and theologians set out to "set the record straight."[2] Their research encouraged others to work toward changing a system that was defined by an exclusively male leadership in exclusively male language descriptive of exclusively male experiences. Women initiated support groups as an aid in appropriating their own history, telling their own stories, and sharing their own religious experiences, thus claiming responsibility for their own self-definition and self-identification.

The changes occurred gradually. One need only recall that women religious in the U.S. saw the need for substantive changes within their community structures as soon as they arrived as teachers and nurses on the American frontiers. Sisters were motivated to adapt to new circumstances not allowed for within their rules and constitutions. And as the women religious helped establish and staff schools, hospitals, orphanages, and retirement homes they helped shape the culture that both sustained and challenged them.[3]

One of the most influential and visionary women's groups that helped to create an atmosphere of renewal within the church was the Sisters Formation Conference established in 1954 and first coordinated by Sister Mary Emil Penet.[4] Convinced that American sisters, for the most part, were lacking in adequate preparation necessary for the taxing demands of teaching and other forms of ministry, women in community leadership initiated collaborative efforts in preparing sisters educationally, spiritually, and psychologically. The well-integrated sister, the leaders argued, could then take her rightful place in responding more adequately to the increasing needs and demands of the American church. Many of the major superiors of that era could aptly be described as the feminists of their time as they argued and fought with bishops, priests, and sometimes their own community members for the right of the younger sisters to be held back from teaching until they could be adequately trained for that profession. This was an important step in the religious women's own perception of themselves, their needs, and the needs of the church. But this was only the beginning of many positive changes that were to occur for the active orders of women in the 1950s and 1960s. The efforts of the Sisters Formation Conference were heartily endorsed by the Sacred Congregation of Religious, which had officially recommended that the sisters' spiritual formation be integrated with intellectual and professional training.

In 1956 the Conference of Major Superiors of Women (CMSW) was organized as a national forum for the interchange of ideas and attempts at collaborative efforts in the sisters' various forms of ministry. It became an official organization of the Roman Catholic church by decree of the Sacred Congregation for Religious and Secular Institutes on December 12, 1959. In 1971 the name was changed to the Leadership Conference of Women Religious (LCWR), and proclaimed as its purpose, "to assist its members personally, collectively and corporately in developing creative and responsive leadership and in undertaking those forms of service consonant with the evolving Gospel mission of women religious in the world through the church."[5] In effect, the Catholic feminist movement was "alive and well" as the LCWR organized its national and regional meetings around such issues as contemporary leadership models for women, "drinking from our own wells" (women's spirituality), corporate moral decision-making, and power and meaning of women's experiences. The LCWR has moved ahead vigorously in studying issues perceived as crucial by its membership.[6] Many important documents have emerged from these studies, documents dealing with themes of solidarity, liberation, and social justice as a global and ecumenical concern. In 1979, Theresa Kane, then president of the LCWR, attempted to initiate dialogue with John Paul II on women's issues. She publicly, but politely, requested that the pope be mindful of women's suffering and be open to their call to be included in greater ministry within the church. In spite of the negative attention that the LCWR and women's communities in the United States have received from the Congregation of Religious and Secular Institutes (CRIS), the LCWR continues to network as a vital Catholic feminist movement. Its membership works collaboratively towards greater commitment to the women's movement, including awareness of and response to the plight of laywomen whose material, psychological, or spiritual poverty is intensified by the lack of any support system. Because of the sisters' increased involvement with a variety of social justice issues, they have both individually and corporately experienced new understandings of authority and leadership in the church. They have encouraged a deeper appreciation of their own leadership abilities and have appropriated for themselves the gift of empowering others to respond radically to the Gospel's demand for justice.[7]

These Catholic feminist sisters have continued to challenge the status quo despite the evidence that this may cause conflict with Vatican personnel and/or some local ordinaries. They have attained a corporate identity as loyal members of the church, opting to remain within the institution while working toward changes necessary for revitalization and renewal.

Within their own religious communities renewal has generally resulted in the replacement of unquestioning obedience with the idea of corporate responsibility in defining and implementing the specific community's mission. This change in the decision-making process became evident in one of the major undertakings of the CMSW in 1965. The group commissioned a study, the National Sisters Survey. Sister Marie Augusta Neal, S.N.D., a Harvard-educated sociologist teaching at Emmanuel College in Boston, spearheaded the study. She and fourteen other trained professionals devised a questionnaire sent to more than 139,000 sisters. The questionnaire's intent was to evaluate where individual sisters from different congregations stood on basic issues of renewal. In effect the data compiled in 1966 helped clarify and articulate an issue that became an increasing concern for sisters: the relation between one's religious beliefs and structural change.[8]

In 1982, the 1966 report was extended to reflect changes that had taken place during the almost twenty years of sisters' struggles and challenges with the renewal processes. Sister Marie Augusta Neal presented the compiled data in a book, *Catholic Sisters in Transition: From the 1960's to the 1980's.*[9] She concluded from the data that major changes had obviously occurred in all facets of life of American sisters since 1950. A complex set of interwoven factors were responsible for the changes, most of them related to cultural trends and changes within society as a whole. What emerges clearly in comparing the data from 1966 and 1982 is that within the almost twenty-year interval sisters had placed more responsibility on their own decision-making capabilities and less upon outside sources. When asked to prioritize causes for action by most administrators, the respondents indicated there was a radical shift from dependence upon outside directives to personal and communal discernment. While in 1966 "decrees of Vatican II" was the most frequently cited course for action (84.3 percent), in 1982 that percentage fell to 38.3, being supplanted by "needs of the human community" (77.8 percent) as the prime determinant. "Ideas of sisters" doubled in value as a determining factor, from 34.9 percent in 1966 to 66.7 percent in 1982. Another decline in perception of influence toward change was "directives of the Sacred Congregation," which fell from 62 percent in 1966 to 18 percent in 1982.[10] The study clearly indicated that women religious had made strides both in individual and corporate self-identification, and were consequently beginning to claim their own power in effecting changes deemed necessary for community renewal and survival.

Sister Charles Borromeo Muckenhirn, C.S.C., contributed greatly to the American sisters' understanding of collegiality or coresponsibility as crucial to the success of an ongoing renewal within the church. She challenged women to reject their conservatism, break their isolation from the mainstream of American life, and become a new and creative voice for the *aggiornamento* ("renewal") mandated by Vatican II. In the book *The Changing Sister*, edited by Muckenhirn, nine sisters discuss the concept of renewal and its urgency for women's communities in the 1960s.[11] The nine essays deal with various communities' thoughtful reflections on American sisters' changing identities and the creative consequences this self-examination could have on American Catholic life. A reiterated theme of the articles is the necessity of the true dialogue if authentic renewal is to take place both within religious communities and throughout the Catholic church generally.

Two years later Muckenhirn, in her book, *The Implications of Renewal*, shared her reflections on the effectiveness of the Second Vatican Council.[12] Her conclusion is that in the two years following the closing of the Council there was great intellectual stimulation in the church, but that in the everyday life of American Catholics the full momentum of the proposed renewal scarcely became visible. She calls upon people, particularly sisters, to "have the courage to say that completely new forms must be envisioned and tried experimentally."[13]

Other authors began to challenge church members to question and to live out their questions as they became involved in the renewal process.[14] Catholic feminist theorists not only called into question their life within the church but extended their study to the full range of human relationships experienced in church life and practice. What began as theologizing about women and women's issues gradually expanded to touch upon the whole of humanity and on almost every contemporary issue.

One group that took a broader approach to serving social justice causes is Network, a Catholic social justice lobby formed to work at influencing the formation of public policy. The group's goals are to persuade Congress to enact laws providing economic justice for the poor, to protect human rights, and to promote disarmament and ensure world peace. Network has successfully lobbied on a wide range of justice issues, for example, tax and budget policies, feminization of poverty, welfare reform, minimum wage, and nuclear disarmament. Volunteers and paid staff keep the public informed of important impending congressional votes through mail and phone alerts. They are a service organization distributing educational resources about political issues that impinge on Christian values.

Carol Coston, one of the founding members and Network's executive director from 1972–1982, has published a monograph, *Feminism: Values and Vision*, in which she presents her definition and evaluation of feminism.[15] She relates how after twenty-five years in religious life and nine years working for Network, she views the rise in feminist consciousness, the development of a feminist perspective, and the utilization of feminist values in working for a just society as today's most hopeful "sign of the times." Along with Francine Cardman and others, she defines feminism as a values-transformation that "values cooperation rather than competition, mutuality rather than hierarchical decision making, and integration rather than dualism."[16]

Other groups and organizations of Catholic feminists have emerged in response to the need for social justice. One of these, the National Assembly of Women Religious (NAWR), was founded in 1968 as an alternative to the Leadership Conference of Women Religious. Many sisters saw the need for a grass-roots organization that would deal more directly with the concerns of the individual, ordinary sister. The name was eventually changed to the National Assembly of Religious Women (NARW) so that laywomen and sisters could work cooperatively in the task of giving prophetic witness, raising awareness, and engaging in public action for the achievement of justice. Both Ethne Kennedy, the first executive director, and Marjorie Tuite, among others, were indefatigable exponents of a new Catholic feminism that predicated action as the lived-out response to theories and ideas. Like Network, NARW has exerted a great influence not only on Catholic women at the grass-roots level, but on leaders at the national level by its relentless activism on behalf of political causes like the poverty of women and children, justice in Latin America, the plight of farm workers, and equality for women in the work force.

Another organization, the National Coalition of American Nuns (NCAN), founded in 1969, has actively espoused feminist causes. The organization is particularly committed to collegiality in leadership and governance, rejecting any civil or ecclesiastical attempts at rule without consultation. Margaret Ellen Traxler, former president of NCAN, has been particularly active in ministry to women in prisons. She is presently director of the Institute of Women Today, a Chicago-based ecumenical group dealing with the historical roots of women's oppression.[17] Many other organizations have been and continue to be formed, each initiated by feminist activists who find that their specific area of interest or concern has not been satisfactorily dealt with by any of the existing groups.[18]

Perhaps more than any other contemporary American Catholic organizations, the Women's Ordination Conference (WOC) and the Women-Church movement have gained national and even international notoriety as embodiments of strong religious feminist movements. The Women's Ordination Conference was first suggested by a Roman Catholic laywoman, Mary Lynch, who discussed with a group of her women friends the question of whether the women's ordination issue should be raised in 1975, the International Women's Year. In January, 1976, the conference was officially established, and subsequently three national women's ordination conferences were held: in Detroit in 1975, in Baltimore in 1978, and in Saint Louis in 1985. The conference proceedings emphasized women's equality in ministry and the need for new models and images of church and of priesthood. The lectures, discussion groups, and rituals were clearly a feminist critique of both church and culture. Dialogue focused on such issues as feminist reinterpretations of tradition; the challenge of feminist reclaiming, appropriating, and reinterpreting women's history; the substitution of male historical and theological bias with a feminist corrective; the formation of new paradigms for ministry, paradigms more reflective of women's experiences; and the need for ongoing renewal that would include collaboration and celebration of male and female alike. The meetings served as support for women interested in the ordination issue but also as pressure to initiate changes of official policies that maintained and fostered sexism within the church.

In November, 1983, approximately, 1,400 women gathered in Chicago for a conference entitled "Women-Church Speaks." The organizers had as their goal to bring women's values to bear on society and church. Distressed by what they perceived as blatant sexism, racism, classism, militarism, and other oppressions in contemporary society, the organization aimed to seek the empowerment of women as church by embodying feminist values in existing institutions. Since 1983 Women-Church groups have proliferated. Some twenty-six groups in the United States have formed a coalition, Women-Church Convergence, which sponsored a second national conference, "Women-Church: Claiming our Power," held in Cincinnati, October 9–11, 1987. The dialogues so integral to the success of the conferences focused on such topics as women's spirituality, information sharing and skill building, strategies for mutual support and networking, lobbying the Catholic church, claiming the creative power within self, women's economic literacy, and creating liturgies with Women Church. The first page of the second national conference brochure invited readers to "Join us in the struggle to empower ourselves as women and to work for a world in which women, men and children may live together in justice and peace."[19] The Women-Church movement is relatively young, but indications are that it is speaking loudly and clearly to many American Catholic women who are beginning to understand that they are church. Their participation in Women-Church allows them to envision a future in which patriarchal authoritarianism and institutional sexism may cease to exist. The solidarity and bonding that follows from participation in the conferences strengthens their self-identification as church, and inspires them to self-determination. Experimentation with new rituals and new liturgical experiences, formation of new friendships and new communities, developing and understanding feminist theories, reinterpreting and reevaluating traditional data, all are means toward developing the individual and corporate identity of American Catholic women. Women are increasingly identifying themselves as active, collaborative participants and leaders in the church rather than primarily observers.

Much of the impetus for U.S. Catholic women's new self-identification and corporate identity derives from feminist authors' articulation of new theories for the reinterpretation of scripture, history, and theology. Catholic feminist scholars are numerous, but the work of three in particular must be recognized because of their successful efforts in formulating feminist hermeneutics that are changing the contours of the church: For many Catholic women, Mary Daly, Rosemary Radford Ruether, and Elisabeth Schussler Fiorenza represent the avant-garde liberation movement as regards the establishment of criteria and theories for "setting the record straight." These women's commitment to scholarship and their application of new and creative feminist theories to the interpretation of texts have given hope to many women and men struggling both inside and outside the church. All three are committed to feminism as a necessary tool, not only to correct what they see as violence against women, but also to change the values and structures of a world society that denies freedom to many peoples, races, and classes. Ruether reminds her readers of this inclusive dimension of feminism: "For me the commitment to feminism is fundamental to the commitment to justice, to authentic human life itself."[20]

Although Mary Daly has left Roman Catholicism because she sees the church as hopelessly and irretrievably patriarchal, she has contributed greatly to the consciousness-raising of women within the church.[21] Her first book on the issue of Catholicism and antifeminism is *The Church and the Second Sex.*[22] Influenced by Simone de Beauvoir's monumental work, *The Second Sex,* Daly sets out to explain how the various forms of discrimination against women within the Catholic church are reflections of a long history of antifeminism. Encouraged by the hope that the Catholic church could be purged of antifeminist notions and practices, she lays out what she observes as the roots of the problem and suggests ways of eradicating the evil. She concludes that though the church alone cannot be blamed for all oppressive situations in the world throughout history, the church's tendency toward absolutist and static policies must be changed radically if it is to be life-giving rather than life-destroying. She calls upon the church to engage in a commitment to a radical transformation of its negative, life-destroying elements. She proposes a theology of hope, calling upon men and women within the church to work together courageously to eradicate the injustices of an antifeminist stance.

> "It is only by this creative personal encounter, sparked by that power of transcendence which the theologians have called grace, that the old wounds can be healed. Men and women using their best talents, forgetful of self and intent upon the work, will with God's help mount together toward a higher order of consciousness and being, in which the alienating projections will have been defeated and wholeness, psychic integrity, achieved."[23]

In the 1975 edition of the work Daly added a "Feminist Postchristian Introduction," which indicated that she had moved from reformist feminism to identify as a radical feminist moving *beyond* the Christianity of the God-Father.

In her second book, *Beyond God the Father,* Daly's loss of hope in a "hopelessly patriarchal" church surfaces.[24] Much of her energy in the text is spent on recreating or reinventing a language that can more adequately define, describe, and help evoke women's experiences. She challenges women to acknowledge that they have had the power of "naming" stolen from them. The power can be restored, she argues, by liberating language, by a reclaiming of the right to name.[25] Hence, the *method* is one of liberation, "a *castrating* of language and images that reflect and perpetuate the structures of a sexist world."[26] She warns women not to canonize method, "one of the false gods of theologians, philosophers, and other academics. . . ."[27] Because of the tyranny of male-devised "methodolatry," women's questions have never been able to be asked or formulated. She urges women "to begin to ask nonquestions and to start discovering, reporting, and analyzing nondata."[28] By doing so, women will free traditions, thought, and customs. By hearing each other, women will make it possible to speak their message. The method is not one of reflection upon social action (false dualism of male methodology) but "rather in the sense of a continual growth, flexibility, and emergence of new perceptions of reality—perceptions that come from being where one is."[29]

Daly here begins the new naming with God, transforming the patriarchal God the Father into a "diarchal" being that she perceives as radically new. That is, God not as one image, the noun *father* (male), but "as the creative potential itself in human beings that is the image of God."[30] God as a noun (male) may have been intended to convey personality, but it fails to convey that God is "Be-ing," the most active and dynamic of all namings. Daly's goal then is to "de-reify" God, to change the conception/perception of God from the supreme being to Be-ing, a process God. With such a God, women are transformed from identification as "the Other" to becoming "I am."[31] And after Daly's death of God the Father, women would bring into being a new meaning context for God-language as they re-create their lives in a new experiential context. The process demands demythologyzing and remythologizing, exorcising from women's consciousness the patriarchal images, symbols, and stories (like the Fall) that religiously reinforced sexual oppression in the world and inhibited women from Being.

Daly's writings have become progressively more radical in their feminism, and in her last two books the empowering force of "Being" and "Goddess" are replaced by feminism.[32] Because Daly has conspicuously and consciously alienated herself from Catholicism, her later works cannot be dealt with as views and theories of a Catholic feminist. However, as she continues her search for sources of transcendence (at times utilizing traditional Catholic concepts) Catholics are undoubtedly still influenced by her message of women's liberation by activating their personal self-power.

Rosemary Ruether has been for many Catholic feminists the most enduring model for attempting to change the system from within. The most prolific of Catholic feminist writers, Ruether was a fore-runner in the Catholic women's movement. Her earliest writings had a strong impact as she expanded the consciousness of men and women regarding sexist language, policies, and practices within the church. In the book edited by Ruether, *Religion and Sexism,* she and other scholars presented evidence of the role religion (particularly Judaism and Christianity) played in shaping the traditional cultural images that have denigrated and suppressed women.[33] The essays present the patriarchal attitudes, ideals, and practices of major historical periods and peoples, demonstrating the effect that patriarchal societies have had on women's self-image. Although the essays are not specifically interested in presenting new theories or methodologies, they have contributed greatly to the consciousness-raising of women who have needed to hear, reclaim, and appropriate their history in order to reshape the injustices stemming from patriarchal religions. *Religion and Sexism* is one of the first bodies of research to enlighten women on the role religion played and has continued to play in legitimating oppressive measures and attitudes against women.

In *New Woman, New Earth: Sexist Ideologies and Human Liberation,* Ruether sketches the basic problems of sexism and the ideologies that have supported it.[34] She broadens the study by an analysis of the interrelationship of sexism with other structures of oppression such as race, class, and technological power, which have been built on the basis of domination and alienation. She does not attempt to develop a feminist hermeneutics for the creation of new paradigms. She reassures the reader that the most one can do is recognize the crisis points of contradiction in the present system and then try to imagine an alternative. She views the women's movement as encompassing all other liberation movements. *New Women, New Earth* lays the groundwork for much of her later work in that in it she scrutinizes the basic interrelation of ideology and social structure in the history of sexism. She reminds women that because domination is society's fundamental model of relationships, liberation of women must be tied to all other liberations, including liberation of ecology.

Ruether's most popular and articulate attempt in developing feminist theory is *Sexism and God-Talk: Toward a Feminist Theology.*[35] Here she offers the most sustained hope for religion through the construction of a feminist theology. She marshals evidence for the content and method of a new, liberating Christian theology. Ruether, like other theologians, claims human experience as the basis for all theology. She ably demonstrates that historically, however, male experience has been the only integrative, interpretative model. An individual's experience allows the creation of a paradigm that may differ from other individuals' cultural and religious traditions. Hence Ruether identifies and justifies her book as an exercise in feminist theology based on a particular selection of human experiences.

She constructs her feminist theology by analyzing "usable tradition" from five areas of Judaic and Christian cultures: Hebrew and Christian scriptures; marginalized or heretical Christian traditions; primary theological themes of mainstream Christian classical theology; non-Christian Near Eastern and Greco-Roman religions and philosophy; and critical post-Christian worldviews. She systematically demonstrates that although all of these traditions are in varying degrees sexist, they do provide "intimations of alternatives" that could lead to options for the revitalization of Christianity.

Her construction of a feminist theology includes an examination of alternatives suggested by usable male and female images of the divine (e.g., parables of Jesus that stress male-female equality, in egalitarian practices in countercultural, minority, and prophetic movements). She argues that individuals need not reject Christianity in their search for viable categories with which to examine human experience and build redemptive communities. The feminist theology she suggests is to replace dominance with a harmonious "ecological-feminist theology of nature."[36]

In her more recent book, *Women-Church: Theology and Practice of Feminist Liturgical Communities*,[37] Ruether invites women to further claim their identity as church by embracing a "liminal religiosity," by standing on the edge and looking backward to options in biblical and prebiblical faiths while also looking forward to new possibilities whose shapes are unclear. The book is written out of a recognition that the institutional churches may wait too long to provide the expressions of faith and worship that women in contemporary society need. Ruether views church as a community of liberation from sexism and offers viable options and guidelines for the development of communities of worship and collaboration. She identifies the work as "an invitation to enter into a process."[38] The process becomes the daily lived-out theory of women's liberation. The book reflects the direction of Catholic feminism in that it encompasses all aspects of life (particularly the bonding at communal worship), it eliminates distinctions between lay and religious, it crosses denominational lines, and it reverences both the prophetic and the social activist stance. It also reflects Ruether's wide range of interests and demonstrates her ability to be highly articulate on and sensitive to all areas and aspects of liberation.

Like Ruether and other feminist theologians, Elisabeth Schussler Fiorenza articulates feminist theology as a critical theology of liberation. In the book *In Memory of Her: A Feminist Theological Recon-*

struction of Christian Origins, Schussler Fiorenza develops a consciously feminist hermeneutics that helps others to identify and reclaim women's experiences in the early church.[39] It is her critical theoretical construction of a feminist hermeneutics that differentiates her work from much other historical data about women in Christianity. She uses the historical-critical method to construct a frame of reference that allows reinterpretation of available sources.

Using Thomas Kuhn's theory of scientific paradigms and heuristic interpretative models, Schussler Fiorenza posits a new feminist paradigm designed to replace androcentric scholarship with *human* scholarship and knowledge, inclusive of all peoples, genders, races, and cultures. This shift implies a transformation of the scientific imagination that has generally not recognized women's actions as an interpretative category. Schussler Fiorenza claims that a truly feminist paradigm has today emerged through the creation of such alternative institutions as women's centers, institutes, and study programs—which Kuhn argues are necessary for shifts to occur.

After rejecting the prevailing androcentric models that both impede and justify a new feminist paradigm, Schussler Fiorenza constructs a "neoorthodox" model by examining and distinguishing form and content, theological essence and historical variables, and language and action within early Christian models. She then reconstructs early Christian history and theology by means of her feminist interpretation of the Jesus movement, the missionary movement in Hellenistic cities, the use of "goddess language and mythology," and the liberating concept of a discipleship of equals. She underscores the fact that women were active participants in the early Christian movements that preceded the gradual formation of the institutionalized, male-dominated church.

Schussler Fiorenza, like Ruether and Daly, has contributed greatly to the women's movement within the church by her scholarship, her creative feminist reconstruction of Christian origins, and her abiding presence on the speaker's platform at many Women-Church gatherings. Schussler Fiorenza's work has encouraged other women both to reclaim their role in history and to work confidently towards collaboration in shaping their future.

Although Mary Jo Weaver could not be categorized as a feminist theorist, her book *New Catholic Women* is an important contribution to the understanding of Catholic feminism and its chief exponents and theoreticians.[40] Her book is particularly germane to this chapter in that she has taken some major theoretical issues and tenets of the women's movement and shown how they intersect with some weighty questions within the American Catholic church. Weaver sets the Catholic feminist movement within the broader arena of feminist issues. She then attempts to demonstrate what is possible when women reimagine the world in their own terms.[41]

Weaver's work is an important study of the new consciousness that has emerged for American women since Vatican II. She traces the development of that consciousness from the early stages of awareness to the contemporary movements within the church that call for renewal and revitalization. The focus throughout is on women's practical, political, and intellectual actions, the consequence of women's consciousness of who they are and what new, creative options are available as a result of this new consciousness and self-identity.

The list of contributors and collaborators who have in one way or another influenced the feminist movement within U.S. Catholicism is long indeed. There are the academics who have presented clear articulations of theories and paradigms, but there are also others whose experiences either within or outside the church have induced them to speak out in their parishes, in support groups, advisory boards, sit-ins and protests, and on parish councils and school boards. Many are extraordinarily active in writing, in presenting and/or attending workshops, and in serving others in creative ways that allow for mutual growth. All have in some way contributed to the inroads made by Catholic feminism. They could be variously categorized as historians (Mary Jo Weaver, Elizabeth Carroll, Ann Patrick Ware), theologians (Anne E. Patrick, Doris Gottemoeller, Rita Hofbauer, Mary Hunt), ethicists (Margaret A. Farley, Joan Timmerman), scripture scholars (Sandra Schneiders, Gloria Durka, Carolyn Osiek, Jane Schaberg), and theorists (Ann Carr, Madonna Kolbenschlag).

Many others who defy categorization are actively engaged in spreading the good news that Catholic feminism and U.S. Roman Catholicism will need to remain in dialogue for some time to come. For most of these women the evolving consciousness cannot be held in check or turned back; its time has come. The initial awareness has given way to commitment to radical change in the language and imagery of God, in the extension and broadening of creative options for ministry, and in continued dialogue and implementation of equality in cooperative decision-making and governance. Mutuality and complementarity are watchwords of the new consciousness, which has gradually expanded its vision so as to include world issues and world ministries. Catholic feminism has had a powerful impact on women's identities as enablers and agents of change in a new church where change is seen as basic for survival. Catholic women's new consciousness indicates a progression from self-identity to self-action to "power with" others, the nurturance of an individual's and an institution's potential to act together for the wholeness of church. Of the "new women" who work towards a renewed church, some are rebels, some pioneers, some leaders, some followers. All are part of the increasing numbers of Catholic women who believe strongly in Vatican II's message of renewal and revitalization of church and society, and who opt to remain within the Catholic church as loving critics with many questions, great hope, and renewed energy.

Notes

Chapter 1 Ideals of American Catholic Womanhood

1. Brent has attracted the attention of chroniclers of Catholic women's exploits over the years, most recently, that of Carr Elizabeth Worland, whose doctoral dissertation, "American Catholic Women and the Church to 1920" (Saint Louis, 1982) alludes to the relevant documents in the archives of Maryland. The general subject of an American Catholic ideology of woman has yet to be explored in a comprehensive fashion. In addition to Worland and sources noted in ensuing chapters, many of which treat briefly of Catholic opinion relative to womanhood and women's issues, surveys that provide a helpful perspective on one or another facet of the topic are George Tavard, *Woman in Christian Tradition* (Notre Dame, Ind., 1973), William B. Faherty, *The Doctrine of Modern Woman in the Light of Papal Teaching* (Westminster, Md., 1950), and Mary Jo Weaver, *New Catholic Women*, (San Francisco, 1985). The American Catholic intellectual community lost an opportunity to express its unique understandings of women when the monumental *Catholic Encyclopedia* finally saw the light of day in 1912: the principal article on "Woman" was assigned to the conservative European priest-scholar, Augustin Rössler. [See *Catholic Encyclopedia* (New York, 1912), vol. 15, pp. 687–94. Also see the subordinate articles by the American, William H. W. Fanning, on "Women in English-Speaking Countries," and "In Canon Law." Ibid., pp. 694–98. These articles did little to mitigate the reactionary erudition of Rössler on the subject.]
2. Protestant and Catholic versions of the cult of true womanhood, and the American context from which it arose, are clearly described by Colleen McDannell, *The Christian Home in Victorian America, 1840–1900*, (Bloomington, Ind., 1986).
3. O'Reilly implied that academy education, especially of the cloistered kind he observed in French Canada, would be acceptable should girls be sent beyond the home for schooling. Higher education of the kind then accessible to American women was out: "mixed colleges" represented a danger for young women; normal schools could be entrusted

with teacher-training only if conducted by nuns as they were then beginning to be in Canada and England. The following quotes are from Bernard O'Reilly, *Mirror of True Womanhood* (New York, 1892), pp. 397ff.

4. I am indebted to David O'Brien for citations in Hecker's diaries and letters. The diaries and letters are in the Archives of the Paulist Fathers, New York; the diaries are hereafter cited as "Diary." On Hecker and his misogynist philosopher friend Brownson, see Arlene Swidler, "Brownson and the Woman Question," *American Benedictine Review* 19 (June 1968):211–19.

5. "Diary," August 26, 1843.

6. Ibid., August 22, 1843.

7. Rober W. Baer, C.S.P., "A Jungian Analysis of Isaac Thomas Hecker." In *Hecker Studies*, ed. John Farina (New York, 1983), pp. 160–63.

8. Hecker to Mrs. Cullen, March 16, 1867, Archives of the Paulist Fathers (hereafter cited as PFA).

9. Hecker to Mrs. Thompson, March 16, 1867, PFA.

10. Hecker to Miss Carey, August 22, 1868, PFA.

11. Robert Fulton, S.J., to Hecker, December 7, 1868, PFA.

12. Carey to Hecker, December 21, 1868, PFA.

13. Cullen to Hecker, September 17, 1868, PFA.

14. Orestes Brownson, "The Woman Question," *The Catholic World* (May 1969).

15. Cullen to Hecker, September 17, 1868, PFA.

16. Hecker to Cullen, April 10, 1867, PFA.

17. This and the following quotations are from addresses and essays dating from 1878 to 1902, as published in collections entitled *Education and the Higher Life* (Chicago, 1890), *Means and Ends of Education* (Chicago, 1895), *Religion, Agnosticism and Education* (Chicago, 1902), and *Socialism and Labor and Other Arguments* (Chicago, 1902). Spalding's critique of the woman question enjoyed a wide currency and served as an inspiration to Catholic women activists of his day. See, for example, the Papers of Mary Kenney O'Sullivan, labor organizer in the late nineteenth century, in which is preserved a faded clipping of Spalding's 1878 Notre Dame University commencement address.

18. "Woman and the Christian Religion." In *Socialism and Labor*, p. 116.

19. Ibid., p. 97; "Women and Education." In *Means and Ends of Education*, p. 109.

20. "Normal Schools for Catholics," *The Catholic World* 51 (April 1890):88–97. Notable also were Spalding's contributions to the evolution of Saint Mary's, Notre Dame, from academy to college in the mid-1890s and to the establishment of Trinity College alongside Catholic University in 1899.

21. See James Kenneally's account of turn-of-the century Catholic episcopal support for woman suffrage in "Eve, Mary and the Historians: American Catholicism and Women," *Horizons: The Journal of the College Theology Society* 3 (Fall 1976):198f. Worland identifies a number of other bishops whose public support of suffrage derived from favorable impressions following passage of woman suffrage on the state level.

22. "A Catholic Sisterhood in the Northwest," *The Church and Modern Society* (Saint Paul, 1904) vol. 2, p. 300. Spalding had touched on this

same theme: "The world in which woman's being may unfold itself is widening and deepening. For her, too, henceforth the career is open to make use of talent;" in keeping with these changes, women's education would need to be serious and not given over to "excessive attention to mere accomplishments" (quoted from "The Victory of Love," *Religion Agnosticism and Education*, p. 278).

23. *Northwestern Chronicle*, April 10, 1891.

24. The Sisters of Saint Joseph of Carondelet, Saint Paul Province, founders of the College of Saint Catherine.

25. The Sisters of Saint Joseph in Saint Paul had early opted for an academy curriculum based on the assumption that women were intellectually equal to men and were capable of high academic achievement, as is evident from catalogs, test records, and reminiscences dating from the 1850's on. Ireland's sister, titled Mother Seraphine (Ellen) Ireland, as superior of the Saint Paul Province 1882–1921, compiled a remarkable record as an inspirational leader and administrator whose watchword, according to one colleague, was "progress." (Letters by Sister Wilfrida Hogan, Saint Paul Archives).

26. School Sisters of Notre Dame, founders of Notre Dame College, Baltimore, which awarded its first baccalaureate degrees in 1896 and thereby earned the right to be regarded as the first Catholic college for women in the United States. Gibbons's most extended comments on suffrage appeared in "The Restless Woman," *The Ladies' Home Journal*, January 1902, p. 6. The second local college he supported was Trinity, founded by the Sisters of Notre Dame de Namur in 1899.

27. Stang's textbook filled a lacuna in seminaries. It was unfortunate so far as balanced attitudes toward the female sex were concerned that earlier English-language seminary manuals, such as Frederick Oakeley's *The Priest on the Mission: A Course on Missionary and Parochial Duties* (London, 1871) did not prevail in American seminaries. To take but one parallel section, Oakeley portrayed the penitent as one meriting the priest's humble and prayerful attention, regardless of sex, for the sake of giving sound advice as well as to extend pardon for sin. Cautions regarding seductive or inane women penitents, derived by Stang from Italian sources, were notably absent.

28. William Stang *Pastoral Theology*, p. 185f. The demeaning advice to ignore ninety-nine women in hopes of snaring one man comes straight from Frassinetti, a nineteenth-century interpreter of Ligouri, who explains the point at greater length: "Should there happen to be both men and women at his confessional," the priest should admit men first, for, "as a rule, their occupations are of more importance than those of women, and moreover they are usually more impatient, so that if they be not heard quickly, they go away and do not return again. Women, on the other hand, in addition to having more time at their disposal, are more patient and wait longer." *The New Parish Priest's Practical Manual*, trans. William Hutch (London, 1893), p. 359. Frassinetti also expatiated on the theme of keeping women humble and ignorant, advising the parish priest to omit in his homilies "all points of doctrine which are superfluous for the people," and giving as an example the foolishness of a priest explaining the just war theory to "a few poor women who were listening to him. . . . He did not reflect that these poor creatures would never have to declare war, except

against the rats and mice which, perhaps, infested their houses" (p. 198). It should be noted that Stang uses the "devout sex" phrase to describe laywomen or nuns whereas the term originally applied only to nuns "devoted" to God by reason of their vows.

29. Alphonsus Ligouri held this opinion. See, for example, "Preaching," in his *Ascetical Works*, trans. Eugene Grimm (New York, 1889), p. 265: the "married woman can, it is true, be holy in spirit but not in body, while a virgin that sanctifies herself is holy in spirit and in body, having consecrated to Jesus Christ her virginity;" and p. 267: "I do not remember to have ever found among married women a single pious person who was content with her state in life."

30. John A. Ryan, *Socialism and Christianity* (New York, 1905).

31. Ryan had not up to this point published anything on woman suffrage, but noted in his 1917 essay that "some twenty-five years ago," that is, in the early 1890s back in his Saint Paul seminary days, he "defended in a classroom essay the proposition that female suffrage had become reasonable and expedient, on account of the large number of women that are otherwise occupied than in the home." John A. Ryan, *The Church and Socialism* (Washington, D.C., 1919), p. 242.

32. Ibid.

Chapter 2   Women in the Convent

1. Many points that I make in this chapter are elucidated in much greater detail in Mary Ewens, O.P., *The Role of the Nun in Nineteenth Century America* (New York, 1978).

2. "Documents," *St. Louis Catholic Historical Review* 2:207.

3. Letters, Thorpe to Carroll, January 16, 1788 and October 18, 1788, quoted in Annabelle M. Melville, *John Carroll of Baltimore* (New York, 1955), p. 170.

4. Joseph B. Code, *Great American Foundresses* (New York, 1929), p. 39.

5. Carroll to Cardinal Antonelli, September 19, 1793, quoted in Peter Guilday, *The Life and Times of John Carroll, 1735–1815* (New York, 1922), p. 490.

6. Ibid., Antonelli to Carroll.

7. Quoted in Melville, *John Carroll of Baltimore*, pp. 172–73.

8. Ibid., p. 162.

9. Quoted in Sister Mary Christina Sullivan, *Some Non-Permanent Foundations of Religious Orders and Congregations of Women in the United States (1793–1850)* (New York, 1940), p. 13.

10. Sister Mary Madeleine Hachard to her father, February 22, 1727, quoted in Henry Semple, *The Ursulines in New Orleans, a Record of Two Centuries, 1729–1925* (New York, 1925), p. 187.

11. Saint Louis Archdiocesan Archives.

12. William Howlett, *Life of Rev. Charles Nerickx* (Techny, Ill., 1915), p. 394.

13. Louise Callan, *The Society of the Sacred Heart in North America* (New York, 1937), pp. 58–59.

14. These anti-Catholic movements are discussed in great detail in Ray Allen Billington, *The Protestant Crusade, 1800–1869* (New York, 1938).

15. Quoted in Ambrose Kennedy, *Speech of Hon. Ambrose Kennedy of*

Rhode Island in the House of Representatives, Monday, March 18, 1918 (Washington, D.C., 1918), p. 33.

16. The work of the sisters who nursed in the Civil War is discussed in greater detail in Ellen Ryan Jolly, *Nuns of the Battlefield* (Providence, R.I., 1927).

17. Charles Daniel, S.J., *History of Blessed Margaret Mary* (New York, 1867), p. 21.

18. I am indebted to Mother Austin Carroll's biographer, Sister Mary Heremina Muldrey, R.S.M., for sharing with me the typescript of her forthcoming biography and many other materials gathered over a period of many years. I base my section on Austin Carroll on this material.

19. *Life of Catherine McAuley* (New York, 1865). *Leaves from the Annals of the Sisters of Mercy*, vol. 1: *Ireland* (New York, 1881); vol. 2: *England, Scotland, Australia, and New Zealand* (New York, 1883); vol. 3: *Newfoundland and the United States* (New York, 1888); vol. 4: *South America, Central America, and the United States* (New York, 1895).

20. Muldrey typescript, p. x-53.

21. Ibid., p. x-51.

22. I am indebted to Edward Ruane, O.P., for this insight from his study, which he has shared in conferences and personal conversation.

23. For examples of the kinds of ideals that were held up to sisters for their emulation in these years, see *The Charity of Christ Presses Us*, ed. Sister Mary Philip, O.P. (Milwaukee, Wisc., 1962).

24. I have described the thrust toward social responsibility at Rosary College, Chicago, during these decades in "Political Activity of American Sisters before 1970." In *Between God and Caesar*, ed. Madonna Kolbenschlag (New York, 1985), pp. 41–59.

25. Debra Campbell is studying this interesting chapter in the history of lay ministry.

26. See, for example, Mary Gilligan Wong, *Nun, a Memoir* and Sister M. Aloysius Schaldenbrand, "Asylums: Total Societies and Religious Life." In *The New Nuns*, ed. Sister Charles Borromeo Muckenhirn (New York, 1967), pp. 115–27.

27. Sister Mary Ann Schintz, O.P., "An Investigation of the Modernizing Role of the Maryknoll Sisters in China," Ph.D. diss., University of Wisconsin at Madison, 1978, p. 129. The Maryknoll China Mission History Project will soon be publishing materials about the Maryknoll China Mission.

28. Mary Jo Weaver, *New Catholic Women* (San Francisco, 1985), pp. 80–81.

29. I base much of my discussion of the Sister Formation on the work of Mary Schneider, who is working on a doctoral dissertation on this topic at Loyola University, Chicago. Schneider has shared her preliminary findings in "The Transformation of American Women Religious: the Sister Formation Movement as Catalyst (1954–1964)." In the *Working Paper Series*, ser. 17, no. 1 (Spring 1986) of the Cushwa Center, the University of Notre Dame.

30. Mary Augusta Neal, S.N.D., *Catholic Sisters in Transition* (Wilmington, Del., 1984).

31. This report was published in the April 20, 1978 issue of *Origins*. I quote it from *Between God and Caesar*, ed. Kolbenschlag, pp. 447–53.

32. Elizabeth Morancy, R.S.M., "Politics as a Mission of Mercy," Ibid., p. 254.

33. Ibid., p. 255.

34. For a detailed discussion of the relevant canons of the Code, see two articles in *Between God and Caesar*, ed. Kolbenschlag; Rosemary Smith, S.C., "Political Involvement and the Revised Code," pp. 104–114, and James H. Provost, "Priests and Religious in Political Office in the U.S.: A Canonical Perspective," pp. 74–103.

35. Ibid., p. 340.

36. Emily George, R.S.M., "Governance, Discernment and Meditation: The Community and Religious in Politics," Ibid., pp. 336–43.

37. Weaver, *New Catholic Women*, p. 98.

38. Weaver's book contains a good discussion of new developments among Catholic women who are examining their roles in the church vis-à-vis the documents of Vatican II.

Chapter 3   Catholic Domesticity, 1860–1960

1. "Maternal Affection," *Catholic Home Journal* (May 1, 1887):3.

2. Willard Thorp, *Catholic Novelists in Defense of Their Faith, 1829–1865* (New York, 1978), pp. 98–99.

3. *Sacred Heart Review* (October 25, 1890):1.

4. Bernard O'Reilly, *Mirror of True Womanhood* (New York, 1892), p. 12. Maurice Lessage d'Hautecoeur d'Hulst, *The Christian Family: Seven Conferences*, trans. Bertrand L. Conway (New York, 1905).

5. Miss Barry, *Sacred Heart Review* (January 25, 1890):9.

6. "French Home Life," *Catholic World* 25 (1877):767.

7. Mrs. I. J. Hale, *Catholic Home Journal* (January 1, 1886):8.

8. Sacred Heart Review (October 2, 1889):11.

9. Mary Teresa Austin Carroll, "A Washerwoman's Household." In *Glimpses of Pleasant Homes* (New York, 1869), p. 177.

10. R. O'K. [*sic*], "A Peasant Home," *Catholic World* 51 (1890):175ff.

11. *New York Irish American* (February 20, 1894):2.

12. Nicholas Walsh, *Woman* (New York, 1904), pp. 29–30. Included in this book is part of the text of Pope Pius X's address to the "Pious Union of Roman Women." His outlook and Walsh's were the same: "It was a good and beautiful thing to see ladies devoting their time and their care to the poor, but woman's greatest influence would always be exercised in her household."

13. *Baltimore Catholic Mirror* (January 14, 1881):3.

14. Stephen V. Ryan, intro. to Wilhelm Cramer, *The Christian Father: What He Should Be and What He Should Do*, trans. L. A. Lambert (New York, 1883), p. 4.

15. "A Mother's Look," *Philadelphia Catholic Standard and Times* (December 13, 1890):7.

16. "A Mother's Influence," *Sacred Heart Review* (July 12, 1890):13.

17. "Home Heroes," *Catholic Home Journal* (November 1, 1886):8.

18. Paul Lejune, *Counsels of Perfection for Christian Mothers*, trans. Francis Ryan (Saint Louis, 1913), p. 40 on rule, pp. 111–12 on not reading mystic writers.

19. Eleanor Donnelly, "A Lost Prima Donna." In *A Round Table of the Representative American Catholic Novelists* (New York, 1897), p. 46.

20. Mary Sadlier, *The Blakes and the Flanagans, a Tale Illustrative of Irish Life in the United States* (New York, 1855), p. 108.
21. *Sacred Heart Review* (June 6, 1886):12.
22. *Catholic Home* (June 4, 1887):1.
23. Francis X. Lasance, *The Catholic Girl's Guide: Counsels and Devotions for Girls in the Ordinary Walks of Life* (New York, 1906), p. 413.
24. Carroll, *Pleasant Homes*, pp. 18–19.
25. d'Hulst, *Christian Family*, p. 69.
26. "A Peasant Home," *Catholic World* 59:179.
27. Eliza G. Herzfeld, *Family Monographs: The History of Twenty-Four Families Living in the Middle West Side of New York City* (New York, 1905), p. 94.
28. Beatrice Griffith, *American Me* (Westport, Conn., 1944, reprinted, New York, 1973), p. 174.
29. Ibid.
30. William I. Thomas and Florian Znaniecki, *The Polish Peasant in Europe and America* (Boston, 1920), p. 228.
31. Paul Wrobel, *Our Way: Family, Parish, and Neighborhood in a Polish-American Community* (Notre Dame, Ind., 1979), p. 47.
32. James Gillis, *The Catholic Church and the Home* (London, 1928), p. 11.
33. Daniel A. Lord, "The Training of Girls for Catholic Action," *The Homiletic and Pastoral Review* 35 (1934–1935):332.
34. H. C. McGinnis, "War-Time Morals Threaten the Sanctity of the Family," *America* (October 17, 1942):43.
35. Andrew M. Greeley, *The Sign* 37 (February 1958):32.
36. Joseph M. McShane, "And They Lived Catholicly Ever After: A Study of Catholic Periodical Fiction Between 1930 and 1950," unpublished manuscript, p. 6.
37. George Kelly, *The Catholic Family Handbook* (New York, 1959), p. 17.
38. Ibid., p. 19.
39. "The Christian in Action" (November 21, 1948) and "The Christian Family" (November 21, 1949). In *Pastoral Letters of the American Hierarchy, 1792–1970* (Huntington, Ind., 1971), pp. 409–10, 416–20.
40. Paul Marx, *Virgil Michel and the Liturgical Movement* (Collegeville, Minn., 1957), p. 270.
41. Marie-Louise and Jacques Defossa, "Family Bible-Reading," *Lumen Vitae* 10 (1955):169.
42. Letters to the Editor, *The Sign* 36 (April 1957):2.
43. Victor J. Donovan, "A Father's Blessing," *Worship* 30 (September 1956):507.
44. Emerson and Arlene Hynes, "Holy Week in the Home," *Worship* 30 (March 1956):262.
45. Kelly, *Catholic Family Handbook*, pp. 265–66.
46. A Carthusian of Miraflores, *The Home and Its Inner Spiritual Life: A Treatise on the Mental Hygiene of the Home* (Westminster, Md., 1952), pp. 156–69.

Chapter 4 Catholic Laywomen in the Labor Force, 1850–1950

1. Rev. Karl J. Alter, "Social Work as a Profession for Women," *National Catholic Welfare Conference Review* 12 (April 1930):12.

2. Edward T. James, Janet Wilson James, and Paul S. Boyer, eds., *Notable American Women, 1607–1950*, 3 vols. (Cambridge, Mass., 1971), hereafter cited as *NAW*. *Notable American Women: The Modern Period*, ed. Barbara Sicherman and Carol Hurd Green (Cambridge, Mass., 1980), hereafter cited as *NAW: The Modern Period*. *Woman's Who's Who of America: A Biographical Dictionary of Contemporary Women of the United States and Canada, 1914–1915*, ed. John William Leonard (New York, 1914), hereafter cited as *WWWA*. *The American Catholic Who's Who*, ed. Georgina Pell Curtis (St. Louis, 1911), hereafter cited as *ACWW*. *The American Catholic Who's Who*, vol. 1, 1934–1935; vol. 6, 1944–1945; vol. 11, 1954–1955; vol. 16, 1964–1965 (Detroit). *The American Catholic Who's Who*, vol. 21, 1976–1977, ed. A. E. P. Wall (Washington, D.C., 1975). Mary S. Logan, *The Part Taken by Women in American History* (reprint of the 1912 ed., New York, 1972). Judith A. Leavitt, *American Women Managers and Administrators: A Selective Biographical Dictionary of Twentieth Century Leaders in Business, Education and Government* (Westport, Conn., 1985). I exclude several groups of women from consideration: (1) women in religious communities; (2) individuals who at some point in their lives severed permanently their ties with the Catholic church; and (3) philanthropists and reformers who were never in the labor force.
3. Hannah Josephson, *The Golden Threads: New England's Mill Girls and Magnates* (New York, 1949), p. 288, and Hasia Diner, *Erin's Daughters in America* (Baltimore, 1983), pp. 74–75.
4. Jay P. Dolan, *The American Catholic Experience: A History from Colonial Times to the Present* (Garden City, N.J., 1985), chap. 5. See also Diner, *Erin's Daughters*, chap. 5.
5. David M. Katzman, *Seven Days a Week: Women and Domestic Service in Industrializing America* (Urbana, Ill., 1981), p. 70.
6. Alice Henry, "Mrs. Winifred O'Reilly: A Veteran Worker," *Life and Labor* 1 (May 1911):186.
7. Mary Jo Weaver, *New Catholic Women: A Contemporary Challenge to Traditional Religious Authority* (San Francisco, 1985), p. 23.
8. S. M. Franklin, "Agnes Nestor of the Glove Workers: A Leader in the Women's Movement," *Life and Labor* 3 (December 1913):372.
9. The connection between union goals and the ideal of womanly purity espoused by their Catholic tradition mobilized unionists like Maloney and Nestor. See Adade Mitchell Wheeler with Marlene Stein Wortman, *The Roads They Made: Women in Illinois History* (Chicago, 1977), p. 82.
10. Alice Timmons Toomy, "There Is a Public Sphere for Women." In "The Woman Question among Catholics: A Round Table Conference," *Catholic World* 57 (August 1893):681.
11. Ibid., p. 678.
12. Agnes Repplier, *Compromises* (Boston, 1904), pp. 178–79. See also Timothy J. Meagher, "Sweet Good Mothers and Young Women Out in the World: Roles of Irish American Women in Late Nineteenth and Early Twentieth Century Worcester, Massachusetts," *U.S. Catholic Historian* 3 & 4 (Summer/Fall 1986):325–44.
13. Comparative figures for Protestant professionals are based upon data from Barbara Kuhn Campbell, *The "Liberated" Woman of 1914: Prominent Women in the Progressive Era* (Ann Arbor, Mich., 1976).

14. Repplier, *Compromises*, p. 34.
15. Weaver, *New Catholic Women*, p. 12.
16. *NAW*, vol. 2, p. 293.
17. Thomas M. Schwertner, "Eleanor Donnelly—The Singer of Pure Religion," *Catholic World* 105 (June 1917):355.
18. Agnes Brady McGuire, "Catholic Women Writers." In *Catholic Builders of the Nation*, vol. 4, ed. C. E. McGuire (Boston, 1923), p. 200.
19. *NAW*, vol. 1, p. 156.
20. Katherine O'Keeffe O'Mahoney, *Famous Irishwomen* (Lawrence, Mass., 1907), p. 182.
21. Helena Modjeska, "Woman and the Stage." In *The World's Congress of Representative Women*, ed. May Wright Seawell (Chicago, 1894), p. 172.
22. Ellen K. Lee, "The Catholic Modjeska," *Polish American Studies* 31 (1974):20–27.
23. *NAW*, vol. 1, p. 277.
24. *NAW*, vol. 3, p. 226.
25. Ibid., p. 503.
26. Cited by Susan Kagan, "Camilla Urso: A Nineteenth-Century Violinist's View," *Signs* 2 (1977):731.
27. Heather Pentland, "Sarah Worthington King Peter and the Cincinnati Ladies' Academy of Fine Arts," *Cincinnati Historical Society Bulletin* 39 (1981):12.
28. Ibid., p. 7.
29. Logan, *The Part Taken by Women*, p. 781.
30. Mary A. Dowd, "The Public Rights of Women: A Second Round-Table Conference," *Catholic World* 59 (June 1894):319.
31. Mrs. Ednah D. Cheney, "The Women of Boston." In *The Memorial History of Boston, Including Suffolk County, Massachusetts, 1630–1880*, ed. Justin Winsor, vol. 4 (Boston, 1881), p. 344.
32. Dolan, *The American Catholic Experience*, p. 143.
33. *ACWW*, 1911, O'Mahoney entry.
34. Barbara J. Harris, *Beyond Her Sphere: Women and the Professions in American History* (Westport, Conn., 1978), p. 99. A few private colleges began to admit women in the 1860s and 1870s, including Antioch, Boston University, Cornell, Oberlin, St. Lawrence, and Swarthmore.
35. Elizabeth P. May, "Occupations of Wellesley Graduates," *School and Society* 29 (February 2, 1929).
36. For an account of the development of Catholic women's colleges, see the editor's introductory essay in *Higher Education for Catholic Women: An Historical Anthology*, ed. Mary J. Oates (New York, 1987).
37. Marion Tinling, *Women Remembered: A Guide to Landmarks of Women's History in the United States* (Westport, Conn., 1986), p. 661.
38. *WWWA*, Maley entry.
39. Wheeler, with Wortman, *The Roads They Made*, p. 90.
40. Dowd, *Public Rights of Women*, p. 320. Reactions of Protestant women to these conflicting pressures were similar. See Joyce Antler, "After College What?: New Graduates and the Family Claim," *American Quarterly* 32 (Fall 1980):409–35.
41. Mary Roth Walsh, *"Doctors Wanted: No Women Need Apply": Sexual Barriers in the Medical Profession, 1835–1975* (New Haven, Conn., 1977), p. 199.

42. Weaver maintains that Nichols did not affect "the landscape of American Catholicism either as it has been defined in the past or as it ought conceivably to be defined in the future" (*New Catholic Women*, pp. 28–29). But the eccentric and exuberant Nichols was well ahead of her times in her causes. "Many of the reforms she advocated in diet, dress, health education, woman's rights, and the relations of the sexes, contained insights whose value has since been recognized" (*NAW*, vol. 2, p. 629).
43. Wheeler, with Wortman, *The Roads They Made*, p. 96.
44. *ACWW*, 1911, Meder entry.
45. "Dr. Lena Edwards: People Lover. An Interview with Sister Anthony Scally," *Negro History Bulletin* 39 (1976):592.
46. Cited by Tinling, *Women Remembered*, p. 377.
47. See A. J. McKelway, " 'Kate,' the 'Good Angel' of Oklahoma," *American Magazine* 66 (October 1908):587–93, and Harvey R. Hougen, "Kate Barnard and the Kansas Penitentiary Scandal, 1908–1909," *Journal of the West* 17 (January 1978):9–18.
48. Arthur Preuss, "Women's Public Rights," *The Review* (August 1, 1894):2. Cited by Samuel J. Thomas, "Catholic Journalists and the Ideal Woman in Late Victorian America," *International Journal of Women's Studies* 4 (1981):96.
49. *NAW*, vol. 2, pp. 350–51.
50. Dorothy A. Mohler, "Jane Hoey and Agnes Regan, Women in Washington." In *Catholics in America, 1776–1976*, ed. Robert Trisco (Washington, D.C., 1976), p. 212.
51. Jonathan Hughes, *The Vital Few: The Entrepreneur and American Economic Progress* (New York, 1986), p. 492.
52. Ibid., p. 462.
53. Ibid., p. 503.
54. *WWWA*, Walsh entry.

Chapter 5   A Question of Equality

1. There are no extended studies of Catholic participation in women's search for equality, and as historians of American Catholicism seldom treat of women one must approach the subject from histories of women. (An interesting account of the phenomena of the missing woman in Catholic history can be found in Mary Jo Weaver's, *New Catholic Women: A Contemporary Challenge to Traditional Religious Authority* (San Francisco, 1985).) Unfortunately, Eleanor Flexner's classic study *Century of Struggle: The Woman's Rights Movement in the United States* (2nd ed., Cambridge, 1975) concludes with the ratification of the Nineteenth Amendment. Among many of the new histories of women that could be used to supplement Flexner are two thoroughly researched and well-written paperbacks: Nancy Woloch, *Women and the American Experience* (New York, 1984) and Lois W. Banner, *Women in Modern America: A Brief History* (2nd ed., San Diego, 1984). Barbara Welter's "The Cult of True Womanhood, 1820–1860," *American Quarterly* 27 (Summer 1966):151–74 is a brilliant analysis of the virtues society believed the ideal woman should possess. Aileen S. Kraditor, in *The Ideas of the Woman Suffrage Movement* (New York, 1965), contends

that these views significantly shaped the arguments used to justify the extension of suffrage and that as a result the ballot was bestowed without a corresponding change in attitudes toward women. James J. Kenneally in "Catholicism and Woman Suffrage in Massachusetts," *Catholic Historical Review* 53 (April 1967):43–57 (reprinted in *Catholicism in America*, ed. Philip Gleason (New York, 1970)), relates the Catholic approach to suffrage with nativism, temperance, and many other issues. His "Women Divided: The Catholic Struggle for the ERA, 1923–1945," *Catholic Historical Review* (forthcoming) focuses on the establishment of the Saint Joan Society in 1943 and the endorsement of the ERA by Cardinal Dougherty. An excellent account of Catholicism and the amendment in recent years is that of Mary Rada Papa, "Catholics on the ERA: Boost It or Blast It," *The National Catholic Reporter* (December 14, 21, and 29, 1979). Brief biographies of many of the women mentioned in this chapter can be found in *Notable American Women 1607–1950: A Biographical Dictionary*, ed. Edward T. James, Janet Wilson James, Paul S. Boyer (3 v., Cambridge, Mass., 1971) and *Notable American Women the Modern Period: A Biographical Dictionary*, ed. Barbara Sicherman *et al.* (Cambridge, Mass., 1980). Kenneally's *Women and American Trade Unions* (Montreal, 1981) is helpful on the relationship between union leaders, suffrage, and the ERA. See also Barbara M. Wertheimer, *We Were There: The Story of Working Women in America* (New York, 1977) on the suffrage question and working women.

2. *Arguments Before the Committee on Privileges and Elections of the United States Senate on Behalf of a Sixteenth Amendment and Protest Against Woman Suffrage to the Same Committee of the United States Senate* (Washington, 1878), pp. 43–45.

3. These concepts of dutiful homebound females were also reflected in most novels of the day by Catholic women. See James A. White, *The Era of Good Intentions: A Survey of American Catholics and Writing Between the Years 1885–1915* (New York, 1978). In his novel, *The Cross and the Shamrock: Or How to Defend the Faith* (Boston, 1853), written for Catholic male and female servants, Hugh Quigley assails "Bloomer" women "and others of a diseased public mind," and asserts that women's rights, which sprang from secularism, were really the effect of Protestantism. See pp. 236–37 and introduction. Also see Colleen McDannell, *The Christian Home in Victorian America 1840–1900* (Bloomington, Ind., 1986).

4. Bernard O'Reilly, *The Mirror of True Womanhood* and *True Men as We Need Them*, (2 vols. in 1, New York, 1887), p. 38. A twentieth century version of this concept is found in the Rev. Irving De Blanc's address to the NCCW: "Your task is clear: woman the lover, the saint, the person, must lead all of us to the Eternal Spouse now and forever." See "The Eternal Woman of 1956." In *Proceedings of the 28th National Convention of the National Conference of Catholic Women* (Washington, 1956), p. 56.

5. *Chicago New World*, July 18, 1903, Feb. 25, 1911. Quoted in Charles H. Shanabruch, "The Catholic Church's Role in the Americanization of Chicago's Immigrants: 1833–1928" (doctoral diss., Univ. of Chicago, 1975), p. 363.

6. *Woman's Journal*, March 24, 1877.

7. *New York Times*, April 11, 1914; *Woman's Journal*, May 2, 1914.
8. *Woman's Journal*, October 13, 1894, Aug. 16, 1913. *The Remonstrance*, January 1917. *New York Times*, December 8, 1916. James Gibbons, "Relative Condition of Women Under Pagan and Christian Civilization," *American Catholic Quarterly Review* 11 (October 1886):658. Idem, "The Restless Woman," *Ladies Home Journal* 19 (January 1902):6.
9. The clergymen were Revs. J. W. Dalton, Edward McGlynn, and Edward Scully, and Bishops Ireland, Spalding, and McQuaid, see *History of Woman Suffrage*, 6 vols., ed. Elizabeth Cady Stanton, et al. (reprint, New York, 1969), vol. 4, pp. 1079–80.
10. For Sherman, see Anna S. McAllister, *Ellen Ewing, Wife of General Sherman* (New York, 1936), and Katherine Burton, *Three Generations* (New York, 1947).
11. For her views on suffrage see Madeline Dahlgren, *Thoughts on Female Suffrage and in Vindication of Woman's True Rights* (Washington, 1871).
12. Dahlgren to James A. Garfield, February 9, 1871, file 129/030, Garfield Papers, Library of Congress.
13. William L. O'Neill, *Everyone Was Brave: The Rise and Fall of Feminism in America* (Chicago, 1969) pp. x, 351, 352.
14. *Woman's Journal*, March 14, 1914.
15. *New York Times*, November 18, 1917, September 13, 1920.
16. New York *Sun* as quoted in *Woman's Journal*, July 13, 1901.
17. John L. Spalding, "Basis of Popular Government," *North American Review* 134 (September 1884):199–208.
18. *Woman's Journal*, June 1, 1901.
19. Austin Dowling, "The Church and the Woman: An Address on the Subject of Equal Suffrage," *Addresses at Patriotic and Civic Occasions by Catholic Orators*, 2 vols. (New York, 1915), vol. 1, pp. 280–85.
20. *Woman's Journal*, March 16, 1889.
21. Ibid., October 19, 1895, January 15, 1896, September 20, 1902.
22. Avery to the Editor, *America* 14 (December 25, 1915):252; Avery to Cardinal O'Connell, February 3, 1914, file M-901, William Cardinal O'Connell Papers, Archives of the Archdiocese of Boston.
23. Katherine F. Conway, "Woman Has No Vocation to Public Life" in "Woman Question Among Catholics—A Round Table Conference," *Catholic World* 57 (August 1895):681–89.
24. Jane Campbell, "Woman and the Ballot." In *Girlhood's Hand-Book of Woman: A Compendium of the Views on Woman's Work—Woman's Sphere—Woman's Influence and Responsibilities*, 2nd ed., ed. Eleanor C. Donnelly (Saint Louis, 1905), pp. 198, 201.
25. The United States Supreme Court used the same rationale, the protection of mothers-to-be, to uphold limitations on the number of hours females could work in a week (see *Muller* v. *Oregon*, 208 U.S. 412). As early as 1894 Rev. John A. Ryan, who would become the leading Catholic exponent of social justice, found suffrage "reasonable because of the large numbers of women working outside the home." See John A. Ryan, "Suffrage and Woman's Responsibility," *America* 22 (December 1917):260–61.
26. James J. Kenneally, *Women and American Trade Unions* (Montreal, 1981), pp. 13–16.
27. Idem, "Catholic and Feminist: A Biographical Approach," *U.S. Catholic Historian* 3 (Spring 1984):239–45.

28. S. M. Franklin, "Elizabeth Maloney and the High Calling of the Waitress," *Life and Labor* 3 (February 1913):36–40.
29. For a few years, due to a second marriage, Valesh was outside the institutional church, however, she always considered herself Catholic. She sent her son to a Catholic boarding school and she was buried from the church. Letter from Marie Valesh to the author, September 28, 1983.
30. Eva Valesh, Reminiscences. Columbia University Oral History Collection, *New York Times* Oral History Program, 1971; Rhoda Gilman, "Eva McDonald Valesh: Minnesota Populist," *Women of Minnesota*, ed. Barbara Stuhler and Gretchen Kreuter (Saint Paul, Minn., 1977), pp. 55–76.
31. Margaret Hinchey, "Thirty Days," *Life and Labor* 3 (September 1913):264–65; Nancy Schrom Dye, *As Equals and As Sisters: Feminism, Unionism, and the Women's Trade Union League of New York* (Columbia, Mo., 1980), pp. 129–31.
32. *Battleground: The Autobiography of Margaret Haley*, ed. Robert L. Reid (Urbana, Ill., 1982), pp. xxiv, 33, 37, 73, 148, 177; Joan K. Smith, "Progressivism and the Teacher Union Movement: A Historical Note," *Educational Studies* 7 (Spring 1976):53–58; David B. Tyack, *The One Best System: A History of American Urban Education* (Cambridge, Mass., 1974), pp. 262–66.
33. Grace C. Strachan, "Our Fight for Equal Pay: New York Women School-Teachers Object to Men Getting Often Twice as Much for Same Work," *Delineator* 75 (March 1910):202, 258; Wayne J. Urban, *Why Teachers Organized* (Detroit, 1982), pp. 94–97, 106, 107, 123.
34. *Woman's Journal*, November 17, 1900.
35. Ibid., September 21, 1912; Reid, *Battleground*, pp. 242–43.
36. Margaret H. Rorke, *Letters and Addresses on Woman Suffrage by Catholic Ecclesiastics* (New York, 1914), pp. 1–2.
37. *Woman's Journal*, September 9, 1911.
38. Ibid., June 10, 1911.
39. *The Tidings*, April 29, 1910.
40. "Archbishop Riordan of San Francisco on Woman Suffrage," *America* 7 (September 1912):528.
41. *Woman's Journal*, September 7, 1912, May 24, 1913, February 24, 1917; *New York Times*, April 12, 13, 1915; *Catholic Citizen*, April 15, 1921; Annie Christitch, "America's Catholic Women Suffragists," *Catholic Citizen*, March 15, 1922:17–18.
42. *Woman's Journal*, February 8, 22, July 12, 1913, July 10, 1915.
43. Catholic Women's League of Chicago, *Annual Announcements 1911–1917* (Chicago, 1911–1917); Shanabruch, "Church's Role in Americanization," 365.
44. *Woman's Journal*, July 31, 1915.
45. A copy of Gallagher's appeal is found in file 37 of the Margaret Foley Papers, Arthur and Elizabeth Schlesinger Library on the History of Women, Radcliffe College.
46. "Woman Suffrage," *Catholic World* 107 (April 1918):134–36.
47. Curran D. Trifanny (her grandson), Life of Teresa O'Leary Crowley, M.S., file 49, Women's Rights Collection, Schlesinger Library.
48. Stanton, *History*, 6:104.
49. Kenneally, "Catholic and Feminist," pp. 245–53.

50. Charles E. Diviney to the author, July 16, 1984.
51. Alice Paul interview quoted in Christine Lunardin, "From Equal Suffrage to Equal Rights: The National Woman's Party 1914–1923 (doctoral diss., Princeton University, 1981), p. 275.
52. Proceedings of Second National Conference of Catholic Women, MS, NCCW Papers, Archives of the Catholic University of America.
53. *Pastoral Letters of the American Hierarchy 1792–1970*, ed. Hugh Nolan (Huntington, Ind., 1971), p. 245.
54. *Our Bishops Speak, 1919–1951*, ed. Raphael H. Huber (Milwaukee, Wisc., 1952), pp. 45–46.
55. Mrs. Michael Gavin, "The National Council of Catholic Women," *Catholic Builders of the Nation: A Symposium on the Catholic Contribution to the United States*, 5 vols., ed. C. E. McGuire (Boston, 1923), vol. 2, p. 371.
56. M. Camilla Mullay, "The Feminist Fight for a Federal Equal Rights Amendment with Particular Reference to the National Council of Catholic Women from 1920–1950" (masters thesis, Catholic University of America, 1961), pp. 19–20.
57. *New York Times*, February 7, June 8, 1925, May 14, 1952.
58. Ibid., October 3, 1929.
59. Hinchey to Leonora O'Reilly, n.d. 1919 as quoted in Dye, *Feminism, Unionism*, pp. 149–50.
60. *New York Times*, January 19, 1926.
61. Ibid., January 13, February 22, 1943.
62. Miller to Alice Paul, October 10, 1943, reel 78, National Woman's Party Papers 1913–1914, Microfilm Edition (Sanford, N.C.: Microfilming Corporation of America, henceforth referred to as NWP Papers).
63. *Equal Rights*, November and December 1941.
64. Dorothy S. Granger to the author, July 11 and September 26, 1984. Apparently in March 1943 Fitzmaurice was asked to make a public statement on the ERA but refused. Nevertheless, his prayer was publicized by Saint Joan's. There is nothing in the archives of the Wilmington diocese on the bishop and the ERA.
65. For Granger's life, Dorothy S. Granger, *The Shipleys of Maryland* (privately published), pp. 1–4.
66. Granger to Caroline Babcock, November 18, 1943, reel 78, NWP Papers.
67. *Our Sunday Visitor*, April 9, 1944.
68. Ethel E. Murrell to Alice Paul, May 9, 1945, reel 86, NWP Papers.
69. Granger to Caroline L. Babcock, April 11, 1944, A-117 folder 95, Caroline L. Babcock Papers, Schlesinger Library.
70. Dougherty to Ethel E. Murrell, December 17, 1943, file 80.7448, Archives of the Archdiocese of Philadelphia.
71. *New York Times*, September 29, 1945.
72. *Catholic Citizen*, May 15, 1964, April 15 and August 15, 1965; Rosemary Lauer, "Women and the Church," *Commonweal* 79 (December 20, 1963):365–68.
73. *New York Times*, December 1, 1973, August 27, 1974; *National Catholic Reporter*, September 6, 1974.
74. *National Catholic Reporter*, February 7, 1975; Rick Casey, "The Church and the ERA—An Update," ibid., April 5, 1974; Elizabeth Alexander and Maureen Fiedler, "The Equal Rights Amendment and Abortion:

Separate and Distinct," *America* 142 (April 12, 1980):314–18; Mary
Jo Weaver, *New Catholic Women: A Contemporary Challenge to Traditional Religious Authority* (San Francisco, 1985), pp. 85, 129, 234.

75. U.S. Senate, Committee on the Judiciary, Subcommittee on Constitutional Amendments, *The "Equal Rights" Amendment*, hearings, the
Ninety-first Congress, 2nd sess, May 5–7, 1970 (Washington, 1970),
p. 662.

76. "Spring Meeting U.S. Bishops Conference," *Origins* 8 (May 25, 1978):
19–20; E. L. Wojtowicz, "Equal Rights Amendment: A Catholic View,"
Our Sunday Visitor, November 9, 1975:1, 6.

77. Antoinette Iadarola, "The American Catholic Bishops and Woman:
From the Nineteenth Amendment to the ERA," *Religion and Social
Change*, ed. Yvonne Y. Haddad and Ellison B. Friendly (Albany, N.Y.,
1985), pp. 470–71; Mary B. Papa, "Catholics and the ERA," *National
Catholic Reporter*, December 29, 1979.

78. Among the signatories to this appeal were Bishop Michael F. McAuliffe
(Jefferson City), who had testified before the Missouri Senate; Archbishops James V. Casey (Denver), Raymond G. Hunthausen (Seattle),
and Rembert Weakland (Milwaukee); and Bishops Maurice F. Ding-
man (Des Moines), L. F. Matthieson (Amarillo), and Walter F. Sullivan
(Richmond). See *National Catholic Reporter*, June 18, 1982.

79. Phyllis Schlafly, *The Power of Positive Woman* (New Rochelle, N.Y.,
1977), p. 12. For her biography, see Carol Felsenthal, *The Sweetheart
of the Silent Majority: The Biography of Phyllis Schlafly* (New York,
1981).

80. Two thoughtful studies dealing with the defeat of the ERA, but hardly
touching the Catholic issue, are *Rights of Passage: The Past and Future
of the ERA*, ed. Joan Hoff-Wilson (Bloomington, Ind., 1986) and Mary
Frances Berry, *Why ERA Failed: Politics, Women's Rights, and the
Amending Process of the Constitution* (Bloomington, Ind., 1986). However, see also *National Catholic Reporter*, November 25, 1983, September 14, 1984; "The U.S. Bishops and the ERA," *Origins* 14 (January
3, 1985):476–79; Douglas Johnson, "ERA and Abortion: Really Separate Issues?" *America* 150 (June 9, 1984):432–37.

Chapter 6   Reformers and Activists

1. The history of American Catholic women's involvement in reform and
social activism has yet to be written. No specialized monographs focus
upon this topic. There are, however, some works in Catholic history
that will be invaluable to future historians examining female Catholic
reformers and activists. Mary Jo Weaver's *New Catholic Women: A
Contemporary Challenge to Traditional Religious Authority* (San Francisco, 1985) lays the groundwork for all future work in this area and
places Catholic women's history in its proper context. Jay P. Dolan's
*The American Catholic Experience: A History from Colonial Times to
the Present* (Garden City, N.Y., 1985) is the first survey of American
Catholic history to take women's experience seriously, and is especially
helpful in its treatment of immigrant women and Catholic participation in the reforms of the progressive era. Mary Ewens's *The Role
of the Nun in Nineteenth Century America* (New York, 1978) remains

the starting point for any examination of sisters' work in activism and reform. Aaron I. Abell's *American Catholicism and Social Action: A Search for Social Justice 1865–1950* (Notre Dame, Ind., 1963) and David J. O'Brien's two books, *American Catholics and Social Reform: The New Deal Years* (New York, 1968) and *The Renewal of American Catholicism* (New York, 1972), along with Robert D. Cross's *The Emergence of Liberal Catholicism in America* (Cambridge, Mass., 1958) sketch the background necessary to place female Catholic reformers and activists in their proper historical context and supply occasional leads on the contributions of women to larger reform movements. Similarly Leo Ward's *Catholic Life, U.S.A.: Contemporary Lay Movements* (Saint Louis, 1959) and *The American Apostolate: American Catholics in the Twentieth Century* (Westminster, Md., 1952), edited by Ward, provide important information on women in the lay apostolate.

Most of the literature available on female Catholic reformers and activists consists of monographs on specific social reform movements or on Catholic immigrants, biographies of individual women, and specialized articles on women or movements. Among the volumes on specific movements, Sister Joan Bland's *Hibernian Crusade: The Story of the Catholic Total Abstinence Movement* (Washington, D.C., 1951), James J. Kenneally's *Women and American Trade Unions* (Montreal, 1981), and Charles A. Meconis's *With Clumsy Grace: The American Catholic Left 1961–1975* (New York, 1979) are the most pertinent to Catholic women reformers and activists. Richard M. Linkh's *American Catholicism and European Immigrants (1900–1924)* (Staten Island, N.Y., 1975) and Hasia Diner's *Erin's Daughters in America: Irish Immigrant Women in the Nineteenth Century* (Baltimore, 1983) contain important material on reform and immigrant women. Dorothy Day has attracted considerable scholarly attention and two works on Day and her movement are especially significant: William D. Miller, *Dorothy Day: A Biography* (San Francisco, 1982), and Mel Piehl, *Breaking Bread* (Philadelphia, 1982). Maisie Ward's two autobiographies: *Unfinished Business* (London and New York, 1964) and *To and Fro on the Earth* (London and New York, 1973), along with Wilfrid Sheed's anecdotal *Frank and Maisie: A Memoir with Parents* (New York, 1985), together describe the network of Catholic women, famous and obscure, who were attracted to Ward's lectures and had links to the Catholic Workers and Friendship House as well.

Information on Catholic women reformers and activists is widely scattered, in single paragraphs and footnotes, throughout the emerging body of scholarship on women and religion. Only occasionally do entire articles appear. James J. Keneally's "Eve, Mary, and the Historians: American Catholicism and Women," a pioneering look at Catholic women's history that makes specific references to reform movements, and Mary J. Oates's "Organized Voluntarism: The Catholic Sisters in Massachusets, 1870–1940," both appear in *Women in American Religion*, ed. Janet James (Philadelphia, 1980). The *U.S. Catholic Historian* has published more articles on Catholic women activists and reformers than any other journal. Besides a double issue (Volume 5, 1986) entirely devoted to Catholic women's history, which contains several pertinent articles, James J. Kenneally's "Catholic and Feminist: A Biographical Approach," *U.S. Catholic Historian* 3 (Spring 1984):229–

53 and Alden V. Brown's "The Grail Movement to 1962: Laywomen and a New Christendom," *U.S. Catholic Historian* 3 (Fall/Winter 1983):149–66 provide especially valuable material on Catholic women's reform and social activism.

2. Bernard O'Reilly, *The Mirror of True Womanhood*, and *True Men As We Need Them* (New York, 1892), pp. 6, 64, 73, 92, 182.

3. Aaron I. Abell, "Introduction," to *American Catholic Thought on Social Questions*, ed. Aaron I. Abell (Indianapolis, 1968), pp. xxiii–xxvi; Dolan, *American Catholic Experience*, ch. 12.

4. Ewens, *Role of the Nun*, p. 104.

5. Ibid., pp. 221–22.

6. Thomas Beer, *The Mauve Decades: American Lives at the End of the Nineteenth Century* (New York, 1926), p. 145.

7. Quoted in Abell, *American Catholicism and Social Action*, p. 77.

8. Harriet Martineau, *Society in America*, quoted in Wendy Kaminer, *Women Volunteering: The Pleasure, Pain and Politics of Unpaid Work from 1830 to the Present* (Garden City, N.Y., 1984), p. 24.

9. William Stang, *Socialism and Christianity* (New York, 1905), pp. 72–73.

10. Virginia Yans-McLaughlin, *Family and Community: Italian Immigrants in Buffalo, 1880–1930* (Ithaca, N.Y., 1971; reprinted, 1977), pp. 248–50.

11. Kenneally, *Women and American Trade Unions*, ch. 8.

12. Bland, *Hibernian Crusade*, pp. 98, 144, 155.

13. *Proceedings of the Twentieth General Convention of the Catholic Total Abstinence Union of America* (Philadelphia, 1890), pp. 22–23.

14. Quoted in Joseph C. Gibbs, *The History of the Catholic Total Abstinence Union of America* (Philadelphia, 1907), pp. 152–53. For more on clerical opposition to Lakes's temperance work, see Bland, *Hibernian Crusade*, p. 209.

15. Alice Timmons Toomy, "There Is a Sphere for Catholic Women," *Catholic World* 57 (August 1893):675.

16. Ruth Bordin, *Frances Willard: A Biography* (Chapel Hill, N.C., 1986), p. 169.

17. Stang, *Socialism*, pp. 182–83.

18. Cardinal James Gibbons, "The Restless Woman," *The Ladies' Home Journal*, January 1902:6.

19. Ibid.

20. Eleanor C. Donnelly, "The Home Is Woman's Sphere," *Catholic World* 57 (August 1893):677–81; Katherine E. Conway, "Woman Has No Vocation to Public Life," *Catholic World* 57 (August 1893):681–84.

21. Martha Moore Avery, "Woman Suffrage," *America* 13 (October 9, 1915):631–32; Martha Moore Avery, "Right Reason the Cure," *America* 14 (November 13, 1915):101.

22. For the distinction between "hard core" (or extreme) feminism and "social feminism," see William L. O'Neill, *Everyone Was Brave: A History of Feminism in America* (New York, 1969; reprint ed., 1971), pp. 142–43.

23. Lelia Hardin Bugg, *The People of Our Parish* (Boston, 1900; reprint ed., New York, 1978), ch. 20; p. 226.

24. *Proceedings of the National Conference of the Society of St. Vincent de Paul Held in Boston, June 4, 5, 6, and 7, 1911* (Boston, 1911), pp. 148–

50; Daniel T. McColgan, *A Century of Charity*, vol. 2 (Milwaukee, 1951), pp. 392–93.

25. Henry Somerville, "The National Conference of Catholic Charities," *Catholic World* 105 (August 1917):587–97.
26. Quoted in Abell, *American Catholicism and Social Action*, pp. 183–84.
27. Warren E. Mosher, "Young Men's Societies," in *Progress of the Catholic Church in America and the Great Columbian Catholic Congress of 1893*, 6th ed. (Chicago, 1897), vol. 2, p. 116.
28. Abell, *American Catholicism and Social Action*, p. 123.
29. Juan Alfred Ede, "The Lay Crusade for a Christian America: A Study of the American Federation of Catholic Societies, 1900–19," (doctoral diss., Graduate Theological Union, Berkeley, Cal., 1979), pp. 239–44.
30. Abell, *American Catholicism and Social Action*, p. 189.
31. Mrs. Michael Gavin, "The National Catholic Council of Women [sic]," in *Catholic Builders of the Nation*, ed. C. E. McGuire (Boston, 1924), vol. 2, p. 369.
32. Martha Moore Avery to David Goldstein, June 16, 1918, David Goldstein Papers, Boston College Special Collections, Chestnut Hill, Mass.
33. Quoted in Brown, "The Grail Movement," p. 150.
34. Pius XII, "Allocution to Italian Women," October 21, 1945 in *The Woman in the Modern World*, selected and arranged by the Monks of Solesmes (Jamaica Plain, Mass., 1959).
35. Dorothy Dohen, *Vocation to Love* (New York, 1950), pp. 26–27, 35–36.
36. Meconis, *With Clumsy Grace*, p. xii.
37. Bugg, *People of Our Parish*, p. 123.

Chapter 7   Catholic Feminism: Its Impact on U.S. Catholic Women

1. This was evidenced in religious communities of women in the 1960s when about one-fourth of U.S. women opted to leave their communities.
2. Several works dealing with research on women in early Christianity have helped women to reclaim their own history and reinterpret some of the sources. See Elaine Pagels, *The Gnostic Gospels* (New York, 1979); Rosemary Rader, *Breaking Boundaries: Male/Female Friendship in Early Christian Communities* (New York, 1983); *Religion and Sexism: Images of Woman in the Jewish and Christian Traditions*, ed. Rosemary Radford Ruether (New York, 1974); and Patricia Wilson Kastner, et al., *A Lost Tradition: Women Writers of the Early Church* (Washington, D.C., 1981).
3. See chapters 1, 3, and 5 of this volume for evidence of the way in which several religious communities and their leaders adapted customs and constitutions to fit the needs of the time. Many communities, especially within the last thirty years, have researched and written accounts of their early foundations and events that forced them to question and change the more traditional aspects of religious life. See, for example, Sister M. Grace McDonald, *With Lamps Burning* (Saint Joseph, Minn., 1957). Lora Ann Quinonez, past executive director of LCWR, does a comparative study of the relationship between the women's movement in general and profeminist attitudes and actions

among women religious, in "The Women's Movement and Women Religious," *Origins* 4 (1974):337–43.

4. For a more detailed analysis of the events leading to the development of the Sisters Formation Conference, see Mary Jo Weaver, *New Catholic Women: A Contemporary Challenge to Traditional Religious Authority* (San Francisco, 1985), pp. 79–92. See also Mary Schneider, *The Sisters Formation Conference: Catalyst for Change* (Notre Dame, Ind., February 1986).

5. *Bylaws of the Leadership Conference of Women Religious of the United States of America*, article 2, section 1, p. 1.

6. Not all religious communities are represented in the LCWR. In 1970 approximately fifty major superiors withdrew from the organization because of its supposedly radical approach to certain issues. These sisters formed their own group, the Consortium Perfectae Caritatis. Another group formed the Institute for Religious Life.

7. The presidents of the LCWR have been particularly articulate about Christ's mandate to his followers to liberate people from oppressive structures and practices, particularly when such oppression is promulgated by religious institutions. Most of the LCWR presidents have continued to speak out for continued empowerment of both women and men in helping to bring about renewal within the church (e.g., Mary Luke Tobin, Margaret Brennan, Elizabeth Carroll, Joan Chittister, Mary Daniel Turner, Margaret Farley).

8. Marie Augusta Neal, "The Relation between Religious Belief and Structural Change in Religious Orders: Developing an Effective Measuring Instrument," *Review of Religious Research* 12 (Fall 1970):2–16.

9. Idem, *Catholic Sisters in Transition: From the 1960's to the 1980's* (Wilmington, Del., 1984).

10. Ibid., pp. 65–66.

11. Sister Charles Borromeo Muckenhirn, C.S.C., *The Changing Sister* (Notre Dame, Ind., 1965).

12. Idem, *The Implications of Renewal* (Notre Dame, Ind., 1967).

13. Ibid., p. 281.

14. See, for example, Thomas Dubay, *Ecclesial Women: Towards a Theology of the Religious State* (Staten Island, N.Y., 1970). Although the author did not deal with specific issues of renewal, his emphasis on religious women as ecclesial served to remind sisters of their responsibility to the church as well-integrated, spiritually and professionally formed witnesses to gospel ideals. A collaborative effort between the editors of *Theological Studies* and staff members of the Washington, D.C.-based Center of Concern resulted in the book *Women: New Dimensions*, ed. Walter J. Burghardt, S.J. (New York, 1975). Especially informative is Anne E. Patrick's chapter "Women and Religion: A Survey of Significant Literature, 1965–1974," pp. 161–89. Patrick traces the development of Catholic theologians' and historians' theories and narratives of women's history. She cites major writings of the period that attempted to develop original systems of thought based on feminist insights. See also Sister Bertrande Meyer, *Sisters for the 21st Century* (New York, 1965), and *Midwives of the Future: American Sisters Tell Their Stories*, ed. Ann Patrick Ware (Kansas City, Mo., 1965), both of which attempt to explain what religious life in the post–Vatican II church has meant to U.S. sisters with regard to personal commitment,

returning to the spirit of founders, and communal response to the world's human condition.

15. (Washington, D.C., 1980).
16. Ibid., p. 2.
17. See Weaver, *New Catholic Women*, pp. 130–31. See also *New Works of New Nuns*, ed. Sister Traxler (Saint Louis, 1968).
18. Two groups of Catholic women, formed to address racism and class discrimination within the church, are Black Sisters and Las Hermanas. Catholics for a Free Choice and New Ways Ministry arose in response to issues of abortion and gay ministry.
19. The brochure for the conference can be obtained from WATER (Women's Alliance for Theology, Ethics, and Ritual), 8035 13th Street, Silver Spring, MD, 20910. WATER, Chicago Catholic Women (CCW), the Quixote Center, and the Center of Concern are part of the Women-Church Convergence. For more information on these groups see Weaver, *New Catholic Women*, pp. 127–136.
20. "Of One Humanity," *Sojourners* 13 (January 1984):19. See also her lengthier analysis of the subject in her book *Liberation Theology: Human Hope Confronts Christian History and American Power* (New York, 1972).
21. See Weaver, *New Catholic Women*, pp. 170–77, for relevant biographical data on Daly and a critique of Daly's writings. I am indebted to Weaver for her analysis of feminist theories and the impact these ideas continue to have on U.S. Catholic women's views on traditional religious authority.
22. Mary Daly, *The Church and the Second Sex* (New York, 1968).
23. Ibid., p. 181.
24. Idem, *Beyond God the Father: Toward a Philosophy of Women's Liberation* (Boston, 1985).
25. Ibid., p. 8.
26. Ibid., p. 9.
27. Ibid., p. 11.
28. Ibid., p. 12.
29. Ibid., p. 11.
30. Ibid., p. 29.
31. Ibid., p. 34.
32. Idem, *Gyn/Ecology* (Boston, 1978) and *Pure Lust* (Boston, 1984). See also Weaver, *New Catholic Women*, pp. 173–77, for a summary analysis of content.
33. See also *Women of Spirit: Female Leadership in the Jewish and Christian Traditions*, ed. Rosemary Ruether and Eleanor McLaughlin (New York, 1979); the essays therein contribute toward an understanding that women *did* make history and that history offers us many paradigms of women's leadership.
34. Rosemary Ruether, *New Women, New Earth: Sexist Ideologies and Human Liberation* (New York, 1975).
35. Idem, *Sexism and God-Talk: Toward a Feminist Theology* (Boston, 1983). Much of my summary appraisal of Ruether's development of a feminist theology was first published in *Signs: Journal of Women in Culture and Society* 10 (Winter 1984):379–80. See also Weaver, *New Catholic Women*, pp. 164–70.
36. Ruether, *Sexism and God-Talk*, p. 85.

37. Ruether, *Women-Church: Theology and Practice of Feminist Liturgical Communities* (San Francisco, 1985).
38. Ibid., p. 6.
39. Elisabeth Schussler Fiorenza, *In Memory of Her: A Feminist Theological Reconstruction of Christian Origins* (New York, 1983). See the analysis of Weaver, *New Catholic Women*, pp. 159–64 and my own, *Signs* 10:378–79.
40. See above, note 4.
41. Sandra Schneiders attempts somewhat the same method in projecting options for communities of women religious, in *New Wineskins: Reimagining Religious Life Today* (New York, 1986).

Index